feeding the starving mind

A Personalized,

Comprehensive

Approach to

Overcoming Anorexia

& Other Starvation

Eating Disorders

DOREEN A. SAMELSON, ED.D., MSCP

New Harbinger Publications, Inc.

Publisher's Note

Care has been taken to confirm the accuracy of the information presented and to describe generally accepted practices. However, the authors, editors, and publisher are not responsible for errors or omissions or for any consequences from application of the information in this book and make no warranty, express or implied, with respect to the contents of the publication.

The authors, editors, and publisher have exerted every effort to ensure that any drug selection and dosage set forth in this text are in accordance with current recommendations and practice at the time of publication. However, in view of ongoing research, changes in government regulations, and the constant flow of information relating to drug therapy and drug reactions, the reader is urged to check the package insert for each drug for any change in indications and dosage and for added warnings and precautions. This is particularly important when the recommended agent is a new or infrequently employed drug.

Some drugs and medical devices presented in this publication may have Food and Drug Administration (FDA) clearance for limited use in restricted research settings. It is the responsibility of the health care provider to ascertain the FDA status of each drug or device planned for use in their clinical practice.

Distributed in Canada by Raincoast Books

Copyright © 2009 by Doreen A. Samelson
New Harbinger Publications, Inc.
5674 Shattuck Avenue
Oakland, CA 94609
www.newharbinger.com

FSC
Mixed Sources
Product group from well-managed
forests and other controlled sources

Cert no. SW-COC-002283
www.fsc.org
© 1996 Forest Stewardship Council

Cover design by Amy Shoup; Text design by Amy Shoup and Michele Waters-Kermes; Acquired by Melissa Kirk; Edited by Elisabeth Beller

Printed in the United States of America

Library of Congress Cataloging-in-Publication Data

Samelson, Doreen A.
  Feeding the starving mind : a personalized, comprehensive approach to overcoming anorexia and other starvation eating disorders / Doreen A. Samelson ; foreword by Robert Graff.
    p. cm.
  Includes bibliographical references.
  ISBN-13: 978-1-57224-584-6 (pbk. : alk. paper)
  ISBN-10: 1-57224-584-0 (pbk. : alk. paper) 1. Anorexia nervosa--Popular works. I. Title.
  RC552.A5S26 2009
  616.85'262--dc22
                                        2008039811

11   10   09

10   9   8   7   6   5   4   3   2   1

First printing

To my daughter, Audrey, whose commitment to the study of medicine makes me so proud, and to my son, Peter, who is proof that disability is not a barrier to a good life.

To my husband, John, whose support and love mean so much. This book would not have been possible without you.

To my best friend, Scott, who has supported me and listened.

To all my patients—the ones who are well and those who are still working on building a life without a starvation eating disorder.

acknowledgments

this book would not have been possible without the help I have received from the many clinicians I have worked with over the years. I want especially to thank Robert S. Graff, MD, who stopped what he was doing and immediately came to my office when I was faced with my first starving patient. I was on call and I had no idea how to begin to deal with that first patient's emaciated state. Watching Dr. Graff with this young adult and her frightened family gave me the direction I needed. Together, Dr. Graff and I successfully treated that first starvation eating disorder patient. I have treated many others since that day.

Many other clinicians have helped me over the years. The late Judy Sobieski, Ph.D., who will be missed by me and by the other eating disorder specialists who worked with her over the years, inspired me to learn more. I am indebted to James Lock, MD, Ph.D., who probably doesn't remember me but who allowed me to present a case during one of his trainings. His work and research have been very important in my work with patients. I am indebted to my fellow Eating Disorder Best-Practice Group members. I am also indebted to the many members of the Academy of Eating Disorders with whom I have talked over the years and whose willingness to share information and ideas has been so important to my practice. I also want to thank the clinicians and staff at my clinic. The clinical team and I have discussed many patient treatment plans over the years, and the team never lets me forget that giving up is never an option. I also want to thank our medical assistant and reception staff. The care they give every patient who comes to the clinic allows me to do what I do. Lastly, thank you to my good friend Pam Van Allen, Ph.D., whose support, mentoring, and confidence in me have meant so much.

As indebted as I am to the many clinicians and staff I have worked with over the years, I have the most gratitude for my patients and their families. Your courage is a constant inspiration to me. I have learned the most from all of you.

contents

STAGE I
education—
starvation eating disorder primer: what we know about starvation eating disorders

STAGE II
getting ready—
commitment, team building, and treatment planning

STAGE III
getting well—
weight restoration

STAGE IV
living—
staying healthy and building a life beyond a starvation eating disorder

foreword

my first encounter with a patient with anorexia nervosa was, at the outset, like my first encounter with a patient with alcoholism. In the case of my patient with alcoholism, I resolved that his problem drinking was obviously due to low self-esteem and too few caring and involved people in his life. During his recuperation from surgery for alcohol-related problems, I, as a dutiful third-year medical student, spent many hours discussing his life with him, never thinking to talk to him about how to stop drinking. I was ebullient when, one day before discharge, he told me he had been thinking about what I had said over the few weeks in the hospital and had decided to stop drinking. I triumphantly related this success to my fellow students. The next time I saw this man, several months had passed and he was lying on a gurney in a VA emergency room with blood flowing from every orifice, thrashing in a state of alcohol-induced liver failure. My fellow students were struggling to insert an IV but couldn't hold him still. He died in just an hour.

That event made me question my approach: Who was I actually caring for while my patient was convalescing from surgery and was a captive audience? Was I helping my patient or was I just indulging my own need to be a wise and caring authority figure without first finding out what would and would not work in the treatment of serious mental disorders?

When I sat with my first patient with anorexia nervosa, I felt a similar urge to help her by being a caring authority figure, but I resisted, deciding after one or two meetings that I had better start to learn what would, and would not, work for this deadly disorder. I began to investigate the basics of anorexia treatment, all of which pointed to the first step—that the patient must eat, period. This straightforward approach surprised me: no long discussions about childhood, no talks about why the patient wants to be thin, no exploration of the social meaning of thinness—just eat food. But how do you make yourself eat? In this book, Dr. Samelson tells you, directly, what you must do to get yourself to eat. She tells you in a way that's understandable and also in a way that emphasizes your part in taking action that will preserve your life.

For people who combine purging with starvation, Dr. Samelson offers specific and concrete steps you must take to regulate your food intake without purging; once again, the burden is on you to take the steps necessary to live a healthy life.

For clinicians, this book is a valuable resource devoted to specific interventions without extraneous theoretical discussions. The focus is on helping very sick people survive this terrible disorder and find ways to contribute to their own lives and the lives of those around them.

—Robert S. Graff, MD

introduction

eating disorders affect an increasing number of people in Western countries like the United States. The most deadly eating disorders involve both starving to lose weight and purging the body of nutrition through vomiting, laxative abuse, or extreme exercise. We call these deadly mental disorders *starvation eating disorders*. They affect the body, brain, relationships with family and friends, and work life. There is no area of life that they can't touch. This book is for people who are affected by a starvation eating disorder.

Along with being the most deadly of all mental disorders, starvation eating disorders can be the hardest to treat (Birmingham and Beumont 2004). If you have such a disorder, not only is your health at risk, but your life is being controlled by your eating disorder. But there is hope—it is possible to beat your disorder and get well. Winning this struggle will require that you educate yourself about the brain and body, learn and practice anxiety-reduction techniques, seek support from others, and commit to getting well. But mostly it will take *food*. The key to recovering from a starvation eating disorder is to eat food and keep the food down. This simple solution is very difficult to accept if you have a starvation eating disorder. This book will help you gain the knowledge and skills you need to develop a plan to apply that simple solution.

I wrote this book because I have seen people beat their starvation eating disorder and get well, one step—one bite of food—at a time. As an eating disorder specialist, I have had the privilege to watch bright, creative people turn the tables on their starvation eating disorder. It takes courage and hope to fight an eating disorder and get your life back, but you can do it. You can have a life without fear of food and fat.

this book is not a substitute for medical care

Starvation eating disorders are associated with multiple medical complications. Of all the mental disorders, starvation eating disorders probably produce the greatest medical risk. This book is not a substitute for receiving good medical care. If you have an eating disorder, you should have regular medical monitoring of your health. Some medical conditions are particularly dangerous. You should seek medical attention as soon as possible if you are currently using syrup of ipecac to purge or if you experience any of the following symptoms or conditions:

- Bleeding when you vomit or cough

- Blood in your stool

- Fainting or becoming very light-headed when you stand up

- Chest pain

- Bone pain

- Easy bruising

- Very low heart rate

the need to be thin

Over the years, I have seen many patients whose desire to be thin has put their health and even their lives in jeopardy. Self-imposed starvation (often combined with purging through vomiting and other behaviors, such as compulsive exercise) is the foundation of starvation eating disorders, a group of serious eating disorders that includes anorexia nervosa. When the need to be thin overrides everything else, losing weight by any means becomes the focus of people's lives. When most people think of an eating disorder, the image that comes to mind is of a young, teenage girl, but older teens and adults, both female and male, can have an eating disorder involving starvation and low weight. Older patients often struggle with starvation and purging for years, leaving them feeling depressed and desperate.

One person who paid a big price for her starvation eating disorder was Amy, a twenty-eight-year-old married woman who had started dieting in earnest at age thirteen after coming home from summer camp. While she was at camp, Amy had compared her body to the bodies of thinner girls. Instead of making new friends, she spent her time going off by herself, worrying that she wouldn't be liked by the thin girls. While her camp experience heightened her anxieties, Amy had started to feel fat before she went to camp. Her brother often teased her about asking for second helpings at the dinner table, and her mother always seemed to be on a diet. Although Amy was not obese, she was a little overweight, and when she came home from camp, her family supported her decision to diet. Amy and her parents thought that she would be healthier if she lost a few pounds. For most thirteen-year-olds, dieting to lose a few pounds would not have developed into an eating disorder. For Amy, who was naturally compulsive in the things she did, dieting quickly got out of control. After losing a few pounds, Amy still felt fat even though her family and doctor told her she was at a healthy weight. Amy continued to diet by severely restricting what she ate, and she lost more weight. Her family became alarmed, and her anxious parents consulted mental health professionals and dietitians who told them not to talk to their daughter about food or weight. Amy, who had been menstruating for only one year when she started to starve, stopped menstruating. When she was sixteen, Amy went to a residential eating disorder program for three months. She gained some weight while in the program but lost the weight again within six months of returning home. Over the next twelve years, her weight fluctuated from a low of 78 to a high of 104 pounds.

When I first saw Amy, her weight was 84 pounds and she was using laxatives and vomiting several times a day. In addition to purging with laxatives and vomiting, she binged on cereal about twice a week, eating as much as half a box of cereal with milk. Amy was married, and her husband wanted a baby. Her obstetrician referred Amy to me because he knew her low weight would interfere with her becoming pregnant. Amy had a serious starvation eating disorder.

Let's look at a second person who is typical of someone with a starvation eating disorder. When I first met her, Grace was a forty-year-old divorced woman who had struggled with an eating disorder since the age of nineteen, when she started dieting for her wedding. She wanted to fit into a size 4 wedding dress, but as a large-boned person, she had to get her weight very low to fit into such a small size. While she was able to lose enough weight to fit into the dress, she quickly gained 10 pounds after the honeymoon. Grace's periods stopped for about six months but started again, and she got pregnant. During her first pregnancy, she worried constantly about her weight. Despite the fact that her doctor told her she needed to gain more weight, Grace dieted throughout the pregnancy and her baby was born one month prematurely. Grace did better during her second pregnancy but started dieting again after her second child was born. She tried vomiting a few times but hated the way vomiting made her feel so she depended on exercise, laxatives, and enemas, as well as restricting how much she ate, to keep her weight low.

When I first saw Grace, she was exercising up to five hours a day and using laxatives and enemas. She refused to allow herself anything to eat before 5 p.m. When she did eat, she kept her food choices to a short list of foods she considered "safe." Grace used laxatives and enemas daily, attempting to get rid of the food she ate each evening. After many years of laxative and enema abuse, she realized that her purging didn't really lead to weight loss, but she continued to use them because she felt fat and bloated when she didn't. Over time Grace felt dependent on this type of purging and was afraid to stop. Like Amy, Grace tended to be compulsive and perfectionistic. Grace's weight was 105 pounds when she first saw me, which put her weight into the borderline-low range for her height. Even though she was not severely underweight, on Grace's larger frame, her 105-pound weight made her look gaunt. She was starving herself. Her menstrual periods became erratic any time her weight was under 120 pounds, and she was only having a period every two to three months. Grace considered her weight of 105 to be high and was surprised when I told her she was at high risk for medical problems like osteoporosis and that she needed to gain weight.

Even though Amy weighed less than Grace, the two women were similar in many ways. They shared many personality characteristics and both engaged in behaviors like starvation and purging (including compulsive exercise), putting them at risk for serious health problems. Amy and Grace spent their lives focused on their weight and shape, and both needed to gain weight to be healthy. This focus cost both women a lot. Grace's husband got tired of Grace spending more time at the gym than with him, and he filed for divorce. Amy's husband was worried that he and Amy wouldn't be able to have children; he wanted her to gain weight, and this was causing daily conflict for the couple. The good news is that both Amy and Grace were able to apply the discipline they had previously used in starving themselves to the process of getting well. This book will explore how Amy and Grace and others have been able to recover from a starvation eating disorder.

who is this book for?

This book is written for people like Amy and Grace. It may also be helpful for family members and friends who are alarmed by a loved one's starvation and purging, as well as for professionals who treat patients with eating disorders.

People with a Starvation Eating Disorder

Starvation eating disorders are the most deadly of all kinds of eating disorders (Birmingham and Beumont 2004). People like Amy and Grace who have to gain weight to be healthy are at higher risk for serious heart problems than people with other kinds of eating disorders. If you're reading this book, you may be like Amy—someone who meets the full criteria for anorexia (officially called *anorexia nervosa*), which, as described in chapter 1, involves more than just low weight. But this book is not just for people who have been diagnosed with anorexia nervosa. You may be like Grace, who doesn't meet the full criteria for anorexia nervosa but still needs to gain weight and stop purging.

Most people with a starvation eating disorder are women, but some men also struggle with an eating disorder. If you are a male who has a starvation eating disorder, you will find that the self-help strategies in this book are just as appropriate for you as they are for women.

Family Members and Friends

As we can see from the lives of Amy and Grace, an eating disorder doesn't just cause stress for the person who has one—eating disorders cause stress for everyone in that person's life. These disorders are particularly frightening for family and friends because a starvation eating disorder threatens the lives of their loved ones. If you are a family member or friend of someone who is starving to lose weight, you know just how stressful caring about that person can be. You may also be angry and confused. For most of us, eating is such a normal and satisfying part of life that it's hard to relate to someone who refuses to eat, spends hours exercising, and engages in other harmful behaviors. The first part of this book will give you a good understanding of what a starvation eating disorder is and how it affects the person who is starving. This information can help you support the starving person in your life.

NONPROFESSIONAL COACH

There is one special role for a friend or family member: you may be asked to be a coach. A coach is a nonprofessional who supports weight restoration. If you are asked and agree to take on this role, you should read the section "Nonprofessional Coaches" (in chapter 7) on how to coach.

Family Members of Children or Teens with Self-Imposed Starvation

If you are living with a child or teen who has a starvation eating disorder, you should get very involved in his or her treatment. The only treatment that has been shown in studies to be effective for children and teens with a starvation eating disorder like anorexia is *family-based treatment* (also called the Maudsley method). You may find some of the strategies in this book helpful, but this book should be considered a supplement to family-based treatment. To find out more about family-based treatment, I suggest you look at the book *Help Your Teenager Beat an Eating Disorder* by James Lock, MD, Ph.D., and Daniel Le Grange, Ph.D. (2005). Lock and Le Grange's book is based on the research they and others have done in treating eating disorders in children.

Professionals and Eating Disorder Treatment Programs

If you are a psychologist, psychiatrist, therapist, or dietitian who treats eating disorders, this book can be used either for individual treatment or as part of group treatment. Much of this book can be used as homework or for discussion during a treatment session. If you are an eating disorder specialist, you know how hard it is to help patients gain weight and stop purging. You probably also know that talking about your patient's feelings about food and the meaning of being thin may fill up an hour's treatment session, but these strategies rarely result in weight gain. This book can supplement more traditional, dynamic talk therapy or form the foundation of cognitive behavioral treatment or specialist supportive clinical management for a patient with a starvation eating disorder.

People with Other Eating Disorders

Starvation eating disorders are not the most common eating disorders seen by psychologists and other mental health professionals. Other eating disorders like *bulimia* (officially called *bulimia nervosa*) and *binge-eating disorder* are more common. If you have one of these eating disorders, you may find parts of this book helpful. However, because this book focuses on gaining weight to be healthy, much of the book will not be relevant to the experience of people with eating disorders that don't involve starvation and low weight. Chapter 1 will look at how eating disorders such as bulimia are different from starvation eating disorders.

how this book is organized

The organization of this book is meant to take you through the treatment process from learning about your starvation eating disorder to developing a life beyond your eating disorder. The book is laid out sequentially in the four stages of treatment that will help you defeat your starvation eating disorder:

- *Stage I: Education—Starvation Eating Disorder Primer: What We Know About Starvation Eating Disorders.* The first stage in defeating your starvation eating disorder is education. As you work through this stage, you will learn what makes a starvation eating disorder different from other disorders and how low weight and purging affects your body and the brain. You will also gain an understanding of how your starvation eating disorder developed. Finally you will learn how your anxiety forms the foundation of your starvation eating disorder.

- *Stage II: Getting Ready—Commitment, Team Building, and Treatment Planning.* This stage is about getting ready to stop purging and gain weight. You will work through the commitment process. Developing your own compelling reasons to get well is an important step; without a reason to get well, you will find it hard to do what it takes to gain weight and stay at a healthy weight. You will also develop a support team in stage II to help you get well. A good support team is important. Going it alone will give your disorder the advantage. Most people with a starvation eating disorder can benefit from having professionals, like a physician or a psychologist, as well as friends and family members on their team. In the last part of stage II, you will discover the essential components of treatment that you will learn to use to get well.

- *Stage III: Getting Well—Weight Restoration.* Everything you learn in stages I and II will prepare you to restore your body to health in stage III. Being able to eat normal amounts of food without purging or engaging in other self-harm behaviors is the key to getting well. Because purging and other self-harm behaviors (like drinking) can keep your starvation eating disorder in charge, you will need to stop these harmful behaviors. Once you have gotten control of your harmful behaviors, you will work through the six phases of weight restoration. To accomplish this, you will need to start eating enough food to gain weight, learn how to challenge your anxiety, and change your thinking about food, weight, and shape.

- *Stage IV: Living—Staying Healthy and Building a Life Beyond a Starvation Eating Disorder.* The last stage of recovering from a starvation eating disorder is to stay healthy by preventing a relapse, improving your body image, and learning how to develop a life beyond your eating disorder. We know that the symptoms of a starvation eating disorder can return even if someone has been well for years. Preventing a relapse of your starvation eating disorder can be as important as getting well.

how to use this book

Each chapter in this book is designed to help you look at your eating behavior, develop a plan to get well, change your thinking about food and weight, and deal with your anxiety about gaining weight. This book can be used as a self-help book or it can be used as part of a professionally facilitated treatment program.

As you work through the chapters, some additional tools will be helpful:

- A spiral notebook or journal

- A highlighter

- A stack of 3 by 5 index cards

Notebook: While there is space to write in each chapter, you will need to keep an ongoing record of what you eat. Your notebook will come in handy for keeping track of what you eat and for writing down how you are feeling about eating and getting well. If you are working with a psychologist or therapist, your notebook can be shared during your psychotherapy. If you are having trouble concentrating because your weight is very low, writing down important points in your notebook will help you remember what you are reading.

Highlighter: Use a highlighter to mark what seems important to you in this book so you can go back and reread the highlighted parts or bring the book to your psychotherapy sessions so you can discuss the highlighted portions.

Index Cards: Keeping on track with your treatment will involve reminding yourself of the following: (1) your reasons for getting well, (2) the useful thoughts you develop that contradict eating disorder thinking, and (3) skills, like self-soothing, that you can use when you become distressed and your eating disorder seems to be getting the best of you. The 3 by 5 index cards are very useful for noting your motivations, thoughts, or skills. As you gain weight and reduce behaviors like purging, there will be times when your starvation eating disorder will be working hard against you. Pulling out the cards can be very helpful at those times, so periodically throughout the book, I will suggest you fill out a 3 by 5 index card that you can use when you need it.

A Special Note on Working in This Book

While this book is meant to be worked through sequentially, there is one important exception to working through this book as it is laid out. If your health is in serious danger and you have been told you need to gain weight immediately, read chapter 1 and then skip to chapters 10 and 11, which deal with gaining weight. If you are under medical care, you should share chapters 10 and 11 with your doctor to make sure you are gaining weight in a way that is medically safe for you and that none of the suggestions in this book contradict instructions from your doctor.

You should also know that if your weight is extremely low, it may be difficult for you to concentrate while reading. Chapter 3 describes the starving brain and why it may be hard to remember what you read when your weight is very low. After you gain some weight, you may need to go back and reread parts of this book in order to get the most out of it.

Source Material

While I have met many people with eating disorders over the years, the stories of Amy, Grace, Joe, and the other people you will meet in this book are composites. I have changed their names and the details of their stories to thoroughly protect their confidentiality. Although these stories do not precisely match any real person's life, they certainly represent the struggles and successes of people living with a starvation eating disorder.

getting well

Recovering from a starvation eating disorder is a process. There will be times when you will want to quit. There will be times when your anxiety will seem unbearable. But getting well is possible. People like Amy and Grace have gotten well, and you can too. Take one step at a time, and if you have to start over, that's okay. If you need help from a professional, get it. If you are lucky enough to have a family member or friend who is willing to learn about starvation eating disorders and support you, accept the support. By starting to read this book, you have taken the first step. Remember the only way your starvation eating disorder can win is if you quit.

STAGE I

education—starvation eating disorder primer: what we know about starvation eating disorders

educating yourself about starvation eating disorders and developing an understanding of your own eating disorder is an important part of working toward being healthy. Two types of treatment that have been shown to be effective in the treatment of starvation eating disorders are specialist supportive clinical management (SSCM) and cognitive behavioral therapy (CBT). You will learn more about SSCM and CBT in chapter 8. For now, know that they have a strong educational emphasis. Consistent with the SSCM and CBT research, stage I of this book lays the educational foundation you will need to get well. As you work through the chapters in this stage, you will have the opportunity to explore the physical changes that occur in the body and brain when someone is starving. You can use this information to help motivate you to get well. You'll also learn how starvation eating disorders are diagnosed and how to tell if you have a starvation eating disorder.

In addition to understanding what a starvation eating disorder is, most people want an answer to the "why" question. You may have asked yourself why you feel such a strong urge to lose weight. In stage I you will learn what we know about why some people develop a starvation eating disorder. By the end of stage I, you will have some ideas about why you might have developed a starvation eating disorder.

CHAPTER 1

what is a starvation eating disorder?

People with starvation eating disorders and people who treat starvation eating disorders have something in common: both groups focus on weight. While the focus is the same, the reasoning behind the focus is different. People with eating disorders focus on weight because they have an intense fear of gaining weight and being fat. If you have a starvation eating disorder or know someone who does, you know just how strong this fear can be. Providers of medical and mental health care also deal with fear, but our fear is that our patients will not gain weight. We are afraid because we know that the lower a patient's weight, the greater the chance that our patient will develop a deadly medical problem such as heart failure. Of course, it's not just weight that can cause medical problems; there are other behaviors in addition to starvation that can lead to serious problems. After starvation, purging is at the top of the list of risky behaviors. "Purging" is the term for a group of self-harm behaviors that have one thing in common—they are always attempts to get rid of food. Most people think of vomiting and laxative or enema abuse when they think of purging, but extreme exercise can also be thought of as a type of purging because it's a way of "purging" the body of calories by burning them off. While not everyone includes extreme exercise in this category, in this book, "purging" refers to vomiting, laxative abuse, enema abuse, and extreme exercise. All types of purging are self-harm behaviors, and all self-harm interferes with getting well while reinforcing the starvation eating disorder. Whatever the purging behavior, it's weight that determines just how risky the purging is.

it's about weight

Most people who have an eating disorder do not have the type of eating disorder that involves starvation and low weight. The hallmark of a *starvation* eating disorder is low weight. To see just how important weight is in determining medical risk, let's look at some examples of people with eating disorders who purge (including exercising to excess).

Joe is nineteen and weighs 90 pounds, which, on his 5'7" frame, makes him severely underweight. Joe imposes strict limits on his intake of calories. On most days, Joe, who is very disciplined, is able to limit his calories to less than 1,000. But several times a week his hunger wins out, and Joe eats more than 1,000 calories. On the days he eats more than his self-imposed calorie limit, Joe vomits to get rid of the extra food. In addition to purging by vomiting, Joe exercises about three hours a day at the gym.

Megan is also nineteen but, unlike Joe, her weight is in the normal range. Like Joe, Megan is very concerned about her weight. She intends to diet every day by severely limiting calories but she invariably gets very hungry and ends up eating more than she planned to eat. This leads to frequent vomiting. Most days Megan vomits at least twice a day. Megan also goes to the gym every day to work out. Megan purges by vomiting more often than Joe does, and they exercise about the same amount.

Although Megan is putting her health at risk with her purging and her attempts at starving herself, her higher weight offers her some protection. On the other hand, Joe is at risk of sudden death from heart failure. His low weight offers no protection from his other harmful behaviors. This is not to say that Megan shouldn't worry about her purging. Megan should stop purging and should eat regular meals. However, if Joe and Megan both came to see me, I would insist that Joe see his primary care provider and stop all exercise immediately. I would be very worried that Joe might develop serious medical problems because his weight is so low. In fact, Joe's so underweight that he might need to be on bed rest. Unlike Joe, Megan wouldn't need bed rest and could continue to go to the gym a few times a week while she worked on stopping her other purging behaviors.

how are eating disorders diagnosed?

In the United States, most professionals use the fourth edition of the *Diagnostic and Statistical Manual of Mental Disorders* (also called the *DSM-IV-TR*; APA 2000) when diagnosing eating disorders. The *DSM-IV-TR* lists the criteria for all kinds of mental disorders. If a patient has enough of the required symptoms, they get the diagnosis; if not, they are not diagnosed with that disorder. This works fairly well for some mental disorders but not so well for others. For example, this approach doesn't work very well for diagnosing anorexia.

Anorexia is the eating disorder most people think of when they imagine someone starving themselves to a low weight. It is a very serious eating disorder, but it's possible to have only a few of the symptoms on the criteria list for anorexia and still have a grave eating disorder involving starvation. Remember Grace from the Introduction? She didn't quite meet the *DSM-IV-TR* criteria for anorexia, but she has a lot in common with people who do meet the criteria. One of the reasons Grace didn't meet the criteria is that she was having a menstrual period at least every three months. As will be described in chapter 2, it's a bad sign if you're a woman whose menstrual periods have stopped because of weight loss, but some women are able to get their weight dangerously low and still have a period every few months. According to the *DSM-IV-TR* diagnostic criteria, if a woman has her menstrual period naturally without the help of birth control pills, that woman does not have anorexia. So, although we use the *DSM-IV-TR* criteria to guide us in diagnosing eating disorders, eating disorder specialists like me know that just because a woman has periods, it doesn't mean she isn't at risk for some of the most serious medical problems low weight can cause. The next section will look more closely at the kind of diagnosis people like Grace might be given, and we'll compare that to anorexia.

Anorexia and EDNOS

If an eating disorder specialist has told you that you meet all the criteria for anorexia, this means you have a very serious starvation eating disorder. Your health is at risk, and if you don't get well, your life will likely be shortened. But what if (like Grace) you don't meet the full criteria for anorexia? You may have been told that you don't have anorexia but do have something called *eating disorder not otherwise specified* (also called *EDNOS*). The problem with EDNOS is that it's not specific. People who are obese and have a binge-eating disorder are given the diagnosis of EDNOS, and so are those, like Megan, who have a bulimic type of eating disorder but don't meet the full criteria for bulimia. Grace's official diagnosis is EDNOS, while Amy's official diagnosis is anorexia. But anorexia and EDNOS are just labels—both Grace and Amy have a starvation eating disorder. The treatment for their eating disorders is the same, and both could use the strategies in this book to improve their health. *The bottom line is this:* to be healthy, both Amy and Grace need to gain weight and change their thinking about weight and eating.

Criteria for Anorexia and Eating Disorder Not Otherwise Specified (EDNOS)	
Summary of the *DSM-IV-TR* criteria for anorexia	**Summary of the *DSM-IV-TR* criteria for EDNOS related to low weight and starvation**
■ You refuse to keep your weight in the normal range for your height. ■ You have an intense fear of being fat or gaining weight even if you are already too thin. ■ You have a distorted body image. You think you are fat when others think you're thin. ■ You don't realize that your low weight is putting your health in jeopardy and is a serious problem for your life and your family. ■ You're a woman who has missed your menstrual period for at least three consecutive months or you have a period only if you take hormones.	■ You're a woman who meets all the criteria for anorexia except you have a period at least once every three months. ■ You meet the criteria for anorexia except that your weight is in the low normal range.

Body Mass Index

The first step in determining if someone has a starvation eating disorder is to look at weight. The most accurate way to do this is by calculating your *body mass index*, or *BMI*. BMI uses your weight and height to come up with a number that tells you if you are underweight, overweight, or at a healthy weight for your height. The easiest way to calculate your BMI is to go online to one of the many BMI calculators. Just put "BMI" in your favorite search engine and you should come up with several BMI calculators. Pick one of the calculators, plug your current weight and height in, and you will get a number. That number is your BMI. Or if you liked math in school and don't want to use an online BMI calculator, you can also calculate your BMI by using the following steps.

BMI Calculation

My weight in pounds: _____
My height in inches: _____

If you don't know your height in inches, just take your height in feet and multiply by twelve, and then add any inches; for example, if you are 5'4", the calculation would look like this:
(5 x 12) + 4 = 64.

Now put your weight in pounds and height in inches into the following formula:
Your weight in pounds ÷ your height in inches ÷ your height in inches x 703 = your BMI.

Using the example above—for someone who is 64" tall and 100 pounds, the formula would look like this:
100 ÷ 64 ÷ 64 x 703 = 17.2

Once you know your BMI, you can see how it compares to the following guidelines:

- BMI less than 18   Underweight

- BMI 18–19   Borderline

- BMI 20–24   Healthy

- BMI 25–30   Overweight

- BMI over 30   Obese

While BMI is a useful way to determine if someone is underweight or overweight, it's not perfect. The BMI guidelines here are general ones. You may find slightly different guidelines if you use an online BMI calculator, but most guidelines are similar to this one. The problem with the guidelines is that they don't take things like bone structure and muscularity into account.

Let's look at Grace again to see how a person's individual characteristics must be taken into account when looking at BMI. Grace is 5'4" and weighs 105 pounds, a weight she considers to be too much. Her BMI is 18, putting her in the borderline normal range. But Grace is also a fairly large-boned person, and her periods are erratic. Putting all of this together means that Grace needs to gain weight. So although Grace does not fall into the underweight category in the BMI guidelines, she is underweight for her body type.

On the overweight end of the BMI scale there are people who are healthy even though their BMI is above 25. Jill is a good example of this. Jill is a college volleyball player. She has large bones and regularly lifts weights. At 5'10" and 183 pounds, Jill has a BMI of 26—just into the overweight category. But Jill, who has regular periods and is naturally a muscular person, is not overweight. Because muscle weighs more than fat and she has a large bone structure, Jill's weight is healthy for her athletic body type, and she does not need to lose weight.

do you have a starvation eating disorder?

Now that you know what your BMI is, you can look at the other symptoms of a starvation eating disorder by completing the Starvation Eating Disorder Self-Assessment. The more items you answer yes to, the greater your risk for having a serious eating disorder.

Starvation Eating Disorder Self-Assessment		
My BMI is under 20, and I don't feel thin.	Yes	No
I have an intense fear of gaining weight.	Yes	No
Even though other people consider me to be thin or a normal weight, I think I should lose more weight.	Yes	No
I spend a lot of time each day thinking about weight and food.	Yes	No
I restrict my eating as much as possible.	Yes	No
I'm a premenopausal female who is not on birth control pills and I don't have regular periods or I was put on birth control pills because my periods were irregular.	Yes	No
I vomit to get rid of food.	Yes	No
I use laxatives at least once a week.	Yes	No
I use enemas to lose weight or get rid of food.	Yes	No
I eat only certain "safe" foods.	Yes	No
I sometimes binge on food because I'm so hungry I can't control myself.	Yes	No
No matter how much I exercise, it never feels like enough.	Yes	No

If your weight is low and you answered yes to at least one of the previous statements, it is very likely that you have a starvation eating disorder. If your weight is normal or high, but you selected one of the statements on the list, it's possible you have an eating disorder, but you probably don't have the starvation type of disorder. You should see a specialist who can evaluate you to determine if you have an eating disorder.

Types of Anorexia and Starvation EDNOS

There are two kinds of anorexia and starvation EDNOS. The types are referred to as the *restricting* type and the *binge-purge* type. These different types can confuse people. I sometimes see patients who come to me thinking they have bulimia because they purge or binge, but after I evaluate them, I diagnose them with anorexia binge-purge type or EDNOS involving starvation and purging. Many people with a starvation eating disorder start out just restricting, but over time, most add purging and, as will be discussed in chapter 3, bingeing is common. While it is true that bulimia is the eating disorder that comes to mind for most people when they think of purging, behaviors like vomiting are common in both anorexia and bulimia. If we compare anorexia and bulimia, we see the following differences.

Is It Anorexia or Bulimia?	
Anorexia or starvation EDNOS	**Bulimia**
Your weight is too low, and you're able to keep your weight very low.	Your weight is normal, or you are overweight. You may be able to briefly get your weight into the low range but you can't keep it that low.
You have eating rituals such as only eating certain foods or cutting foods in a certain way.	You don't have eating rituals.
You may have true binges but usually you binge on "safe" foods. Your "binges" may not always be true binges but you think of them as binges because you eat more calories than you planned to eat. Your binges are most likely triggered by starvation.	When you binge, it's usually foods high in carbohydrates, and your binges are not centered around "safe" foods. Your binges may be triggered by stress or hunger but not by starvation.
You have obsessive and perfectionistic personality characteristics.	You are less likely to have obsessive or perfectionistic personality characteristics.
You have experienced medical problems associated with low weight, such as osteoporosis.	You haven't experienced low-weight medical problems.

Although it is rarely confused with anorexia or starvation EDNOS, binge-eating disorder is another type of eating disorder. People with binge-eating disorder binge but don't purge and are usually overweight or obese. Binge eating is associated with a number of serious medical problems such as diabetes.

THE DEADLIEST EATING DISORDER

Starvation eating disorders are the least common of all the eating disorders. While there is a lot we don't know about starvation eating disorders, there is increasing interest in research into how to treat self-imposed starvation. This interest is driven by the fact that starvation eating disorders cause more medical problems than any other eating disorder. When we compare anorexia to other mental disorders we find that anorexia is the cause of more deaths than major depression or schizophrenia. In fact, of all types of mental disorders, starvation eating disorders have the highest mortality rate (Birmingham and Beumont 2004).

to sum up

Eating disorders are diagnosed based on how many criteria for a disorder you meet. Anorexia nervosa is the most well-known starvation eating disorder. As described in this chapter, some people, like Grace, can have a serious starvation eating disorder without meeting the full criteria for anorexia, and this makes those criteria problematic because they leave out people who have a serious starvation eating disorder. For people like Grace, the diagnosis is eating disorder not otherwise specified (EDNOS)—a catchall diagnostic term that includes people with binge-eating disorder. The risk of a catchall diagnosis is that someone like Grace may need to gain weight as much as someone who is diagnosed with anorexia, but without that diagnosis, the need to gain weight may not be recognized. While all eating disorders can cause medical problems, starvation eating disorders are the type associated with more risk for serious medical problems—and your weight is a critical determinant of how high your risk is for medical problems. While there are some similarities between bulimia and starvation eating disorders, low weight and the tendency for people with starvation eating disorders to be obsessive and perfectionistic distinguish starvation eating disorders (like anorexia) from bulimia. If you think you have an eating disorder, you should be evaluated by someone with specialized knowledge of eating disorders and you should also go to your primary care doctor for a physical examination. The next chapter explores how starvation and purging affect your body.

CHAPTER 2

the starving body

much of what we know about how starvation affects the body is from a starvation experiment the U.S. government conducted during the 1940s (see Tucker 2006). Not surprisingly, what we learned from this research is that our bodies need a certain amount of fuel to function, and if our bodies are not getting enough fuel, we will experience medical complications. The medical complications of starvation can be as benign as dry skin and as dangerous as heart failure. Purging has its own risks, independent of low weight. And when you combine low weight and purging, your medical risks increase dramatically. Let's look at what we learned from the 1940s starvation experiment—one that could never be conducted today because of its severe effects on the study participants.

the world war II starvation experiment

During World War II, the U.S. government conducted an experiment that is now considered unethical. The government gave healthy young men the option of participating in a starvation experiment in lieu of serving in the military. The purpose of the experiment was twofold: (1) to study how starvation affects healthy individuals and (2) to determine how to refeed people who need weight restoration. Most of the men who volunteered for the study did so because they were pacifists whose religious beliefs were inconsistent with serving as a soldier. The men were recruited with the promise that the knowledge gained in the experiment would help the starving people of the world.

The results of this experiment, documented in Todd Tucker's book *The Great Starvation Experiment* (2006), tell us a lot about what starvation does to the brain and body. For six months the subjects in the starvation experiment were allowed to eat only about half the calories that the average young man needs to maintain a healthy weight. In addition to this very low-calorie diet, the men were required to walk twenty-two miles a week on a treadmill. The starvation phase of the experiment was designed to lead to a 25 percent reduction of weight for each man. During the starvation phase, the men were subjected to many physical and psychological tests intended to monitor the effects of starvation and weight loss. Among the physical effects observed in the men were swelling of the feet, decreased ability to do tasks involving dexterity, difficulty keeping warm, and fatigue.

The psychological effects were just as numerous as the physical effects and included strong urges to binge on food, obsessive thinking, and a decreased ability to concentrate. Depression was also often observed in the men. Chapter 3 will explore the psychological effects of starvation. Luckily for the men, after six months of starvation, each subject entered the second phase of the experiment, which consisted of three months of refeeding in order to restore weight and health.

Even though the duration of the experiment was limited, the results were so devastating to the men's health that no human-subjects review committee would allow this kind of experiment to be done today.

If you have a starvation eating disorder, your body and brain have probably been starving for much longer than six months. You may also purge regularly, something the men in the starvation experiment did not do. These differences may make your health risks even greater than were those of the men who chose to starve rather than go to war.

In addition to the World War II experiment, there have been other studies that contributed to our knowledge of the medical and psychological effects of starvation and refeeding, but the World War II experiment probably resulted in the most comprehensive understanding of the effects of starvation. The next section provides a closer look at the physical symptoms of starvation.

physical symptoms of starvation

Many of my patients with a starvation eating disorder say they want to be healthy and that being thin is healthy. In fact, patients like Amy (first mentioned in the Introduction) report that in the beginning, dieting was motivated by a desire to be healthier. After all, we all know that being overweight is not healthy. Amy, like many people who develop a starvation eating disorder, was a little overweight when she first started to diet. Ironically for Amy, what may have started out as a way to lose a few extra pounds to improve her health turned into a self-imposed starvation experiment that harmed her instead.

Let's look at how starvation impacts health. We can divide the physical effects of starvation into two categories. There are the physical effects that you can easily notice, like feeling too full every time you eat even a small amount of food, and the effects that require a medical professional and testing to diagnose, like having fragile bones.

Noticeable Symptoms of Being Too Thin

Noticeable symptoms can give you valuable information about what your starvation eating disorder is doing to your body. Read through the following list of noticeable symptoms. Check off those symptoms you have experienced in the past or are experiencing now.

- ☐ Constipation

- ☐ Gastroesophageal reflux disorder (GERD)—stomach acids coming up into your throat

- ☐ Feeling too full after eating a small amount of food

- ☐ Having difficulty sleeping—particularly waking up too early in the morning

- ☐ Dry skin

- ☐ Edema (swollen ankles and hands)

- ☐ Feeling light-headed, particularly when you stand up too fast

- ☐ Feeling tired

- ☐ Bruising easily

- ☐ Muscle weakness

- ☐ Dental problems

- ☐ For women: not having a period or having erratic periods

- ☐ Fine hair growth on your body

- ☐ Hypothermia or feeling cold all the time

How many symptoms did you check off? Look back at the symptoms you checked off; which three symptoms do you feel make the biggest impact on your life? On the next page, write down these symptoms and what bothers you most about them.

What Bothers You Most
Example: *Dental problems—I hate going to the dentist all the time and I'm embarrassed by how my teeth look.*
1.
2.
3.

making a motivational card: Motivational cards can help you keep focused on your reasons for getting well. Write down on a 3 by 5 card the most bothersome symptoms you identified. You can put the card on your bathroom mirror or someplace else where you will see it every day, or you can carry the card with you in your purse or wallet for easy review. As you continue to work through the book, you'll have other opportunities to make additional motivational cards.

Symptoms That You Can't See

Symptoms that often go unnoticed until you are experiencing major medical problems are listed next. A good example of a symptom of starvation that could go unnoticed is *osteoporosis*, a condition causing bone loss, which leads to fragile bones. Osteoporosis or the milder form of bone loss, *osteopenia*, have no noticeable symptoms in the early stages. Without a medical test, called a *bone mineral density test*, you won't know that you are losing bone mass until you have lost enough to cause pain or a broken bone.

Look over the following list and check off any symptoms you have been told you have now or have had in the past.

- ☐ Osteoporosis or osteopenia (fragile bones)

- ☐ Heart rhythm problems, including a very low heart rate

- ☐ Electrolyte disturbances (an imbalance of salts, such as too little sodium, potassium, calcium, or magnesium)

- ☐ Hormonal imbalances

- ☐ High cholesterol

- ☐ Blood abnormalities

Some of these symptoms, like a low heart rate, are clear messages to you and your doctors that your life could be shortened by your starvation eating disorder.

motivational card: On a 3 by 5 card, list any medical problems your doctor has told you that you have.

All of the symptoms on both of these lists are signs of starvation, purging, or both. Noticeable symptoms (such as constipation or feeling too full after you eat even a small amount of food) might not be life threatening but can confuse you into thinking you need to eat even less or purge more. The following discussion of these confusing symptoms will focus on why the symptoms are really signs you need to eat more, not less. *The bottom line is this:* with all of the symptoms you are experiencing, your body is trying to tell you something. Understanding what your body is telling you about your health can help you commit to getting well. One way to gain a better understanding of the messages your body is sending you is to look at how starvation and purging affect different systems in the body.

how starvation eating disorders affect the body's organ systems

Our bodies are made up of different systems with each system centering around a major organ, therefore often called *organ systems*. There are ten major organ systems. The following discussion addresses the effect of starvation on the six organ systems that are most closely associated with the medical problems seen in starvation eating disorders—the digestive, endocrine, cardiovascular, nervous, muscular, and integumentary systems. Aspects of two additional systems, the skeletal and reproductive systems, will be discussed along with the endocrine system. As you read though the descriptions of the different organ systems, use your highlighter to mark the organ system effects that you have experienced.

Digestive System

When you're not eating enough or you're purging, your body will probably react with digestive problems. I hear two common complaints from my patients. The first is that eating even a small amount of food leads to an uncomfortable, overly full feeling. The second complaint is constipation. If you have experienced these problems, you may have responded by limiting your food intake even more or increasing your use of laxatives. It makes sense that if you feel all "clogged up," you would either put less into your digestive system or use some kind of bowel stimulant like an over-the-counter laxative to get rid of that clogged-up feeling. The problem is that restricting what you eat, using laxatives, or both will make digestive problems worse.

When you starve or purge, your stomach and intestines get "lazy." A lazy stomach causes food to stay in your stomach longer than it should. This is called *delayed gastric emptying,* and it is a very common bodily response to starvation and vomiting. If you have delayed gastric emptying, even eating a few ounces of food makes you feel uncomfortably full. You may also experience mild nausea after you eat. Restricting the amount you eat will only continue to promote delayed gastric emptying. The only way to resolve this problem is to eat solid food so that your stomach gets used to food again.

Constipation is also caused by slowed functioning in your digestive system. In this case it's your intestine, not the stomach, that is stuck on slow. There are two reasons for the slowdown: (1) your body is trying to get all the fuel it can from what you are eating and (2) one of the normal signals used by the intestine to control movement is missing. The first reason makes a lot of sense. Think of it this way: if you're not taking in enough food, your body will try to compensate by getting every bit of nutrition out of the food you do eat. Unfortunately this doesn't work very well because once the food gets into the lower intestine, all the nutrients have been used up. What is left is just waste your body can't use, but when you are starving, your body does the best it can. The second reason involves the trigger provided by the physical stimulation of food—the "bulk" that is provided by vegetables and fiber. If you don't have much material in your intestine, there's little to trigger this movement and this leads to constipation. Laxative use just makes it worse. When you use a laxative on a regular basis, your body becomes dependent on the stimulation from the laxative. Over time, laxative use decreases the normal motility of the bowel, which leads to more constipation. If the constipation then causes you to use laxatives more often, a vicious cycle of laxative dependency is set up. The only way out of this vicious cycle is to give your bowel the opportunity to start working again without the laxative. Over time, without laxative stimulation, your bowel motility will return.

Endocrine System

Our bodies depend on dozens of hormones produced by many glands in the body. These hormones do everything from determining height to governing fertility and much more. Glands such as the pituitary gland respond to starvation by changing the amount of hormone the gland produces. As a result, some hormone levels decrease while, at the same time, other hormones increase. For example, levels of thyroid hormone usually decrease while levels of growth hormone often increase (the increase in some hormones may be the body's way of trying to compensate for starvation). Changes in levels of hormones that affect the skeletal system can lead to problems with bones; changes in those that affect the reproductive system can result in problems with fertility. In general, we can say that starvation throws off the balance of hormones that is needed for our bodies to work properly. Let's look at some of the major ways in which a starvation eating disorder plays havoc with our hormones.

WOMEN'S HORMONES

Many women who have a starvation eating disorder find that their periods become erratic or go away altogether. Some of my patients have even told me that not having a period is one of the things they like about having low weight. If you don't want to get pregnant, the loss of your periods may seem like "no big deal" or even a plus. However, if you want to have a baby, you may find that, like Amy, you can't get pregnant.

Whether viewed positively or negatively, not having regular periods is a sign that your body is not producing enough hormones. Consider, for example, one of the major female hormones—estrogen. A woman's body produces estrogen in several ways. You may have learned in biology class that estrogen is produced by a woman's ovaries. This is true—a woman's ovaries are one of the major sources of estrogen—but what your biology teacher may not have mentioned is that another major source of estrogen is a woman's fat cells. You might be thinking, "I don't want to get pregnant, so what's the big deal about having enough estrogen?" The answer is that estrogen is tied to many healthy body functions having nothing to do with pregnancy. Here are some of the reasons why estrogen is a young woman's best friend:

- *Osteoporosis is associated with low estrogen.* Weakened bones can lead to fractures and bone pain. We usually think of osteoporosis, or the milder osteopenia, as something that happens to old women, but if your periods stop because of an eating disorder, this is an indicator that you could develop bone loss at a very young age. Research tells us that up to 50 percent of women with anorexia will develop osteoporosis (Miller et al. 2006). If your weight is low and you're not having regular periods, you can expect to lose about 2.5 percent of your bone density a year. Unfortunately, studies have also shown that osteoporosis associated with low weight does not respond to hormone treatments, calcium supplements, or the prescription medications used to treat osteoporosis in older women. Weight gain is the only effective osteoporosis treatment for women with a starvation eating disorder (Miller et al. 2006).

- *There may be a loss of interest in sex.* Not surprisingly, healthy hormonal levels, including estrogen levels, are important for a satisfying sex life. Women with low weight often report a lack of interest in sex.

- *Infertility can be caused by low estrogen and the other hormonal changes that happen with a starvation eating disorder.* We used to think that fertility automatically returned when a woman with a starvation eating disorder gained weight, but more recent research suggests that for some women this might not be the case. Consistent with this research, many eating disorder specialists like me have stories about patients who gained enough weight to get into the normal weight range and yet their periods did not return—and they couldn't get pregnant. It may be that the longer the reproductive system is not working properly, the more likely it is that regular periods will not automatically return when you gain weight (Garner 1997).

MEN'S HORMONES

Starvation eating disorders (particularly anorexia) are much rarer in men than in women, so fewer studies have been done with men who have starvation eating disorders. Still, it appears that male hormones are also affected by low weight. Here are some of the problems men with low weight experience:

- *Starvation decreases testosterone (the major male hormone).* This decreases the size of a man's testicles.

- *Fertility is affected.* Men with a starvation eating disorder may find they are producing too few sperm to father a child.

- *There may be a loss of interest in sex.* Even young men, who should be experiencing an increased interest in sex, report a lack of interest in sex, with severe weight loss.

■ *Muscularity in men is significantly supported by testosterone.* Without testosterone, a man will not be able to build muscle and will find his muscles wasting away.

LOW THYROID FUNCTION

Both men and women with a starvation eating disorder experience other hormonal problems. One common problem is a condition involving low thyroid function called *hypothyroidism*. Insufficient thyroid hormone leads to fatigue and dry skin and contributes to constipation and just generally feeling unhealthy.

GROWTH PROBLEMS

Growth hormone is also affected by starvation. Growth hormone levels can actually increase with starvation. This may be the body's way of trying to compensate for starvation. Despite this compensation, puberty can be postponed and growth can be permanently stunted for children with a starvation eating disorder. This is one of the reasons why a starvation eating disorder in a child needs to be addressed very quickly.

Cardiovascular System

As organs go, the heart is pretty simple: it's basically just a big muscle. Starvation eating disorders affect every muscle in the body, so it's not surprising that they negatively affect the heart as well. When the body is starving, the need to keep the brain going becomes the body's first priority, so the body takes energy from any fat available. When the fat is used up, the body starts to use the energy stored in your muscles, including your heart. The effects of starvation on the heart include slowed heart rate (called *bradycardia*), difficulty recovering between each beat (leading to altered heart rhythm or *arrhythmias*), and wasting away of the heart (*cardiomyopathy*), making your heart too small to function.

During the World War II starvation experiment, one of the cardiovascular symptoms that confused both the men and the doctors was the swelling of feet and ankles most of the men experienced. This swelling (*dependent edema*) is caused by poor cardiovascular function, which leaves fluid in your feet and ankles. Basically, the heart and the rest of the cardiovascular system, the veins and arteries, can't move fluid around very well if you're not taking in enough food. The farther the fluid is from your heart, the more work is required to move it around. So if your heart is struggling, fluid can be left in the feet and ankles because of their greater distance from your heart. If you have a starvation eating disorder and you notice that your ankles are getting big, your ankles are not "fat"; this edema (fluid buildup) is a sign that your heart is struggling. Anorexia has the highest rate of mortality of any mental disorder, and heart problems are one of the leading causes of death (Birmingham and Beumont 2004).

The effect of starvation on your heart is why exercise can be so dangerous for you. Remember Joe from chapter 1? Joe spent hours at the gym each day. If Joe's weight had been in the normal range, his dedication to exercise would have been healthy. However, Joe's low weight put him at risk for heart failure even when he wasn't exercising. In fact, the daily trips to the gym increased Joe's risk of dying many times over. *The bottom line is this:* if you have a starvation eating disorder, you need to have a physical exam to determine the health of your heart and you should not exercise until you gain weight.

HIGH CHOLESTEROL

One of the symptoms of starvation that confuses a lot of people is having high cholesterol. Fat and high cholesterol are bad, right? We've all seen TV advertisements for cholesterol-lowering drugs, and those ads tell us that if our cholesterol is high, we should eat less fat. But we all need fat in our diets. As mentioned, fat cells play an important part in hormone production. Another reason we need fat is that our body uses it to make *cell membranes.* Our bodies are made up of trillions of cells—little packages of DNA and enzymes that perform our body functions. Cell membranes form a container that keeps the insides of our cells in and protects that content from material that's outside of our cells. That membrane is also a filter that lets only certain things through. One of the building blocks of the membrane is a double layer of fat molecules. Without fat, we can't make new cells or replace those cells that become worn out.

"Okay," you might be saying, "fat is good, but I have high cholesterol, and that means I eat too much fat and so I must have enough fat and need less fat, right?" If you have a starvation eating disorder and you have been told that your cholesterol is high even though you eat very little fat, the answer is *not* to eat less fat. It's not known precisely why people with very low weight often have high cholesterol, but, like many other things about starvation, your body's balance gets disrupted, and things that should be low can be high and things that should be high can be low. Luckily the solution to the cholesterol problem is clear. People with a starvation eating disorder find that gaining weight brings their cholesterol into the healthy range. Unlike people who are obese and may need to eat a very low-fat diet, if you have a starvation eating disorder, you should include fats in your diet.

Nervous System

The brain, spinal cord, and nerves make up the central nervous system, but it's the brain that is most affected by starvation. Most of us would agree that who we are is largely determined by the brain. The body's job is to keep the brain alive and functioning. There is only one kind of fuel that our brains can use—sugar in the form of glucose. The body takes anything we eat and makes it into glucose for the brain. So if you are starving your body, your brain is also being starved. Chapter 3 will describe how the starving brain experiences distorted and slowed thinking, how emotions also get distorted from starvation, and, perhaps scariest of all, how the starving brain gets smaller.

Muscular System

All muscles are affected by starvation. As shown in the exploration of the cardiovascular system, the heart is a muscle and starvation can lead to wasting of the heart muscle. Other muscles in the body also waste away when someone is starving. The result of this wasting is small, "flabby" looking muscles that have little tone. Over time, if enough of the large muscles in the legs and torso are wasted, it can be hard for someone who is starving to stand or walk. Weight lifting will not tone muscles that are wasted. The only way to tone the muscles is to feed the muscles.

Integumentary System

Our skin, hair, and nails are part of a system called the *integumentary system*. You may have noticed that your skin is very dry and that you have fine hair growing all over your body. The dryness and the fine hair (called *lanugo*) are common symptoms of starvation. Hair loss and brittle nails are another common problem. All of these problems are a direct result of not eating enough. The changes in skin can be particularly dramatic: longer-term starvation can make your skin look twenty or more years older than you actually are.

the effects of purging

It's not just starvation that causes medical complications—purging causes its own problems. As described earlier in this chapter, the combination of purging and low weight is very risky. But even if your weight is in the normal range, purging affects the body. Common ways to purge are laxative abuse, vomiting, and extreme exercise. While each way to purge has its own set of problems, if you combine laxative abuse and vomiting, the combination increases your risk for medical complications. Adding extreme exercise increases your risk even more. In addition, the frequency of vomiting, the amount of laxatives, and the amount of time you spend exercising are all factors that increase risk. *The bottom line is this:* the more you purge, the more dangerous it is.

To learn more about how purging affects the body, let's look at the specific medical problems caused by different types of purging.

Vomiting

The most common complication caused by vomiting is gastroesophageal reflux disorder (GERD). If you have GERD, you may have experienced minor symptoms such as heartburn or regurgitation (stomach acids coming up into your mouth). Over time, regurgitation can damage the esophagus and lead to more serious symptoms, including damage to the cells lining the esophagus, causing inflammation. The esophagus can become scarred or even rupture (Mitchell et al. 1987). There is also concern that these cellular changes can lead to cancer of the throat or esophagus (Vesper et al. 2008).

Vomiting also damages teeth by eroding the tooth enamel, promoting cavity development, and damaging gums (Birmingham and Beumont 2004). Visible signs that your teeth have been affected include discoloration of your teeth and receding or bleeding gums. Some of my patients have spent countless hours at the dentist and thousands of dollars in an effort to prevent tooth loss. Losing teeth is not uncommon, and once the damage is done, it is very hard to correct.

Laxative Abuse

As described earlier in this chapter, laxative abuse just leads to more constipation and dependency on the laxative. Ironically, the total loss of calories associated with laxative abuse is no more than 4 percent of the calories eaten in any day, so it's a very ineffective weight-loss strategy. The more serious effects of laxative abuse include gastrointestinal bleeding, protein loss, and permanent damage to the bowel (Birmingham and Beumont 2004).

Extreme Exercise

For people with a starvation eating disorder, exercising for hours is a common way to compensate for food eaten. Some of my patients report that they feel the urge to exercise constantly throughout the day in the same way that others feel the urge to vomit many times a day. While going to the gym daily is one way to engage in extreme exercise, some people also try to burn as many calories as possible by staying in constant motion, rarely sitting, constantly tensing muscles, or finding other ways to burn calories without being noticed. This can be thought of as *covert extreme exercise*. A few of my patients have even said they feel like exercise is an addiction. While not an addiction in the true sense, the urge to exercise, like the urge to engage in other self-harm behaviors, is often very strong. Extreme exercise depletes the calories your brain and body need to function normally, and if your heart rate is too low, your heart may not be able to keep up with the stress of exercise. Sudden death while you are exercising can occur if your heart can't keep up. In addition, exercising for long periods of time without giving your body sufficient time to rest in between can make you more prone to injuries. *The bottom line is this*: extreme exercise, even if it is covert, will interfere with gaining weight and getting well and should be addressed as a form of purging.

Syrup of Ipecac

Eating disorder specialists like me are becoming increasingly concerned about another twist on purging. Syrup of ipecac is being used by some people to purge. *Syrup of ipecac* causes vomiting and is meant to be used when someone ingests a poison. The usefulness of ipecac is in question and some experts are not recommending its use in cases of accidental poisoning. Taken repeatedly, syrup of ipecac can cause damage to the heart, which makes this form of purging the most dangerous of all the purging methods.

Syrup of ipecac's effects on the heart include wasting of the heart muscle, arrhythmia, and heart failure (Lock and Le Grange 2005). We don't know exactly how much ipecac it takes to damage the heart, but using ipecac more than once or twice for emergencies is dangerous.

While it appears that if you stop using ipecac, your heart can recover, we don't know how long a heart needs to recover, and sudden death from ipecac abuse has been documented (Silber 2005). If you have used ipecac recently, you should go to your doctor and let her know that you have been using ipecac to purge.

Evaluating Your Purging Risks

While we can't predict if you will definitely experience a particular medical problem based on your method and frequency of purging, we know that the more often you purge and the more ways you purge, the higher your risk will be for serious medical problems. The following questions will give you an idea of how risky your purging behavior is.

Vomiting, over the last two weeks:

☐ I purged by vomiting at least once but not more than two days each week (1 point).

☐ I vomited three to four days each week (2 points).

☐ I vomited every day or nearly every day (3 points).

For the days you did vomit, circle the average number of times you vomited.

Once	**Two to three times**	**Four or more times**
Lower risk (1 point)	Moderate risk (2 points)	High risk (3 points)

Laxative abuse, over the last two weeks:

☐ I used laxatives at least once a week (2 points).

☐ I used laxatives three to four times a week (3 points).

☐ I used laxatives every day or nearly every day (4 points).

On days when you did use laxatives, circle the average number of doses you took each day.

One	**Two or three**	**Four or more**
Lower risk (1 point)	Moderate risk (2 points)	High risk (3 points)

Exercise, over the last two weeks:

☐ I exercised one to two hours, several times each week (1 point).

☐ I exercised one to two hours each day (2 points).

☐ I exercised two to three hours each day (3 points).

☐ I exercised more than three hours each day (4 points).

Syrup of ipecac, over the last two weeks:

☐ I used ipecac once in two weeks (3 points).

☐ I used ipecac twice in two weeks (5 points).

☐ I used ipecac two or more times in two weeks (8 points).

Scoring note: If you use ipecac, you will need to add incidents of vomiting to the incidents of ipecac use when you add up your points. So, for example, if you use ipecac once a week, you will have 3 points for that as well as points for the number of times you vomited, with ipecac and without.

Now add up your points. Total points: _____

In general, the lower your total points, the lower your relative risk for having medical complications from purging.

Relative risk:	Low	Moderate	High
Total points:	3 or below	4–7 points	8 or above

Remember, "low risk" doesn't mean you won't have any purging-related medical problems. But the less you purge, the lower your overall risk for serious medical problems will be. If you scored in the moderate or high-risk categories, decreasing the number of times you purge each day can make an important difference. Purging leads to more purging and interferes with weight gain. You will have the opportunity to develop a plan to address purging (see Self-Harm-Reduction Plan in chapter 9). By getting your purging under control, you will lay a good foundation for successful weight gain and decrease your risk for medical problems.

"but I feel fine"

If you have a starvation eating disorder, you may be thinking that starving yourself or purging is not hurting your health because you feel fine. But as described in this chapter, some medical complications are not noticeable until the symptoms become serious. A related problem is that people with starvation eating disorders often ignore physical symptoms that indicate starvation or purging are causing problems. This makes sense because if you ignore the signals your body is giving you, it's easier to continue to starve and purge.

Listening to your body can give you valuable information about what your starvation eating disorder is doing to your physical health. Listening to your body can also help you make a commitment to getting well. Complete the next exercise, Listening to Your Body, to zero in on how your starvation eating disorder has affected your body.

Listening to Your Body

Ask yourself the following questions and write down what you have noticed about your body after each question. The more complete your answer is, the more you can learn from listening to your body.

An example from Grace's answers:
Am I tired when other people aren't? *Yes, I'm having trouble keeping up with my children. My friends don't seem to have the same level of fatigue I have. I am going to bed earlier and earlier because I'm so tired.*

■ Am I tired when other people aren't?

_____

■ Is my skin drier than it used to be?

_____

■ Do I wake up in the early morning before I have had enough sleep?

_____

■ For women: Have my periods stopped or are they irregular?

_____

■ Is my hair falling out?

_____

■ Are my ankles and hands puffy even though people consider me to be thin?

_____

■ Do I feel cold all the time even when other people are feeling warm?

_____

How many times did you answer yes? Each "Yes" answer is your body trying to tell you that you need to eat more and stop purging.

motivational card: Here's another opportunity to make a motivational card. Write down your answers to Listening to Your Body on one or more 3 by 5 cards.

to sum up

Starvation eating disorders affect every organ system in the body. Some of the effects of starvation, like constipation or dry skin, are very noticeable. Other symptoms of starvation and purging can go unnoticed until a major medical problem, like a heart rhythm problem, occurs. The medical complications caused by starving and purging not only put you at risk for an early death but can affect your quality of life. Being too tired to enjoy activities, spending a lot of time at the dentist's, and losing interest in sex are all changes that can decrease your quality of life. Getting in touch with how your starvation eating disorder has affected your body can help you make the decision to get well. The next chapter will explore how starving and purging can affect your brain.

CHAPTER 3

the starving brain

Our brains are complex, and there is much that is unknown about how they work, but we do know that starvation affects the brain in profound ways. Our brains use both chemical and electrical signals to function. For example, thoughts are made up of signals within brain cells and between brain cells. Chemical and electrical signals from the brain also make our bodies move and control how our organs function. In order to send these various signals, brains need fuel, and the fuel our brains need is glucose. Human brains are greedy when it comes to glucose. While the brain accounts for only about 2 percent of body mass, it uses up about half of the glucose our bodies make. *The bottom line is this*: our brains need a lot of fuel.

Improvements in brain imaging allow us to see some of the effects of starvation on the brain. For example, starvation reduces both the total volume of brain tissue and the blood flow to the brain (Frank et al. 2007). We also see cognitive or intellectual problems when a brain is deprived of glucose. Cognitive issues can include problems with memory, concentration, doing complex mental tasks, or reasoning. Our emotions are affected by a lack of fuel too. Depression and anxiety are common results of a starving brain. While it appears that when weight is restored, brain volume and blood flow return to normal, researchers don't yet know if all cognitive and other problems resolve fully with weight gain. The next section will take a more detailed look at how starvation causes emotional and intellectual problems.

the psychological effects of starvation

Remember the World War II starvation experiment? At the start of the experiment, these men (who as pacifists had strong religious and political views on war and social policy) spent much of their time discussing the war and politics. But after just a short time in the starvation phase of the experiment, the men's conversations became almost exclusively focused on food. Starvation turned all of the men, who had entered the experiment as articulate and engaged men, into people who could only think about food (Tucker 2006).

From the World War II experiment and from studying people who have a starvation eating disorder, we have learned that the following psychological symptoms are caused (or made worse) by starvation:

- Emotional problems, including depression, anxiety, and moodiness

- Obsessional thinking, including preoccupation with food

- Strong desire to binge eat

- Compulsive behaviors, including food rituals

- Distorted thinking, including thinking you are overweight or that you have to do everything perfectly

- Withdrawal from social activities

Let's look at a few of these symptoms in detail.

Depression, Anxiety, and Moodiness

If your weight gets low enough, you are guaranteed to feel at least some symptoms of depression and anxiety. Emotions from a starving brain are driven by two factors:

- Starvation eating disorder thinking (which will be examined later in this chapter)

- The effect on the electrical and chemical signals when your brain doesn't have enough fuel to function properly

Think about what your car needs to run smoothly. It needs gasoline and oil, and if it doesn't have enough of either, it will run rough and then just stop. If your brain isn't getting enough fuel, you will have a hard time keeping a steady mood and may find that you move back and forth between feeling down and anxious. Purging just adds to the depression and anxiety that starvation causes. Moodiness is a common problem for people with eating disorders, and many people with a starvation eating disorder experience significant depression.

Anxiety may be a more significant problem than depression. Most people with a starvation eating disorder find that anxiety is a constant companion while the brain is starving (for example, ruminating about weight-related concerns is a common problem). You may have tried to control your anxiety about weight by eating less and purging more. The problem is that starvation and purging just make anxiety, like depression, worse. Anxiety is such a core feature of starvation eating disorders that chapter 5 will focus on its role. For now, take the survey below to see if you are experiencing symptoms of anxiety or depression.

Are You Experiencing Depression or Anxiety?		
Depression		
Do you feel down, sad, or depressed most of the time?	Yes	No
Have you lost interest in activities you used to enjoy?	Yes	No
Do you feel more down in the morning than at other times of day?	Yes	No
Do you feel hopeless or think about dying?	Yes	No
Anxiety		
Do you ruminate about things other than food or weight?	Yes	No
Does worry interfere with your sleep?	Yes	No
Do you sometimes feel so panicky that you avoid doing normal, routine things like driving on the freeway or going to the mall?	Yes	No
Do you wash your hands over and over again or check and recheck doors, locks, and appliances many times?	Yes	No

If you are having problems with your anxiety or depression, you may wonder which should be treated first, the eating disorder or the mood problem. In the case of a starvation eating disorder, the answer is clear. If your brain is starving, you will not feel emotionally good until your brain has enough fuel to function properly, so treating a mood problem without gaining weight will not be helpful. It would be like putting oil in your car but not adding gas and then expecting your car to run. Without enough fuel, your brain can't produce a normal mood no matter what else you do to try to feel better. This is why treatments that focus on emotions (for example, talk therapy or taking antidepressant drugs) are usually ineffective for people with very low weight. That is not to say that it's not helpful to talk about how you feel once you gain weight—it just means that if your weight is very low, you will feel depressed and anxious regardless of how much you talk about your feelings.

Obsessional Thinking, Preoccupation with Food, and Binge Eating

Most people with a starvation eating disorder started out worrying about weight and thinking about food before weight loss. Amy (first described in the Introduction) was certainly typical of someone who was concerned about her weight before she started starving herself. What Amy didn't realize was that her extreme dieting only increased her obsession with food and weight. Starvation intensified Amy's natural tendencies to be perfectionistic and to worry about her body weight and shape. By the time I saw Amy, she had been starving for fifteen years and her obsession with weight and food had taken over her life.

The focus on food and weight makes sense from the brain's point of view. As the starving body struggles to make enough fuel, the brain sends a starvation message to the body. We can think of this as the "feed me" message. The less the body is able to feed the brain, the louder the "feed me" message becomes until all the starving brain can think about is food. If you have a starvation eating disorder, you know how strong the "feed me" message can be. This message can lead to binge eating or to an overwhelming fear that once you start eating, you won't be able to stop. In the starvation experiment, when the men were finally able to eat, they binged on food. Binge eating is also what happened when starving prisoners were released from the concentration camps at the end of World War II. All of this tells us that binge eating is the normal response to starvation.

When Amy's brain started to send out the "feed me" message, this conflicted with Amy's anxiety about being fat and eating too much. This set up a war inside Amy, and after a short time she was thinking almost exclusively about eating, food, being fat, getting rid of food, and how she was being weak if she ate more food than she planned. This internal conflict and the effects of starvation on the chemical and brain circuitry caused Amy to become completely obsessed with food and weight.

Compulsive Behaviors and Food Rituals

In addition to food obsession, we know from the World War II experiment and from talking to people with starvation eating disorders that a starving brain will increase compulsive behavior. The men in the study didn't start out being picky about how they cut their food or the order in which they ate food. But during the starvation phase of the experiment, many of the men became compulsive about how they ate. Compulsive behavior is not restricted to food; once the brain becomes more compulsive about food, the tendency to be compulsive spills over to other things. Here are some of the ways compulsivity is expressed when the brain is being starved; check off any behaviors you engage in:

- ☐ *Food rituals:* Eating only certain foods prepared certain ways, cutting food into small pieces and arranging it on the plate, or only eating at certain times of the day

- ☐ *Perfectionism:* Being a perfectionist about school, work, personal care, or housekeeping

- ☐ *Rigidity:* Having difficulty with change and wanting to keep to a rigid schedule

As will be described in chapter 5, having perfectionist or obsessive-compulsive personality traits may make someone more likely to develop a starvation eating disorder. And, in the same way that anxiety intensifies once the brain is starving, so obsessive-compulsive tendencies are amped up when you starve your brain.

Starvation Eating Disorder Thinking

Although we don't know exactly how thoughts are formed in the brain, we do know that lack of glucose affects both the chemical and electrical signals in the brain that are involved in thought patterns. Starvation can also lead to brain-cell death. Perhaps for these reasons, starvation causes *distorted thinking*, sometimes called *eating disorder thinking* or *anorexic thinking*. When you think something over and over, it becomes a thought habit. If your brain is starving, the thoughts you think over and over again will be distorted. Over time, the distorted thinking becomes more and more automatic until all your thoughts are affected. This explains why even after the brain has enough fuel to function, some distorted thoughts persist. Chapter 12 will look at how to change distorted thinking about food and weight into healthy thinking. However, the techniques you will learn in chapter 12 will only help you change your thinking if your brain is getting enough food.

The connection between thoughts and feelings is strong. Thoughts about gaining weight will cause anxiety just as thoughts about being a failure can make us feel sad. This strong connection between thoughts and emotions means that if your thoughts are distorted, your emotions will be distorted too, and distorted emotions then cause more distorted thoughts. Figure 1 shows this cycle of distorted thoughts and emotions. We can see this in Grace's thinking. Whenever Grace was faced with eating any kind of high-calorie food,

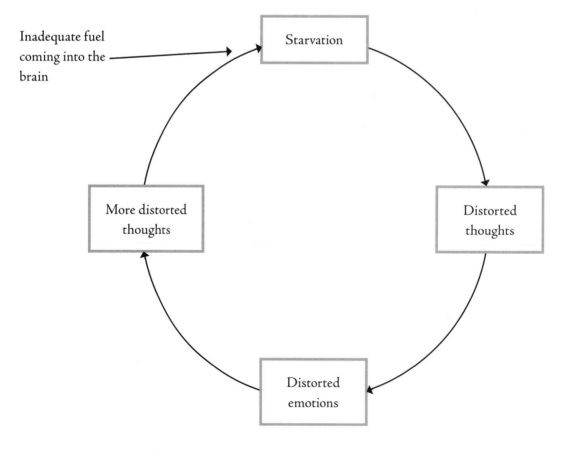

FIGURE 1: The vicious cycle of starvation

such as ice cream, she immediately had distorted thoughts about being too fat, which led her to feel very anxious. Grace's anxiety then triggered more thoughts about being overweight.

Withdrawal: Food and Weight Become Everything

Having a starvation eating disorder can also be a lonely experience when food and weight become everything. You may have noticed that you avoid social situations and have withdrawn from life since your starvation eating disorder took control of your life. Eating is a social activity for most of us, so fear of eating in public or concern that others will try to get you to eat can cause you to isolate yourself and withdraw from your family and friends. Grace found that her life became dominated by food and weight. Her marriage suffered, and she stopped seeing her friends. When she did socialize, she found that she spent more time thinking about her weight and worrying about eating in front of others than she did about the people she was with. To see if you are withdrawing from life, look over this list of ways people with starvation eating disorders avoid normal social situations. Check off any of the descriptions on the list that fit you.

- ☐ Only eating alone

- ☐ Helping in the kitchen—getting people food or doing dishes so you don't have to eat or sit at the table with others

- ☐ Declining invitations to go to restaurants or saying you have already eaten or are just there to keep others company

- ☐ Avoiding eating with your family by giving excuses like, "I got up early and ate" or "I'm still full from lunch and I'll eat later"

- ☐ Staying in your room away from family members

- ☐ Spending a lot of time alone at the gym

- ☐ Turning down invitations to socialize because you don't want to change your exercise schedule to go out with friends or family

If you saw yourself in any of these descriptions, you are probably withdrawing from others. Isolating yourself from your family and friends will make your eating disorder worse and isolation will add to any depression you are experiencing. As you get well, you will learn to reconnect with others.

what scares you the most?

At this point you should have a good idea of how your starvation eating disorder is affecting your physical and psychological health. As you read through the problems that starvation and purging can cause, was there anything that really scared you? For Amy it was thinking she might never be able to be a mother. Joe was worried about his heart. One of my patients who was a writer used her answers to What Scares You the Most to remind herself what could happen to her ability to write if she continued to starve her brain. Answer the following questions to see what worries you the most.

What Scares You the Most

Physical symptoms: Rank the physical complications from starvation and purging (from 1 for the most anxiety provoking to 9 for the least anxiety provoking for you).

_____   Having problems with my heart

_____   My hair falling out

_____   My bones being brittle

_____   Not being able to have a baby

_____   Losing my teeth

_____   Small, flabby muscles

_____   Loss of sex drive

_____   Old-looking skin

_____   GERD

Psychological symptoms: Rank the psychological complications from starvation and purging (from 1 for the most anxiety provoking to 7 for the least anxiety provoking for you).

_____   Being depressed

_____   Losing brain cells

_____   Not being able to work because my eating disorder has taken over

_____   My anxiety getting out of control

_____   Being so caught up in my eating disorder that I don't think about my family

_____   Not being able to think well enough to do the things I want to do (for example, go to school, write)

_____   Losing my friends

---

motivational card: Look at the motivational cards you have already made. Are your worst fears reflected in what you have written on the cards? At this point your fear can be your best friend because it can motivate you to continue your commitment to being well and free of your starvation eating disorder. As you work through this book, you will have to commit yourself to doing frightening things. The fear of what might happen if you don't get well can help you face the fear you have about eating and gaining weight.

to sum up

Starvation eating disorders don't affect just the body. Starvation and purging have powerful effects on the brain. Starvation causes depression and anxiety, and, unless you gain weight, it's unlikely that your symptoms of depression or anxiety will resolve. A starving brain is also the perfect environment for distorted thoughts. These thoughts help to keep your starvation eating disorder strong and promote obsessive thinking and compulsive behaviors like food rituals or checking your weight many times a day (which, in turn, just make starvation eating disorders worse, as will be described in chapter 5). Over time, food, weight, and shape become everything, and you may isolate yourself from family and friends.

Staying motivated means keeping in touch with the damage that starvation and purging can do to your body and brain. Review your motivational cards when you start to think that you don't need to gain weight or stop purging. You can start to talk back to your starvation eating disorder with the knowledge you have gained in these chapters.

CHAPTER 4

how did I get this way?

Starvation eating disorders are confusing. Particularly in the United States, where obesity is on the rise and most Americans have difficulty saying no to the readily available range of food, self-imposed starvation is the exception. If you have a starvation eating disorder or love someone who is starving, you have probably asked why, when a lot of Americans are eating too much, are some people eating too little?

what causes starvation eating disorders?

The nature versus nurture debate is alive and well for all psychological disorders—and eating disorders are no exception. It's easy to use the culture's emphasis on thinness, the media, parents, traumatic life events, or the need for control to build an argument for each of these factors being the cause of eating disorders. Despite the surface logic of these arguments, there's little research data to support the idea that culture, media, parents, trauma, or the need for control cause starvation eating disorders. This does not mean that factors like overprotective parents or advertising are not involved at all, but it is clear that these factors alone do not cause starvation eating disorders. The truth is that all psychological disorders are caused by a combination of (1) the genes we inherit from our parents, (2) how we are raised, (3) the culture we grow up in, and (4) the events that happen to us. So the question is never, "Is it nature or nurture?" but rather how much of a disorder is caused by genes, how much is environmental, and what is the interaction between our genes and our environment.

Biology

As with many other psychological disorders, the impact of biological factors on starvation eating disorders is strong (Lock and Le Grange 2005). The most likely explanation for why people develop eating disorders like anorexia is that biology provides a strong vulnerability or predisposition to developing an eating disorder and then other factors add to a person's vulnerability. Biological factors include genetic factors and, possibly, things we might be exposed to, such as infectious disease. Eating disorders are complex, and there are multiple factors that might make a person susceptible to developing an eating disorder, but probably the strongest single factor is genetics. Few if any psychological disorders are purely genetic; no one develops schizophrenia, for example, because of one or two genes, and it's the same with starvation eating disorders. But heritability studies have shown that the heritability of starvation eating disorders is at least 50 percent, meaning that genes inherited from parents are at least 50 percent responsible for the development of a starvation eating disorder (Gorwood, Kipman, and Foulon 2003). This includes inheriting personality traits like perfectionism, which can make you vulnerable to developing a starvation eating disorder, as well as inheriting the ability to lose weight quickly. Being able to lose weight quickly is an important biological factor. Eating disorder specialists like me often see patients who are trying to lose enough weight to become underweight but just can't do it. Some of these patients may go on to develop a different type of eating disorder, but they don't often develop a starvation eating disorder. If you don't drop weight quickly, it's very easy to go back to eating more, but if you're the kind of person who loses weight as soon as you start restricting calories, you'll be much more likely to continue engaging in a behavior that you perceive to be helping you succeed in your goal.

In the same way that the ability to lose weight quickly can set the foundation for a starvation eating disorder, personality traits can also be an important factor. For example, a perfectionist is likely to be able to stick to a plan of eating only so many calories a day. Because personality traits play such a large role in starvation eating disorders, you will have the opportunity later in this chapter to look at how your personality traits probably make it easier for you to engage in imposed starvation.

PANDAS

In addition to genetically based factors, other biological factors have been investigated in the search for what causes starvation eating disorders. One that may play a role is strep throat. Strep throat is caused by a bacterium called group A beta-hemolytic streptococcus (GABHS). In some children, if the infection goes untreated, the GABHS bacteria can cause an autoimmune reaction. This autoimmune reaction is called pediatric autoimmune neuropsychiatric disorder associated with streptococcal infection (PANDAS). PANDAS is thought to be a contributing factor in some psychological disorders such as obsessive-compulsive disorder (OCD). As will be described in chapter 5, obsessive thinking and compulsive behavior are very common in people with a starvation eating disorder. We also know that if you have a starvation eating disorder, you are at higher risk for developing OCD than someone without a starvation eating disorder. This connection between OCD and starvation eating disorders has led to research into a possible link between anorexia and PANDAS. This research, which is ongoing, has resulted in some evidence that PANDAS could be involved.

While it is unlikely that PANDAS cause most cases of anorexia, it may be a factor for some people who have a starvation eating disorder (Puxley et al. 2008).

At this point you may be saying that if even genes and biological factors like strep throat are involved, don't factors like a thin-at-any-cost culture reinforced by Western media, parents, or traumatic events make people want to get as thin as possible? Let's take a look at these factors to see how environment might affect the development of a starvation eating disorder.

Culture and Media

We are all aware of Western culture's emphasis on thinness. All we have to do is pick up a fashion magazine to see the influence of the "thin culture." Many fashion models are too thin to be healthy, and if a model is not thin enough, no problem—digital technology can thin out her legs and make them longer at the same time. Public awareness of eating disorders among high-fashion models has increased recently, but it's not just what we see in advertising or on the runway that emphasizes thinness—every time we turn around, someone is proposing some new diet to lose weight. Talking about losing weight, the latest diet, or the size of one's thighs is more socially accepted than talking about politics or money! Despite this emphasis on losing weight, obesity is on the rise. If our thin-at-any-cost culture caused starvation eating disorders, you might expect a lot more people to be suffering with a starvation eating disorder. But the truth is, the rise in obesity has more closely tracked the emphasis on thinness in our culture and media than has the incidence of starvation eating disorders.

While obesity has been steadily on the rise, the data on prevalence of starvation eating disorders is more complex. A fifty-year study in the Midwest of the incidence of anorexia (starting in 1935 and ending in 1984) showed that anorexia had increased in adolescents but not in adults (Lucas et al. 1991). One might expect, given the cultural pressure to be thin, that more recent studies would show an increase in adult cases of anorexia, but a 2003 review of research found that the prevalence of anorexia increased somewhat in the 1970s and then stopped increasing (Hoek and van Hoeken 2003). So it would appear that most of the teens in the fifty-year study had an episode of starvation that did not extend into adulthood. Complicating the picture even more, rates of anorexia in England, a country that is as obsessed with thinness much as is the United Sates, have remained very stable (Currin et al. 2005).

It is not just the prevalence and incidence studies that tell us that culture on its own isn't the driving force behind the development of a starvation eating disorder. Another piece of evidence is that self-imposed starvation existed before thin was "in." The first known description of anorexia is in a medical text from 1689, and there are other descriptions, from the 1700s and 1800s, of patients with anorexia. The only differences between these historic cases and modern cases of anorexia are the reasons patients give for self-imposed starvation. The first description of anorexia in a seventeenth-century woman provides a good example. In the 1600s in Europe, the large curvy woman with extra fat on her body was considered beautiful, as can be seen in the art of the time. This early patient didn't explain her starvation by saying that she didn't want to be fat; instead, she reported religious reasons for her self-imposed starvation (Silverman 1997). So her rationale differed, but her symptoms were the same as someone with a starvation eating disorder today.

Although it's clear that culture does not cause starvation eating disorders, it's not accurate to say that culture has no effect. Culture likely has a role in encouraging larger numbers of adolescents to diet and in the trends toward thinner fashion models. For someone who has an eating disorder, culture also likely affects the thoughts you have about why you need to be thin rather than your starvation eating disorder itself. Also, once you have an eating disorder, our culture reinforces the push to lose more weight. Culture can also reinforce behavior through social pressure. For example, being told, "Wow, how did you lose weight? I wish I could lose weight!" might reinforce your weight loss and encourage you to lose more. I have been surprised to hear that many of my patients get comments from people like, "I wish I had the problem of being too thin." These comments not only reinforce distorted starvation thinking but also totally invalidate the emotional pain starvation eating disorders cause.

But it's not just the comments people make that reinforce starvation eating disorders; cultural icons like fashion models also give us the idea that being very thin is a good thing. We don't realize when we look in a fashion magazine that pictures have been altered to make a model's legs look even longer and thinner or that some of the models are starving themselves; we just see a body that is supposed to be ideal.

And if fashion isn't enough to make us think we need to be thin, the ready availability of weight-loss information in books, online, and on TV can make us feel that everyone is—or should be—dieting.

It's hard to get away from all the messages our culture is giving us about losing weight and being thin. So, while living in a culture that emphasizes thinness does not cause starvation eating disorders, culture can make it harder to get well. Complete the How Culture Is Reinforcing Your Eating Disorder exercise to see how it's affecting you.

How Culture Is Reinforcing Your Eating Disorder

Social pressure:

What comments do you get from others that you make you feel you need to lose more weight or stay very thin? _____

_____

Social icons:

How does comparing your body to the typical fashion model affect you? _____

_____

Diet information:

How much time do you spend reading about diets, talking about diets, or trying new diets? How does this affect your thinking about food and your weight? _____

_____

Parents

Parent-blaming is a time-honored tradition for all psychological disorders. There was a time when schizophrenia and autism were thought to be caused by bad mothering (at the time, only mothers were thought to be the root of these severe disorders, leaving fathers out of the blame theories). We now know that both of these disorders are largely biological in nature and not caused by mothers, good or bad. Family dysfunction or bad parenting can make us vulnerable to developing a wide range of problems including depression, anxiety disorders, asthma, obesity, or an eating disorder, but "bad" parenting does not cause most disorders. As with schizophrenia, there is no evidence that starvation eating disorders are *caused* by bad parenting or family dysfunction (Benninghoven et al. 2007). Most people with a starvation eating disorder do not report bad childhoods, but, like autism or schizophrenia, a starvation eating disorder can create family problems. It's not hard to imagine how confused parents, watching a child starve, would blame each other or even their child. Family conflict is often a consequence of parents' confusion and fear.

Although parents do not cause starvation eating disorders, there are a few family characteristics that are associated with such disorders. If you have a starvation eating disorder, it is more likely that your parents were anxious or overprotective. Anxiety is a core symptom of starvation eating disorders. In addition, a family focus on thinness or being perfect can make it harder for a child who is at risk for developing a starvation eating disorder. Answer the following questions to see how your family may have influenced you.

Anxiety, Perfection, and Focus on Thinness		
Do you have a close biological relative who is very anxious or has been diagnosed with an anxiety disorder such as obsessive-compulsive disorder?	Yes	No
Did your parents tend to be overprotective?	Yes	No
Do you have a parent who is a perfectionist?	Yes	No
Growing up, did you get the feeling you had to be perfect?	Yes	No
Was one or both of your parents concerned with being thin?	Yes	No

If you answered yes to two or more questions, it's likely that your parents' anxiety, perfectionistic tendencies, or concern about weight influenced your starvation eating disorder.

Trauma

While there is an association between trauma and some psychological disorders, few disorders, with the exception of *post-traumatic stress disorder* (PTSD), are caused by trauma. And even in the case of PTSD, there may be biological factors that make someone vulnerable to developing it in the aftermath of trauma. Starvation eating disorders are less associated with trauma than is bulimia, and even bulimia is only weakly associated with trauma (Lock and Le Grange 2005). This does not mean that if you have experienced trauma in your life, your experience hasn't affected you. It's just that most people with a starvation eating disorder have not had a traumatic experience (such as a rape), and there is no reason to believe that trauma causes eating disorders. If you have experienced some kind of trauma that you feel you need to work through in psychotherapy, you should gain weight first. Trying to come to terms with a trauma when your brain is starving is nearly impossible.

Control

A need for control has been proposed as a possible factor in starvation eating disorders. Needing to be in control is often an attempt to deal with anxiety. It makes sense to think that if you can control your environment, you can prevent bad things from happening. Wanting control is also related to personality. Some people are naturally more inclined to want control while others are happy to "go with the flow." To see how important control is to you, answer the following questions.

Control
Rate how strongly you agree or disagree with each statement.

Not being able to control my weight seems very dangerous to me.

Strongly disagree				Strongly agree
1	2	3	4	5

When I eat something I didn't plan to eat, I feel out of control.

Strongly disagree				Strongly agree
1	2	3	4	5

Any weight gain makes me feel that I am so out of control that I'll keep gaining weight until I'm obese.

Strongly disagree				Strongly agree
1	2	3	4	5

People have told me I'm controlling.

Strongly disagree				Strongly agree
1	2	3	4	5

Change in my normal routine makes me feel like I'm losing control.

Strongly disagree				Strongly agree
1	2	3	4	5

Total score: _____

The higher your score, the more need for control you have. If you answered most of the questions with a 4 or higher, your need for control is likely helping to maintain your starvation eating disorder.

Other Environmental Factors: Toilets, Drug Stores, and the Internet

Some environmental factors don't cause starvation eating disorders but may help support them. For example, the modern toilet plays a role in how someone expresses their starvation eating disorder. The simple truth is that bathrooms make it easier to purge. It's hard to vomit if you don't have access to a modern commode. Purging is also made easier when you can easily buy over-the-counter laxatives.

The Internet has further complicated the complex picture of starvation eating disorders. The Internet is both a positive and negative influence on self-imposed starvation. There is a lot of good information online that can help you get well, but there are also websites that promote starvation. These websites (called *pro-anorexia* or *pro-ana* websites) have one purpose—to help your starvation eating disorder win! We don't know if these websites have a role in helping a person develop a starvation eating disorder, but if you have one already, pro-ana websites will not help you get well. As you can see by these common pro-ana website themes (Norris et al. 2006), these sites attempt to normalize self-imposed starvation, and they reinforce unhealthy behavior.

Pro-Ana Website Themes

- *Control:* You need to lose weight to maintain control of your life.

- *Success:* The only way to measure success is by how much weight you can lose.

- *Perfection:* You need to be perfect. The only way to be perfect is to be very thin.

- *Isolation:* You need to stay away from anyone who encourages you to gain weight.

- *Sacrifice:* You need to focus solely on your starvation eating disorder. It should be the most important thing in your life, and you should be willing to give up everything for your eating disorder.

- *Coping:* The only way to cope with life's difficulties is to lose more weight.

- *Deceit:* You need to learn how to hide your weight loss so your family and friends won't try to get you to eat and gain weight.

- *Solidarity:* You should support the efforts of others with a starvation eating disorder to lose more weight.

- *Revolution:* People with starvation eating disorders should channel their strengths to convince society that starvation is a good thing. Help others starve!

---

personality traits

Like everything else about us, our personality is shaped by both nature and nurture, but biology plays a very strong role in most personality traits. *Heritability of a trait* refers to how much genes contribute to the development of that particular trait. The heritability of traits varies, but many traits are 50 percent (or more) heritable, meaning that it would be very difficult to develop a particular personality trait like perfectionism without the genes for perfectionism. Perfectionism, obsessiveness, and compulsiveness are personality traits that are associated with starvation eating disorders. The genetic contribution toward having these traits is high. There is also good evidence from studies of personality and starvation eating disorders that these personality traits are stable and that they persist after weight gain (Wagner et al. 2006). This is good news because it means these personality traits can help you get well. For example, taking advantage of your tendency to be compulsive can help you keep food logs and stay on your weight restoration plan. *The bottom line is this:* you can use your personality traits to get well or to increase the power of your starvation eating disorder.

Complete the Personality Trait Survey to see if you have personality traits that are contributing to your starvation eating disorder.

Personality Trait Survey

Rate how strongly you agree or disagree with each statement.

I am very particular about how things are arranged at my house or at work.

Strongly disagree   Strongly agree

1	2	3	4	5

I tend to be a careful person.

Strongly disagree   Strongly agree

1	2	3	4	5

I like order.

Strongly disagree   Strongly agree

1	2	3	4	5

I believe that if you are going to do something, you should go all the way and do it right.

Strongly disagree   Strongly agree

1	2	3	4	5

I tend to make lists.

Strongly disagree   Strongly agree

1	2	3	4	5

I think about things before I do them.

Strongly disagree   Strongly agree

1	2	3	4	5

I am particular about the way I dress.

Strongly disagree   Strongly agree

1   2   3   4   5

People have told me I'm a perfectionist.

Strongly disagree   Strongly agree

1   2   3   4   5

Total score: _____

The higher your total score, the more likely you are to have the common starvation eating disorder personality traits. Listed below are the personality traits that are most often seen in people with starvation eating disorders. Look at each trait and check off the ones you think apply to you.

Common Personality Traits		
☐	High perfectionism	You feel that everything you do needs to be perfect. You strive for personal perfection.
☐	High obsessiveness	You think about things carefully. You spend a lot of time considering options. You ruminate about things that you feel are important. (And if your brain is starving, this trait becomes even stronger.)
☐	Low novelty seeking	You like sameness.
☐	High harm avoidance	You are careful and don't put yourself in risky situations.
☐	High persistence	You don't give up or give in very easily. Once you decide to do something, you stick to it.
☐	Low self-directedness	You are influenced by others or culture.
☐	Low impulsivity	You think carefully before you act.

Which of these traits do you think made you the most vulnerable to developing a starvation eating disorder? Here is how Amy answered the question.

I am a very careful person who tends to be perfectionistic in everything I do. When I decided to lose weight, I wanted to do it the right way—the perfect way. I also like to have a routine that I stick to, so once I started restricting or exercising, I didn't want to stop. I like to eat the same thing every day; I never liked trying new foods very much. I'm a very persistent person and I don't like to give up. When I give in to hunger, I feel like I'm giving up. These personality traits also made me a very good student when I was in high school, but they really helped my eating disorder take over my life too.

In the space below, write how you think your personality traits set you up for developing a starvation eating disorder.

How Your Personality Traits Set You Up for Developing a Starvation Eating Disorder

Now it's time to see how your personality traits can be used to help you get well. Let's look again at the common traits to see how they helped Amy get well.

Amy's Use of Personality Traits to Get Well	
High perfectionism	I can use my tendency to be perfectionistic to make my body more perfect in a healthy way. I can change my idea of what a perfect body is. I know I have to be careful, though, not to go too far with perfectionism in any direction.
High obsessiveness	I need to use my ability to think about things carefully to study how starvation is hurting me. I can also use my obsessiveness to help me keep good food logs.
Low novelty seeking	I hate to eat breakfast. If I eat the same (healthy) thing every morning, I think eating breakfast will be easier.
High harm avoidance	I can use this trait as motivation to avoid medical problems.
High persistence	I can use this trait as motivation to not give up on getting healthy.
Low self-directedness	I know this trait makes me more vulnerable to the "thin-is-in" culture but I can also take direction from my doctors.
Low impulsivity	I tend to go on fad diets. I can use my carefulness to keep me off the diets that are bad for my health.

Like Amy, you can use your personality traits to help you get well. Next, write down how you think your personality traits can help you. Most people with a starvation eating disorder will have the personality traits listed here even if they have a mild form of the trait (Crane, Roberts, and Treasure 2007). But if you don't think a particular trait applies at all to you, leave the space for that trait blank.

Your Use of Personality Traits to Get Well
High perfectionism
High obsessiveness
Low novelty seeking
High harm avoidance
High persistence
Low self-directedness
Low impulsivity

low weight promotes more of the same

Lastly (and as shown in chapter 3), low weight affects thinking, so if your weight is too low, your brain will mistakenly tell you that even a small amount of food is too much and that even a weight gain of a couple of pounds will make you fat. This means that after you gain some weight and your brain is no longer starving, you will be able to work on thinking healthy thoughts about your weight and shape. In chapter 10 you will start weight restoration. After you gain weight, you will learn in chapter 12 how to how to change your distorted starvation thinking.

to sum up

It appears that if you don't have the genes for a starvation eating disorder, other factors, like culture, won't be enough to cause you to develop one (Birmingham and Beumont 2004). The biological/genetic contributions to the development of a starvation eating disorder include genes for losing weight easily and for personality traits. The most likely explanation for the development of eating disorders is that biology provides a strong vulnerability or predisposition to developing an eating disorder and then other factors add to a person's vulnerability. But without the biological factors, other factors (the kind of parents you had, our thin-at-any-cost culture, trauma, or your need for control) won't lead to the development of a starvation eating disorder.

By now you probably have some understanding of why you developed a starvation eating disorder. But perhaps you're still not sure. The good news is that you don't have to know exactly why you have a starvation eating disorder in order to get well. Getting well requires action not explanation. You will take your first action step in the next chapter by learning how to deal with the anxiety that is associated with a starvation eating disorder.

CHAPTER 5

fear: obsessive thinking and compulsive behaviors

the hallmarks of a starvation eating disorder are an extreme focus on weight and food and an attempt to control anxiety through starvation. The anxiety that people with starvation eating disorders experience leads to obsessive thinking about weight and to obsessive behavior, such as compulsive exercise. In this chapter, you will look at how this focus, and the underlying anxiety, endanger your health and help maintain your starvation eating disorder and how your starvation eating disorder is interfering with what is important to you.

core anxiety

Fear and anxiety about body shape, being fat, and eating certain foods all lead to starvation and purging (including compulsive exercise). Anxiety is such a core feature of starvation eating disorders that some eating disorder specialists, like me, think starvation eating disorders are closely tied to anxiety disorders.

That there is a relationship between anxiety and starvation eating disorders is supported by research showing that people who go on to develop a starvation eating disorder like anorexia tended to be very anxious as children (Raney et al. 2008). There is additional evidence for the relationship: it is common for people with starvation eating disorders to also have an anxiety disorder, and anxiety often persists after weight gain (Strober et al. 2007). Lastly, we see a high frequency of anxiety disorders in the relatives of people with starvation eating disorders, indicating some kind of genetic predisposition to anxiety in the families of people with starvation eating disorders (Strober et al. 2007). So it's possible that people with starvation eating disorders are, in part, expressing anxiety by starving and purging. Complete the Anxiety Self-Assessment to see if you tend to be an anxious person outside of your anxiety about food and weight.

Anxiety Self-Assessment		
1. Did you experience school anxiety when you were a child (that is, were you more anxious than your peers about going to school)?	Yes	No
2. Have others described you as a worrier?	Yes	No
3. Would you describe yourself as someone who worries a lot?	Yes	No
4. Have you been diagnosed with an anxiety disorder?	Yes	No
5. Are you compulsive about things having nothing to do with weight or food (for example, do you feel you have to organize your house in a certain way)?	Yes	No
6. Do you have a family member(s) who has been diagnosed with an anxiety disorder or who is very anxious?	Yes	No

If you answered yes to at least two questions, chances are good that you have a tendency to be an anxious person.

Anxiety is often expressed in layers. For example, someone might be anxious about not being as successful as a sibling, and they might express that anxiety physically by having frequent headaches. The headaches might then keep that person from going to work. If not at work, that person can't then fail at work. If we look under the layers, we might see that fear of being seen as a failure as compared to the sibling might be at the core of the headaches. For someone with a starvation eating disorder, fear can be expressed through starvation and purging. To see how your core anxiety may be expressed through your starvation eating disorder, it is helpful to look at what it means to you to be thin.

What Does It Mean?

"What does it mean?" is based on a cognitive therapy technique developed by David Burns (1999). "What does it mean?" will help you identify what is underneath your anxiety about food and weight by looking at your thoughts about both. Answers from Grace, Amy, and Joe show how the exercise works.

Start "What does it mean?" by asking yourself the question, "If I gain weight, it means I am. . . ." When Grace asked herself this question, the first thing that came to her mind was the thought, "If I gain weight, it means I am a weak person." The first thing that comes to your mind is rarely the closest to your core anxiety, so Grace took that statement and used it to answer the next question, "If it's true I'm a weak person, this means that I won't be able to protect myself or my family from bad things that could happen." Grace kept going, asking, "What does it mean?" until she felt she had gotten to the worst thing she could think of. As her answers show, for Grace this was "having no value as a person." Read the answers that Grace, Amy, and Joe gave to "What does it mean?" to see how each of them got to the thoughts associated with their core anxiety.

What Does It Mean If I Gain Weight?
Grace's answers
<ul><li>If I gain weight, it means I am: *a weak person.*<ul><li>If that is true, it means: *I won't be able to protect myself or my family from bad things that could happen.*<ul><li>If true, it means: *I can't control what happens, and if something bad happens to me or my family, I have no value as a person.*<ul><li>If true, it means: *having no value as a person is the worst thing I can think of.*</li></ul></li></ul></li></ul></li></ul>
Grace's last thought (that she had no value if she couldn't control everything that happens) was the worst thing she could think of, so that thought was the closest to her core anxiety. Grace realized she was expressing her anxiety about control—and her worry that something bad could happen to her or her children—by controlling her weight. When she thought about this pattern, Grace realized that starving and spending large amounts of time at the gym actually made her less able to prevent bad things from happening.
Amy's answers
<ul><li>If I gain weight, it means I am: *out of control.*<ul><li>If that is true, it means: *I won't be able to stop eating and I will be obese.*<ul><li>If true, it means: *I will be like my mother.*<ul><li>If true, it means: *I will be unloved. This is the worst thing I can think of.*</li></ul></li></ul></li></ul></li></ul>
Amy's last thought surprised her. She was unaware that she feared being like her mother. After her parents divorced when she was very young, Amy was raised by her father, and her mother was ostracized by the family. Amy, who was an anxious person like her father, grew up hearing negative things about her mother. While Amy did not develop a starvation eating disorder because her parents divorced or because her father raised her, the fears she had of being like her mother gave her a reason to starve. After Amy gained some weight and started working on changing her thinking, she decided to target her thoughts about her mother as something to work on first.

Joe's answers

■ If I gain weight, it means I am: *a slob.*
 	
  ■ If that is true, it means: *people will reject me.*
 	
  ■ If true, it means: *I'll be alone.*
 	
    ■ If true, it means: *no one will help me when I need it.*
 	
    ■ If true, it means: *I won't be able to make it. I can't cope on my own. This is the worst thing I can think of.*

Joe's last thought that he couldn't cope without people to help him was the closest thought to his core anxiety. Joe's core anxiety was tied to his fear of being rejected and not being able to cope without help. Being very thin made Joe think he was safe from rejection and all the fears that rejection held for him. Joe realized that, ironically, his starving and compulsive exercising also meant he spent less time with his friends and family.

Now it's time for you to look at what is underneath your anxiety about gaining weight. While there is rarely one underlying cause, the "What does it mean?" technique can help you explore your anxiety. If you use this technique more than once, you may come up with additional core anxieties. In fact, "What does it mean?" can be used to explore just about any question that is important to you and which you think may have its root in anxiety. In chapters 12 and 13, you will get the opportunity to explore how to turn your core anxiety about food, weight, and shape around by changing your thinking or by facing the anxiety through a behavioral technique called worry exposure, but for now, focus on discovering what is at the core of your anxiety.

What Does It Mean If I Gain Weight?

■ If I gain weight, it means I am:
 	
_____
 	
  ■ If that is true, it means:
 	
  _____
 	
  ■ If true, it means:
 	
    _____
 	
    ■ If true, it means:
 	
    _____

Look at your last answer. Below, write down what you have learned about your core anxiety about gaining weight.

_____

_____

_____

food and weight obsessions

Weight and shape concerns are common in most Western countries. But for most people, these concerns do not become obsessions. *Healthy concerns* lead to adaptive behavior. For example, for someone who has diabetes, a healthy concern about what to eat is adaptive: the diabetic person with a healthy concern will avoid foods that lead to unstable blood glucose (also called blood sugar) and eat multiple small meals every day to keep blood glucose at a safe level. *Obsessive concerns* are over-the-top concerns that dominate a person's thinking. If a person with diabetes is obsessively thinking about their blood glucose so that they can't think about anything else, that diabetic person will probably become extremely anxious. Extreme anxiety is not compatible with making healthy choices.

For someone with a starvation eating disorder, thinking about food, weight, and shape becomes obsessive. You may have noticed how your thinking is dominated by your eating disorder; focusing on issues other than food, weight, and shape can be difficult for someone with a starvation eating disorder. For instance, Joe dropped out of college because he found he spent most of the time in class worrying about his weight and thinking he should be at the gym. He couldn't concentrate on what the professor was saying. His obsessive thinking about exercise, how many calories he could eat, and the size of his stomach took over his thinking.

Common obsessive thoughts that people with starvation eating disorders have are listed next. Check off the obsessive thoughts you have. If you have a frequent thought or thoughts that are not on the list, write them in the space at the end:

- ☐ Worrying that you are too fat

- ☐ Thinking that if you start eating, you will never stop

- ☐ Feeling that one or more body parts (like your stomach) are too big

- ☐ Thinking about how much to eat

- ☐ Planning ways to get around eating

- ☐ Believing that eating leads to weakness

- ☐ Counting calories in your head while you eat

- ☐ Planning and replanning the food you are going to eat

- ☐ Obsessing about food and recipes

- ☐ Calculating approximately how much exercising you need to do to burn off calories you've eaten

- ☐ Focusing on how much you weigh

- ☐ Other thoughts: _____

_____

food and weight compulsions

Obsessive thoughts lead to compulsive behaviors—those behaviors we think we have to do in order to avoid something very negative. Compulsions are usually an attempt to control anxiety. For people with a starvation eating disorder, that very negative thing they obsess about is usually gaining weight. When we engage in compulsive behaviors, it often feels like we have to do the behavior over and over again in order to decrease our anxiety.

To see how obsessions are a response to anxiety, let's look at Joe's experience. Joe obsessed over how many calories he ate each day. He would feel more and more anxious each time he thought about what he had eaten. In order to decrease his anxiety, Joe compulsively and repeatedly added up the day's calories. He did this to reassure himself that he hadn't gained weight. It's often the case that just one compulsive behavior won't be enough to decrease anxiety. In addition to rechecking how many calories he ate, Joe checked the size of his stomach several times a day to make sure it didn't look bigger.

Other compulsions commonly seen in people with starvation eating disorders include getting on the scale many times a day, obsessively exercising, or getting online to read about the latest diets. Check off your starvation eating disorder compulsions and, as you did for obsessive thinking, write in any additions at the end of the list:

- ☐ Checking your weight multiple times a day

- ☐ Checking your shape in the mirror

- ☐ Checking your weight by pinching yourself in your waist or other areas to see how much you can pinch

- ☐ Performing eating rituals like cutting up your food in certain ways

- ☐ Eating only certain foods

    ☐ Counting calories

    ☐ Exercising a certain amount of time or doing a certain number of repetitive exercises (like doing five hundred sit-ups a day)

    ☐ Reading about diets

    ☐ Other behaviors: _____

    _____

Like your obsessive thinking, all of these compulsive behaviors serve to keep your starvation eating disorder in charge of your life. Obsessive thinking and compulsive behaviors also take up a great deal of time and interfere with relationships. Remember Grace? Grace's husband got tired of Grace spending all of her time at the gym. He felt that she wasn't engaged in their marriage. While this may not have been the only factor that led to the divorce, Grace's obsessive thinking and compulsive exercising contributed to the end of her marriage. In the next section you will have the opportunity to see just how much time you are losing to your starvation eating disorder's obsessions and compulsions.

obsessive thoughts and compulsive behaviors are time robbers

The Obsessive-Compulsive Log will allow you to see how much of your time is spent in obsessive thinking or behaviors. Let's look at Joe's Obsessive-Compulsive Log, which follows, to see what can be learned from keeping track of obsessions and compulsions for two days. In the first hour, Joe spent fifteen minutes checking his weight and looking at his stomach in the mirror to see if it looked too big. He also spent more than thirty minutes planning his eating for the day and twenty-five minutes worrying about his stomach being too fat. Because Joe's worry overlapped with his checking, his total minutes per hour could even exceed sixty minutes; he was often totally absorbed with his eating disorder. Joe's multitasking continued later in the day, when he went to the gym. Joe spent almost all his time there thinking about how many calories he was burning or how fat he felt while he exercised. At the end of two days, Joe discovered he'd spent almost all of his waking hours thinking about or engaging in compulsive behaviors connected to his starvation eating disorder. Before completing his log, Joe was aware that he spent time on being concerned about his weight and body shape, but after he finished the log, he realized his eating disorder had taken over his life.

Joe's Obsessive-Compulsive Log—Day 1

Thinking

Thoughts about food and calories (for example, what to eat, what not to eat, counting calories, or projecting how many calories you are burning)

Hour	1	2	3	4	5	6	7	8	9	10	11	12	13	14	15	16	17
Minutes spent	35	50	45	60	30	30	40	50	40	45	50	20	50	40	50	50	30

Thoughts about body shape or size (for example, being fat, needing to lose weight, or wanting part of your body to be smaller)

Hour	1	2	3	4	5	6	7	8	9	10	11	12	13	14	15	16	17
Time spent	25	10	10	20	15	30	20	10	20	10	5	40	10	15	10	10	5

Behaviors

Checking (for example, checking your weight, checking in the mirror, or checking how loose your clothes are)

Hour	1	2	3	4	5	6	7	8	9	10	11	12	13	14	15	16	17
Time spent	15	10	20			10				15	10		10		30	10	

Exercising (for example, sit-ups, lifting weights, or "fat burning" exercise)

Hour	1	2	3	4	5	6	7	8	9	10	11	12	13	14	15	16	17
Time spent				60	60	60			15					60	10		

How to Fill Out the Obsessive-Compulsive Log: Completing the Obsessive-Compulsive Log takes a two-day commitment. You don't need to log two days in a row, but the days should be within the same week. Each hour you're awake, record how much time you spend thinking about your weight, shape, calories, or food, and how much time you spend engaging in starvation eating disorder behaviors like checking your weight or cutting your food into small pieces. The log provides seventeen one-hour spaces that you can fill in; assuming you sleep seven to eight hours in twenty-four, you should record at least sixteen times a day. "Hour 1" is the first hour after you wake up. Because you can think about weight at the same time that you are exercising or engaging in other obsessive behaviors, some hours you will spend time doing both. Joe's log is a good example of this kind of multitasking: the entire time he was exercising, Joe was also calculating how many calories he was burning and worrying about his stomach being too fat.

It's helpful to set a timer or use a watch with an alarm to remind you to log at the end of each hour. If you miss an hour, just fill it in as soon as you remember. Even if you think you know how much time you spend in starvation eating disorder thinking or behaviors, you will learn important information by completing the log, so don't skip this activity. After the two-day log period, you should have a good idea about how much time your starvation eating disorder is taking away from you.

Obsessive-Compulsive Log—Day 1

Thinking

Thoughts about food and calories (for example, what to eat, what not to eat, counting calories, or projecting how many calories you are burning)

Hour	1	2	3	4	5	6	7	8	9	10	11	12	13	14	15	16	17
Minutes spent																	

Thoughts about body shape or size (for example, being fat, needing to lose weight, or wanting part of your body to be smaller)

Hour	1	2	3	4	5	6	7	8	9	10	11	12	13	14	15	16	17
Time spent																	

Behaviors

Checking (for example, checking your weight, checking in the mirror, or checking how loose your clothes are)

Hour	1	2	3	4	5	6	7	8	9	10	11	12	13	14	15	16	17
Time spent																	

Exercising (for example, sit-ups, lifting weights, or "fat burning" exercise)

Hour	1	2	3	4	5	6	7	8	9	10	11	12	13	14	15	16	17
Time spent																	

Obsessive-Compulsive Log—Day 2

Thinking

Thoughts about food and calories (for example, what to eat, what not to eat, counting calories, or projecting how many calories you are burning)

Hour	1	2	3	4	5	6	7	8	9	10	11	12	13	14	15	16	17
Minutes spent																	

Thoughts about body shape or size (for example, being fat, needing to lose weight, or wanting part of your body to be smaller)

Hour	1	2	3	4	5	6	7	8	9	10	11	12	13	14	15	16	17
Time spent																	

Behaviors

Checking (for example, checking your weight, checking in the mirror, or checking how loose your clothes are)

Hour	1	2	3	4	5	6	7	8	9	10	11	12	13	14	15	16	17
Time spent																	

Exercising (for example, sit-ups, lifting weights, or "fat burning" exercise)

Hour	1	2	3	4	5	6	7	8	9	10	11	12	13	14	15	16	17
Time spent																	

What You Learned

Now that you've finished your Obsessive-Compulsive Log, you will want to spend some time carefully looking over it. When Joe looked at his log, he realized he was spending more time in "checking" behavior than he'd thought. Joe knew he was getting on the scale every morning, but he didn't realize how much time he spent looking at his stomach in the mirror each day. Now it's time for you to record what you have learned by answering the following questions to see how obsessive thinking and compulsive behaviors are running your life.

- How much total time per day did you spend in obsessive thinking or compulsive behaviors? ____

- Even when you were not engaging in compulsive behavior, were you thinking about your weight, shape, or food?　　Yes　　No

- How much time did you spend checking your shape or weighing yourself? _____

- How much time did you spend exercising? _____

Next, rate how much you think compulsive behavior or obsessive thinking is interfering with your life.

Minimal interference				Extreme interference
1	2	3	4	5

When Joe learned how much time he was spending checking the size of his stomach, he started to think about how much his eating disorder was taking away from him. Joe realized that his eating disorder was interfering with his ability to spend time studying or seeing his friends and family. Write down the insights you got from your log.

What You Learned from Your Obsessive-Compulsive Log

anxiety disorders

Anxiety disorders are a group of psychological disorders characterized by debilitating anxiety that interferes with a person's functioning. This chapter has explored the connection between starvation eating disorders, core anxiety, weight obsessions, and compulsions. Beyond the relationship between starving oneself and anxiety, there is a risk for a person with a starvation eating disorder of having a true anxiety disorder that is separate from an eating disorder.

Not surprisingly, the anxiety disorder most associated with starvation eating disorders is obsessive-compulsive disorder. In addition, panic disorder and social phobia are also seen in people who have starvation eating disorders. Because this association goes beyond the effects of starvation, it's important to include a short discussion about each of these anxiety disorders.

Obsessive-Compulsive Disorder

Despite the similarity in names, obsessive-compulsive disorder (OCD) and the obsessive-compulsive personality traits discussed thus far are distinct from each other. OCD is a true anxiety disorder involving behaviors such as compulsive hand washing or checking. People with OCD may engage in these behaviors so often that there is little time for anything else.

OCD with contamination fear is a good example of such interference. Imagine being as afraid of germs as you are of gaining weight. The fear of germs leads to compulsive hand washing and hours of cleaning. Hand washing fifty or more times a day, scrubbing the body in the shower for more than an hour, even using bleach to clean the skin are not uncommon activities for someone with OCD. In addition, people who suffer with contamination OCD often spend hours cleaning their homes, frequently cleaning and recleaning the same area of the house over and over. Similarly people who suffer with the checking types of OCD spend hours checking doors, windows, stoves, and even drive back and forth over the same part of a road to make sure they haven't run over something.

Symptoms of OCD are seen in people with very low weight but also in people who have recovered from their starvation eating disorder and are completely weight restored. OCD is also seen more often in people with starvation eating disorders than in people with other types of eating disorders, indicating a relationship between OCD and starvation eating disorders (Godart et al. 2006).

Even though the obsessive and compulsive personality traits common in people with starvation eating disorders are not the same as symptoms of OCD, the combination of these personality traits and low weight can make it look like someone has true OCD. Further, obsessive or compulsive personality traits (like harm avoidance) may make someone more susceptible to developing OCD. For these reasons, it is very hard to know if someone who is starving has OCD in addition to a starvation eating disorder, so if you have symptoms of OCD, you will probably have to wait until you gain weight to determine if you really have true OCD.

Panic Disorder

The defining feature of panic disorder is fear of anxiety, specifically, fear of the strong physical manifestation of anxiety, called a *panic attack*. Panic attacks are characterized by symptoms such as racing or pounding heart, difficulty breathing, and feeling dizzy. People with panic disorder become so concerned that they might have a panic attack that they start avoiding any situation that might trigger panic. This avoidance can result in being afraid even to leave the house. Panic disorder is seen in people with starvation eating disorders and also in people with bulimia. Interestingly, the risk for panic disorder is not increased for people who have a binge-eating disorder (Godart et al. 2006).

Social Phobia

Social phobia involves feeling so embarrassed in social situations that the social phobic person avoids all or most social situations. This avoidance causes an isolation that can result in significant impairment. Like OCD, social phobia is associated with starvation eating disorders and is seen less often in people with other types of eating disorders. Like OCD and panic disorder, social phobia can persist after weight gain (Godart et al. 2006).

How Do You Know If You Have an Anxiety Disorder?

Because the symptoms of OCD, panic disorder, and social phobia can be associated with low weight, it can be hard to determine if you have an anxiety disorder separate from your starvation eating disorder. *The bottom line is this:* as with depression, you have to gain weight before it can be determined if you have an anxiety disorder. If the symptoms persist after you have gained weight, you may need treatment for one of these anxiety disorders. As with treatment for depression, weight gain should come first. See the Helpful Resources appendix for anxiety disorder treatment self-help resources.

to sum up

Starvation eating disorders are powered by anxiety. Understanding what being thin means for you can help you understand your core anxiety. Core anxiety is the innermost layer of anxiety. Core anxiety can be so powerful that it leads to obsessive thinking. Obsessive thinking leads to compulsive behaviors, which are an attempt to escape the anxiety. The obsessions with weight and shape take over, and compulsive starvation eating disorder behaviors (like overexercising) consume large amounts of time. In this way, time that might have been spent with family or friends or doing other important things is spent maintaining the starvation eating disorder.

You should now have a basic understanding of starvation eating disorders and be ready to move to stage II. The chapters in stage II will prepare you for weight restoration by giving you the opportunity to strengthen your commitment, pull together a support team to help you get well, and explore what is involved in successful treatment by looking at treatment components.

STAGE II

getting ready—commitment, team building, and treatment planning

getting well will mean making a commitment, but making a commitment is not something you do just once. Recovering from a starvation eating disorder will require that you recommit to getting healthy over and over again. Your eating disorder will challenge your commitment every step of the way.

Getting well will involve doing the opposite of what your starvation eating disorder thinking is telling you to do. It will also mean going in the opposite direction of where your anxiety is taking you. We call doing the opposite of how we think and feel *opposite action*. This is a concept that comes from dialectical behavior therapy, developed by Marsha Linehan (1993). In chapter 6, you will have the opportunity to focus on committing yourself to opposite action. The commitment activities you complete in chapter 6 will help you do what you need to do to get well. As you work through the rest of this book, you will be able to renew your commitment to a new life and good health by completing additional commitment activities. In chapter 7, you will also learn how to mobilize your support team—which can include friends, family, and health care professionals—to help you when you feel like quitting.

Chapter 8 covers the components of a treatment plan, describing what you will need to get well. By the end of stage II, you will have what you need to start the active treatment phase of getting well. As you work through these three chapters, remember that the only way you can fail to get better is to quit.

CHAPTER 6

making a commitment
to opposite action

*a*t this point you may be saying to yourself that you want to feel better but you don't want to gain weight. You may even feel you need to lose more weight. Or perhaps, like one of my patients, you are saying to yourself, "I feel fine, so all of those medical complications are for other people to worry about." Perhaps you have even avoided looking at the motivational cards you have made so far so that you don't have to think about what might happen if you don't gain weight. All of these feelings are perfectly understandable. I have never talked to a person with a starvation eating disorder who wanted to gain weight, and many of my patients do tell me they want to lose more weight.

But to get well, you will have to do the very thing you don't want to do, which is called opposite action. No one wants to take opposite action—as human beings, we want to go with our feelings, to do what feels good and right to us. Opposite action means going against your feelings, and for someone with a starvation eating disorder, it means going against your starvation eating disorder thinking. If you have tried to get well in the past and failed, it's likely that you weren't able to do opposite action.

While opposite action is hard, to be effective in life, we have to go against our feelings sometimes. Look at these examples of opposite actions and check off any you have taken in the past:

☐ Doing your taxes or paying the bills

☐ Studying for a test

- ☐ Walking away from the perfect dress because it cost too much even though you really wanted it badly

- ☐ Visiting your in-laws

- ☐ Doing housework or laundry

- ☐ Reading this book

- ☐ Other examples: _____

_____

All of the exercises in this chapter are designed to help you commit to the opposite actions that will lead to getting well. But to gain weight, most people need a compelling reason to do opposite actions. During past treatment attempts, if you didn't have a compelling reason to eat and to stop purging, your treatment was headed for failure from the beginning, but looking over your treatment history can give you insight into how to make treatment a success this time around.

your treatment history

You have probably tried to gain weight before—perhaps many times. Examining what happened when you did try to gain weight can give you important information that will help you be successful now. Like many people with a starvation eating disorder, Amy had gained enough weight to restore her health only to lose the weight again. Although she'd once kept most of the weight on for over one year, she had never given up purging. Here's how Amy answered the questions I first asked her about her history with weight restoration.

Your Weight Restoration History
Amy's answers
How many times have you gained enough weight to have a BMI of at least 18? *I reached a BMI of 18 when I was a teenager, and the last time I gained weight, my BMI got up to 19.*
How did you gain the weight each time (for example, a residential program, an outpatient program, on your own)? *The first time was when my parents put me in a residential treatment program. The second time was when I went into outpatient therapy after being in the hospital with heart problems. The dietitian gave me a food plan each week, and I followed the plan.*

Why did you gain weight each time?
The first time was because my parents said I had to stay until I gained weight. I knew I would lose the weight again as soon as I could get out of the program. The second time I gained weight because I was scared—my doctor said I would have to go back in the hospital if I didn't gain weight.
What is the longest period of time you've been able to keep your BMI at 18 or above?
About 18 months.
Why do you think you were able to keep your BMI at 18 or more for that period of time?
I did it because I was scared. I almost died. I was in the ICU for a week, and the doctor told me I might never be able to have a child.
Did you stop purging each time you gained weight?
I never stopped except when I was in the hospital. I couldn't purge then because I couldn't even get out of bed. After I got out of the hospital, I didn't purge for a few days but then I started again.

Analyzing your weight restoration history can provide valuable information that you can use to be successful with weight restoration now. Let's look closely at Amy's history to see what there is to learn.

- *Did Amy ever gain weight for herself?* It appears that the only time Amy gained weight and kept the weight on was when she was worried about her health.

- *What were the other reasons Amy gained weight?* Amy's weight gain when she was an adolescent was strictly a way to get out of a residential program.

- *Did Amy ever stop purging?* With the exception of a few days, the only time Amy didn't purge was when she was in the hospital.

- *What opposite actions did Amy take?* Amy did eat, so that was an opposite action, but she never used opposite action with purging.

When Amy and I analyzed her history, we came up with several important considerations for making her next weight restoration attempt a success.

- Amy was motivated by her health. She could use having a healthy heart and being healthy enough to have a baby as motivators. She made sure she added these reasons to her motivational cards.

- Because Amy continued to purge after she gained weight, her starvation eating disorder stayed in control. It was very important that Amy learn how to control her purging; this is where she needed to focus her opposite action.

Now write down your weight restoration history.

Your Weight Restoration History
How many times have you gained enough weight to have a BMI of at least 18?
How did you gain the weight each time (for example, a residential program, an outpatient program, on your own)?
Why did you gain weight each time?
What is the longest period of time you've been able to keep your BMI at 18 or above?
Why do you think you were able to keep your BMI at 18 or more for that period of time?
Did you stop purging each time you gained weight?

Answer the following questions about your weight restoration history:

■ *Did you ever gain weight for yourself?* _____

    ■ If you did, what was the reason? _____

       _____

■ *What were the other reasons you gained weight?* _____

    _____

    _____

■ *Out of all the reasons you gained weight in the past, do you think any could motivate you to gain weight now?* _____

    ■ If you answered yes, put these reasons on a 3 by 5 motivational card.

- *Did you ever stop purging?* _____

- *What opposite actions did you take when you were in treatment?* _____

_____

Look over your answers. What have you learned that will help you be successful this time around?

_____

_____

_____

why do people make commitments?

You might ask, "Why do people commit to doing things they don't want to do?" Every day someone somewhere makes a commitment to do something their thoughts and feelings tell them not to do. Generally there are two reasons people are willing to make a commitment to opposite action. The first reason is that the benefit of opposite action outweighs the cost. The second reason is that the person has a strong value that is upheld by taking the opposite action. I once met a woman who worked at a job she absolutely detested for ten years, and she never missed a day of work. When I asked her why she got up every day and went to a job she hated, she said she had made a commitment to put her son through college. Her job paid very well, and in her small town, she couldn't find another job that paid as well. Her commitment to the job allowed her to keep her commitment to her son. The woman's strong value that parents should make sacrifices for children reinforced her commitment. It cost this woman a lot to go to work, but for her, the benefit was worth it and she felt good about herself because taking an action that went against what was comfortable for her was in line with her value system as a mother. Doing what you don't want to do requires that the benefit outweighs the cost and that the opposite action fits your value system.

Cost Analysis

Doing this cost analysis will give you a picture of how much your eating disorder has cost you and your family. Starvation eating disorders demand a heavy price. A cost analysis looks at the following:

- *Costs to your relationships:* The effects of a starvation eating disorder on relationships range from interfering with time with family or friends to loss of relationships.

- *Costs to your family:* Starvation eating disorders affect the entire family. A child may have to grow up fast because a parent's eating disorder makes the parent unavailable to that child. Partners may have increased financial burden if the starvation eating disorder interferes with employment.

- *Costs to your physical health:* As described in stage I, starvation eating disorders have serious implications for physical health. A starvation eating disorder can literally rob you of your life.

- *Costs to your emotional health:* Starvation eating disorders promote anxiety, depression, and poor self-esteem.

- *Costs to your occupational life:* Starvation eating disorders rob you of your ability to focus on your career. Whether that career is as a homemaker or a doctor, if you can't focus on doing your job because of your starvation eating disorder, your occupation will be negatively affected. In cases where the starvation eating disorder causes significant physical or emotional problems, working is sometimes not even an option.

An examination of Grace's cost analysis can show us how a starvation eating disorder demands a cost in each of these areas.

Cost Analysis: What Has Losing Weight and Staying Thin Cost You?
Grace's answers
Costs to my relationships
<ul><li>*When I was married, my husband and I fought all the time about my eating and not spending time with him. When he asked for a divorce, he told me he was sick of my eating disorder.*</li><li>*My friends don't invite me out for girls' night because I refuse to eat in restaurants. I want to go out with them and have fun, but they don't invite me anymore.*</li><li>*I don't date because I don't like to eat in front of people.*</li></ul>
Costs to my family
<ul><li>*My daughter was born one month early because I didn't gain enough weight when I was pregnant.*</li><li>*My mother is worried about me all the time.*</li><li>*I don't go to family gatherings because I know food will be there. My sister tells me my dad is upset every year at Thanksgiving because I'm not there. My sister has to deal with my parents' distress about this, and my children have missed seeing their grandparents on most major holidays.*</li><li>*My youngest daughter is embarrassed by my use of laxatives and enemas. Once when she was in the store with me, she got upset when I went down the personal-care aisle. She thought I was going to buy laxatives. She started crying and left the store. After that I tried to hide my use of laxatives and enemas, but she knows that I still do these things.*</li><li>*My oldest daughter has a lot of anxiety about her weight. She isn't fat but she worries a lot about her weight, and my ex-husband and parents blame me.*</li></ul>

Costs to my physical health

- *My doctor has told me I am developing osteoporosis.*

- *I feel tired much of the time.*

- *I have had to go to the hospital several times because my potassium was too low and I was dehydrated. It was embarrassing to have to admit to the doctor in the emergency room that I purge.*

Costs to my emotional health

- *I feel anxious and depressed a lot. I can't stop thinking about my weight and food. I don't sleep very well and have panic attacks.*

- *I never feel happy about my body.*

Costs to my occupational life

- *Two years ago I started to go back to school for a master's degree, but it was too stressful to miss my work-outs. I just can't go to the gym, work, and school. I dropped out of school after two weeks. I know I would be in a good position to move up in my company and make more money if I had the degree, but when I think about giving up going to the gym each day to go to school, I get panicky.*

Grace paid a big price in damage to her relationships, professional life, and her health in an effort to lose weight. In addition, she has paid a big emotional price. Grace needed to take opposite action and gain weight. In order to do opposite action, Grace stayed in touch with the cost that her eating disorder was demanding from her.

Now it's time for you write down the price you have paid for being thin or trying to get thinner.

Cost Analysis: What Has Losing Weight and Staying Thin Cost You?

Costs to my relationships

_____

_____

_____

_____

Costs to my family

Costs to my physical health

Costs to my emotional health

Costs to my occupational life

Look over your answers. Have you paid a big price? Some things are worth a big price. Remember the woman who worked at a job she hated for ten years? She paid a big price, but it was worth the benefit she received when her son graduated from college. Has the price you have been paying to be very thin been worth it?

motivational card: Take five 3 by 5 cards and label each with one of the areas of your life (relationships, family, physical health, emotional health, and occupation), then list the price(s) you have paid in each area.

Does Starvation Fit Your Values?

As described in chapter 5, starvation eating disorders are time robbers. How we use our time says a lot about what we value. If I value my relationship with my children, I will find a way to spend time with them. Sometimes we get in a situation where something we don't value takes up all of our time, leaving little time for what is important. In chapter 5 you discovered just how much time your starvation eating disorder takes up in a day. You may want to go back to your Obsessive-Compulsive Log to remind yourself just how much time that is.

In the last activity, you examined how much your starvation eating disorder is costing you and the people close to you. Now it's time to make a list of things that are important to you. Because you have a starvation eating disorder, we know that your weight, shape, and the food you eat seem important. You might even feel like these are the most important things in your life. But there are probably other things that are important to you, too. When Joe made a list of what was important to him, these were the first three things he came up with:

1. Finishing my degree

2. Spending time with my friends

3. Traveling

Joe then wrote down how his eating disorder was interfering with each of his important items. Let's look at Joe's answers to see what he discovered.

How Your Eating Disorder Interferes with What Is Important to You	
Joe's answers	
What's important to you	How your eating disorder has interfered
1. *Finishing my degree*	*I dropped out of school because I found it hard to concentrate on the schoolwork. When I was in class, I was adding up calories and planning my workouts. I still think about finishing my AA degree.*
2. *Spending time with my friends*	*My friends don't call anymore, and I never call them. I'm too busy with my eating disorder to see very many people. My friends are important to me, and now I have lost touch with everyone.*
3. *Traveling*	*I have always wanted to travel but I don't because I'm afraid I won't be able to exercise enough and I don't want to take a chance on the food I might have to eat in other places.*

You may remember in chapter 5 that when Joe used the "What does it mean?" technique, he realized that a component of his core fears was being left alone. Ironically, when Joe looked at how his starvation eating disorder was interfering with what was important to him, he saw that he had given up time with his friends in order to be thin. Rather than making him less alone, being thin had made him more alone.

Now it's time for you to make a list of what is important to you. If you have been living with a starvation eating disorder for a very long time, it might be hard to think of what is important other than being thin. Reviewing your cost analysis and asking yourself what goals you had before you developed an eating disorder can help. When Grace reviewed her cost analysis, she realized that spending time with her daughters and helping her oldest daughter focus less on weight was important to her, and this was the first thing she put on her list. If you are struggling with what is important to you, complete the following questions:

- Of all the costs you have paid to be thin, what hurts the most? If you haven't already put this on a motivational card, you should do this now.

  - _____
  - _____
  - _____

- Before you had an eating disorder, did you have goals that you have since given up? What were these goals?

  - _____
  - _____
  - _____

- What activities do you engage in that don't have anything to do with your eating disorder? Would you like to do these things more?

  - _____
  - _____
  - _____

Instructions for What Is Important to You: As you fill out the next exercise, try to be as detailed as possible. The more detail you can provide, the more insight you will gain, and this will help later in this chapter when you develop your compelling reasons for gaining weight. Review your responses to the questions you just answered and spend time thinking about what you would be doing if you didn't have an eating disorder.

How Your Eating Disorder Interferes with What Is Important to You	
What's important to you	How your eating disorder has interfered
1. _____ _____	_____ _____ _____
2. _____ _____	_____ _____ _____
3. _____ _____	_____ _____ _____
4. _____ _____	_____ _____ _____
5. _____ _____	_____ _____ _____

finding your compelling reasons to get well

By now you should have some idea of what derailed your treatment in the past and why it's important to you to gain weight and stop purging. A compelling reason to get well can help you do opposite action and eat without purging. For Grace, it was her daughters that provided her with her most compelling reason. When we reviewed her list of what was important to her, spending more time with her family and being more available to her daughters were the first things Grace wrote down. For Joe, it was the realization that his eating disorder was leading to the thing he was the most afraid of—being alone in the world. Amy wanted a better relationship with her husband and to be able to get pregnant. These were *compelling* for Grace, Joe, and Amy—these reasons were personal for them and therefore evoked emotion.

Write down the top one or two most compelling reasons you can think of to get well:

1. _____

2. _____

Sometimes it can take more than one try to come up with a compelling reason. Review your reasons; do these reasons evoke an emotional response? Ask yourself how you would feel if you failed. When Grace thought about failing to improve her relationship with her daughters, she cried. Her strong reaction meant that being closer to her daughters and providing a good role model for her oldest daughter (who struggled with weight issues) were compelling reasons for Grace.

If the one or two reasons you wrote down don't prompt emotion, these reasons may not be powerful enough. Sometimes we think we have to do something because someone else wants us to. Lorrie was one of my patients who at first came up with a reason that didn't elicit an emotional response. Lorrie told me she wanted to get well so she could join the family business. When I asked her how she had felt when she told me her reason, she said she'd felt neutral. It turned out that Lorrie said "join the family business" because she knew that's what her sister and father wanted her to do.

Lorrie wanted to be a writer. When she looked back at what her starvation eating disorder had cost her, what stood out to her was not being able to write because her low weight made it hard for her to concentrate. Then she looked at her list of what she valued and she saw that writing wasn't even on her list. She had made a list of things she thought other people wanted her to do. She loved her family and liked spending time with her sister, but she was not very interested in helping her sister manage the family's large dry-cleaning business. Lorrie could see herself helping out part time while she worked on her writing, but her compelling reason for making a commitment to get well wasn't dry cleaning—it was writing. So if you are like Lorrie and the reasons you wrote down don't seem compelling, go back and try again. Look over your answers to your cost analysis and to How Your Eating Disorder Interferes with What Is Important to You. What jumps out at you? Do any of your answers make you feel sad or regretful? Your emotions can help you identify what your compelling reasons might be.

There is one important caveat to developing a compelling reason: If your weight is so low that you feel nothing at all, you might need to gain a little weight and come back to this chapter later. In fact, to get you started, consider your compelling reason to be gaining enough weight so that you will be able to determine what is important to you. So if you need to gain 5–10 pounds to feed your brain, move on to stage III now, and then, after you have gained a little weight, come back to this chapter and figure out what is important to you.

motivational card: Make a motivational card with your compelling reasons for getting well.

sticking to your commitment

Making a commitment is almost always easier than sticking to it. Your motivational cards can help. You should now have motivational cards for the following:

- What your eating disorder has cost you

- What you value

- Your compelling reasons for getting healthy

At this point you should have about a half-dozen cards. You can carry these cards in your purse or pocket, or put them on your bathroom mirror so you see them every morning. You can even make more than one copy of each card so you can carry one set and put the other set someplace in your house where you will see them every day. The cards won't help if you don't review them, so make sure you don't just stick your cards somewhere and forget about them. It is normal for someone with a starvation eating disorder to be overwhelmed by distorted starvation thinking. Reminding yourself of your reasons for gaining weight and for decreasing purging will help you keep your commitment to opposite action.

A Room That's Free of Starvation Eating Disorder

In order to decrease purging, you will have to tolerate being anxious. Your motivational cards can help by reminding you of why you want to get well, but the cards will probably not be enough. Another way to keep yourself motivated and to tolerate the anxiety you will feel when you don't purge is to imagine a life without your eating disorder. Imagine a room where your eating disorder can't go. When you are in the room, you won't worry about food or think about being fat. What would that room look like? Who would you like in the room with you? What would you do in a room that was free of your starvation eating disorder? How would you feel when you were in the room? Let's look at Grace's description of her room that's free of starvation eating disorder.

Grace's Room That's Free of Starvation Eating Disorder

My room is a large room with lots of mirrors, and I don't mind the mirrors. Everywhere I look I can see myself, and it never even occurs to me that I need to lose weight. There is no exercise equipment in the room, and I don't even think about going to the gym. My children are there with me, and we spend our time playing games and talking about everything except eating disorder stuff. My daughters and I eat lunch in the room and enjoy what we are eating. I don't even care about the calories; I am just enjoying being with my daughters. I feel free.

Instructions for Your Room That's Free of Starvation Eating Disorder: Now it's time for you to imagine your room as it would be if free of starvation eating disorder. Find a quiet place to sit. Look over your cost motivational cards and imagine getting rid of all those problems. None of them are allowed in the room; instead you have what you value in your room. Now imagine that you don't think about your weight or how many calories you are eating when you are in your room. Imagine all the people you want to spend time with in the room with you. Think about how it would feel to be with the people you love, eating food with them, and not thinking about your weight or shape. Write down your room description.

Your Room That's Free of Starvation Eating Disorder

What does your room look like? Who is there with you? What do you do in the room? How do you feel?

_____

_____

_____

_____

_____

_____

_____

_____

_____

_____

_____

_____

_____

_____

_____

_____

_____

_____

You can have that room if you beat your eating disorder. To remind yourself how your starvation eating disorder makes you feel, write down the most important thing about your room on a 3 by 5 card. Add this card to your other motivational cards. You now have motivational cards citing what your eating disorder has cost you, what you value, your compelling reasons for getting well, and a description of your disorder-free room. These cards can help you keep your commitment to getting well. Anxiety about gaining weight and eating will still be with you, but you can use your cards to help you move on to weight restoration.

to sum up

This chapter has explored making a commitment to getting well. Commitment involves opposite action. We need to have strong reasons to do the opposite of what our thoughts and feelings are telling us. Examining yout treatment history and what your starvation eating disorder is costing you, looking at what you value, and developing your most compelling reasons for getting well can help you make the commitment. To keep the commitment, you will have to remind yourself why it's important. Some days you may need to get out your commitment cards and read them over and over to get through the day. It's anxiety provoking to eat and to stop purging (discussed in more detail in chapter 9). Committing yourself to gaining weight is the most extreme opposite action a person with a starvation eating disorder can take. But following through on your commitment will bring improvements in your health, relationships, self-esteem, and overall quality of life. In chapter 9 you will learn other skills that will help you do opposite action, including self-soothing when your anxiety gets very high. A good support team can also help you do opposite action, so the next chapter will look at who to have on your team to help you get well.

CHAPTER 7

who's on your team: health care providers and nonprofessional coaches

many mental disorders carry medical risks. Like a handful of other disorders, starvation eating disorders are distinct in that they are associated with severe medical complications that can lead to death (Birmingham and Beumont 2004). This means that a good relationship with your health care team is essential. The decision about who will be on your team is an important one. While some team members, like a primary care provider, will be indispensable and will have an ongoing long-term relationship with you, other professionals you might see only once. This chapter will start with an overview of all the potential members of a health care team and then look at the option of working with a nonprofessional coach and at how your family and friends can support you.

health care team members

Some people will work with health care teams made up of three or four professionals, while others with a starvation eating disorder will work with only one professional and one nonprofessional coach. Regardless of how many people you have on your team, you will need to work with a primary care provider (PCP). Here are other potential members of your professional team:

- Psychologist

- Psychiatrist

- Social worker

- Marriage and family therapist

- Registered dietitian

- Dentist and oral surgeon

- Eating disorder specialist

- Nonprofessional coach

Because a primary care provider is essential, the examination of the PCP's role on your team is the place to start.

Primary Care Providers

A PCP is the health care provider who will take care of your basic medical needs. It will probably be your PCP who orders the lab tests and other medical tests (like a bone density test) that you may need. Most often it will also be your PCP who gives you information about your overall health and prescribes supplements you might need if you are anemic.

A PCP can be a physician or a nurse practitioner. PCPs who are physicians are usually internists or family practice physicians. These physicians either have an MD or a DO (doctor of osteopathy) degree. Nurse practitioners usually have a master's degree, although an increasing number have doctoral degrees in nursing. More important than whether your PCP is an MD, a DO, or a nurse is the experience your PCP has in treating eating disorders. Depending on your medical insurance policy, you may or may not have a lot of choice in picking a PCP. If you have a choice, ask to be assigned to someone who has some experience with eating disorders.

Alternatively, you may already have a PCP. Perhaps you have a PCP who has cared for your medical needs for some time and you feel very comfortable with him. If this is case, you don't need to change PCPs, but you should have a discussion with your PCP about what experience he has with starvation eating disorders. Most PCPs who don't have experience with eating disorders are willing to consult with an eating disorder specialist. Consultation can help you and your PCP make informed decisions about your medical care.

The ideal PCP, in addition to having experience with eating disorders, will be accessible. Because starvation eating disorders are associated with many medical problems, you'll want to work with a PCP who can answer your concerns as they come up. An increasing number of PCPs are using electronic means to communicate with patients. E-mail can be a useful way to communicate concerns or questions you have as well as a way for your PCP to keep you up to date on your latest lab results.

Common Medical Tests

Your PCP will probably want you to have regular blood draws for laboratory tests and may order other medical tests to monitor for medical complications. Lab tests are used to monitor the electrolytes and minerals in your blood as well as to look for signs of malnutrition. In addition to lab tests, your PCP may order other medical tests to determine the health of your heart or bones. Common medical tests that are used to monitor the health of people with starvation eating disorders are listed here. Talk to your PCP about which tests are appropriate for you and how often she wants you to have these tests.

Blood tests

- Perform complete blood count to monitor you for malnutrition.

- Determine if you have the right balance of electrolytes (salts) and minerals; if you purge, your PCP will probably want to monitor your levels of calcium, magnesium, and potassium.

- Determine your hormonal levels.

Urinalysis

- Urine tests are used to monitor protein levels in your urine. Extreme exercising can cause increased protein in your urine. Increased protein can also be an indication of kidney problems.

Other medical tests

- An electrocardiogram (EKG) determines if your heart is beating too slowly or with an abnormal rhythm.

- Bone density tests determine the health of your bones.

- Gastrointestinal (GI) tests (like upper or lower GI X-rays) determine problems related to vomiting or laxative abuse.

Source: Birmingham and Beumont (2004)

Because it will be your PCP who monitors your health, picking the right PCP is very important. If you don't already have a good working relationship with a PCP, consider this list to determine what characteristics you want in a PCP:

☐ Female PCP

☐ Male PCP

☐ Background in eating disorders

☐ Part of a group practice with other professionals, like psychologists and dietitians

☐ Accessible by e-mail

☐ Other things I want in a PCP: _____

_____

Psychologists and Psychiatrists

Many people get confused about the difference between psychologists and psychiatrists. Psychiatrists are medical physicians who have either an MD or DO degree; psychologists also have doctoral degrees—either a Ph.D., Ed.D., or Psy.D. One of the major differences between the two is that in most of the United States, psychiatrists can prescribe medication while psychologists cannot. In two states (New Mexico and Louisiana) and in the military, psychologists can prescribe medication; so if you live in one of these states or are being cared for in the military, you can see either a psychologist or a psychiatrist for psychotropic medications (like antidepressants). However, because starvation eating disorders don't respond well to antidepressant and other psychotropic medications, it's not necessary to see someone who can prescribe.

Psychotherapy, sometimes called *counseling,* includes all behavioral and talk therapies. While both psychologists and psychiatrists can do psychotherapy, it is becoming increasingly difficult to find a psychiatrist who does psychotherapy. In general, as with a PCP, it's probably most important to find someone who has experience in treating eating disorders within either category of these providers or among other practitioners of psychotherapy, including clinical social workers and marriage and family therapists. Most psychotherapists do not have eating disorder expertise, but some are eating disorder specialists and can help you with weight gain as well as with the treatment of any other mental health concerns you have.

Choosing a Psychotherapist

If you decide that you want to work with a psychotherapist, look for the following:

- Experience treating starvation eating disorders

- Experience providing cognitive or cognitive behavioral therapy (this type of therapy specializes in helping you change your thinking and your behavior)

- Some training in nutrition as well as experience helping people gain weight (if you are not working with a dietitian)

- Specialized training in the cognitive behavioral treatment of anxiety disorders (which can help you deal with your core anxiety), because anxiety is such a driving force in starvation eating disorders

---

Social Workers and Marriage and Family Therapists

Depending on the state you live in, social workers and therapists specializing in working with couples and families (called marriage and family therapists in many states) can provide psychotherapy. Both social workers and marriage and family therapists have master's degrees and are licensed by whatever state the therapist practices in. Generally, their scope of practice is more limited than a psychologist's, but, again, the most important factor will be how much experience the therapist has with eating disorders.

Registered Dietitians

A registered dietitian (RD) who has experience working with starvation eating disorders can help you with weight gain and maintaining a healthy weight. However, most RDs don't have much experience with such disorders, so you may have difficulty finding an RD who is also an eating disorder specialist. It's usually not helpful to work with a dietitian who focuses on calories and healthy foods; while this approach can be very helpful for someone dealing with obesity or even bulimia, it's much less helpful for someone with a starvation eating disorder. On the other hand, a dietitian who understands starvation eating disorders can be a helpful member of your team by supporting you in trying new foods, monitoring your weight, and getting you away from calorie counting.

Dentists and Oral Surgeons

Starvation eating disorders can cause oral problems. If you purge by vomiting, you may have damaged your teeth and gums. A dentist who understands starvation eating disorders and knows that you purge will be an important part of your treatment team. If you have significant gum damage, you may also need an oral surgeon. Talk with your dentist about how often he wants to see you. *The bottom line is this:* for many people with a starvation eating disorder, more frequent trips to the dentist are necessary.

Eating Disorder Specialists

An eating disorder specialist can be a psychologist, psychiatrist, social worker, or registered dietitian who also has specialized training and experience in treating eating disorders. Most eating disorder specialists belong to a professional organization such as the Academy for Eating Disorders (AED) or the International Association of Eating Disorder Professionals (IAEDP). Both of these organizations have a referral service that can help you find an eating disorder specialist in your area (for more information about AED and IAEDP, see the Helpful Resources appendix).

nonprofessional coaches

A nonprofessional coach is someone who can help you with weight restoration. A coach can encourage you, help you analyze your food log, think of useful thoughts to substitute for your distorted starvation eating disorder thoughts, and remind you why you need to gain weight. When a child has a starvation eating disorder, a parent or guardian becomes the child's coach to help the child gain weight. We don't allow a child to starve even if that is what the child wants to do. As an adult, you have the right to starve or purge if that is what you choose to do. But if you are working your way through this book, it means you want to be healthy; starving and purging do not equate with health. A coach can help you stick to your decision to choose health. A nonprofessional coach can be a friend or a *peer coach* (someone you know who has successfully recovered from a starvation eating disorder). To decide if having a coach might be a good choice for you, review the role of a coach described next.

A coach provides general support by doing the following:

- Helping you analyze your eating to determine eating problems, such as using caffeine to avoid eating

- Giving you ideas for foods to eat

- Helping you keep on track by reviewing your food logs with you and encouraging you to eat new foods

- Supporting you as you work through this book

- Acting as a cheerleader

The bottom line is this: a coach cannot tell you what to eat or make you get better—you have to do that for yourself—but a coach can support and encourage you. If you decide on a nonprofessional coach, consider getting a copy of this book for your coach. You should meet with your coach before starting weight restoration and make sure both you and your coach understand what you need to do to gain weight.

Choosing a coach can be a little tricky. Your coach needs to be someone you have a good relationship with but also someone who is in control of her own feelings about your eating disorder. In other words, your coach needs to be someone who is not so affected by your eating disorder that she becomes too distressed or overly invested in any setbacks you might have. Here are some general guidelines:

- Children (even young-adult children) should never be coaches. Having a parent with any kind of eating disorder is stressful for children, and the responsibility of being a coach is not fair to a child (or a young adult).

- Spouses or partners usually don't make good coaches. This is because the spousal relationship is too close. Most couples have conflicts about a variety of issues, including money and raising children. If you have a starvation eating disorder, your weight, eating, or purging has likely been a source of conflict. Having your spouse act as your coach will probably put too much stress on your relationship. Spouses are also affected very personally by their loved one's eating disorder and can become very emotional when there are setbacks, making them too vulnerable for the coach role.

- Parents (like spouses) are not usually effective coaches for an adult. For children, the role of a parent-coach is powerful. This is because the parent has the power to enforce eating even if the child doesn't eat. Sometimes this might even mean agreeing to have a child tube fed if parents cannot get their child to eat. Our relationships with our parents change when we become adults, and it's not appropriate for parents to tell adult children what to do. So if you are eighteen or nineteen and still living with your parents, you might consider asking one of your parents to coach. In some cases this can work. But before your parent agrees to be your coach, you should sit down and discuss how the role of a coach is different from the normal parent role. If you are twenty years old or older or no longer living with your parents, you should consider choosing someone else as a coach.

- Siblings sometimes make good coaches. If you plan to ask an adult brother or sister, consider if the coach role will cause problems for your family. If your sister is your coach and your anxious mother is calling her every day to see how you are doing, this may not be a very healthy situation for your family.

- Friends often make the best coaches. A friend is removed enough from you that he can bring an outside perspective to your weight restoration. If you have a friend who has recovered from an eating disorder, you are lucky. These peers often make the best coaches. Friends who have experience with 12-step programs can also be very good coaches. Programs such as Alcoholics Anonymous have a sponsor system where one person sponsors or "coaches" a new 12-step member. Because the concept of coaching is not that different from sponsoring, most people in 12-step programs understand what it means to be a coach. So if you have a 12-step friend, consider asking her to be your coach.

Advice for the Nonprofessional Coach

Someone you care about has a starvation eating disorder and has asked you to act as a coach. If you decide to take on the role of a coach, you will want to understand what a starvation eating disorder is. The early chapters in this book can give you the information you need to understand self-imposed starvation. As a coach, you will provide emotional support and cheerleading through the difficult task of weight restoration. Here are some basic ground rules to follow as the coach of an adult with a starvation eating disorder:

- Coaches give suggestions but they don't give advice.

- Coaches are not therapists.

- Coaches offer encouragement and remain nonjudgmental.

- Coaches cannot *make* someone eat.

- Coaches are not responsible for weight gain or loss.

- Coaches listen and they act as sounding boards.

- Coaches may help with analyzing the baseline food log.

- Coaches may review weight restoration food logs during weight restoration and may make suggestions.

- Coaches who find the coaching role too stressful have the right to say so and to give up the role.

- Coaches should not give medical advice.

Review this advice for coaches with the person you want as your coach. Make sure you both understand that if it doesn't work, either of you has the right to make a change. You and your coach should read the next few chapters together. This will give you the information you both need to decide what exactly you want your coach to do. The role your coach plays in your treatment is up to the two of you. Some people will want a coach to just help with food ideas or only offer encouragement. Others may want a coach to be more involved. In chapter 10 you will find a Coach Agreement. You and your coach can use this agreement to decide what your coach is going to do for you.

support from your family and friends

Your family and friends can support you as you get well, but only you can decide what kind of support you need from family and friends. There are four factors that keep family members or close friends from supporting you. The first factor is how much your eating disorder has cost the family member or friend. If your starvation eating disorder has cost the person a lot emotionally, it may be difficult for him or her to support you now.

Lorrie's oldest adult son, Jim, was in this situation. As the oldest, Jim felt his mother's eating disorder had cheated him out of his childhood. Jim's anger was understandable, but that anger kept him from supporting his mother. Having been through several failed treatment attempts with Lorrie, Jim made it very clear that he didn't want to talk to his mother about treatment. Rather than ask her son for support, Lorrie agreed not to talk with her son about her eating disorder or treatment. Lorrie got her support from a good friend instead who was able to listen to Lorrie's concerns about how slowly her treatment was going. Lorrie and her son connected over other things in their lives, but it wasn't until Lorrie was well that her son was willing to talk about his mother's eating disorder. If you have a situation like Lorrie's, you may want to connect with your loved one around issues other than your eating disorder.

Occasionally someone in the life of a person with a starvation eating disorder feels that the starvation eating disorder has hurt them so much that they need time completely away from the eating disorder, which means no or very limited contact with the person with the eating disorder. Lorrie's son did not feel this way; he wanted to see his mother on a regular basis but just didn't want to talk about his mother's eating disorder. If you have a situation where someone in your life has told you they can't see you until you are well, the best thing to do is to accept the decision. You can make a motivational card for this if reestablishing the relationship after you get well would be motivating for you.

The second factor that interferes with a family member or friend supporting you is any kind of abuse. If you have been in an abusive relationship with someone and that relationship continues to be abusive, that person will not be able to support you now, and you shouldn't ask him or her. Even if the relationship is no longer abusive, if the two of you haven't come to some kind of peace over the past, that person will likely not be able to support you as you get well.

The third factor is that there may be people in your life whose own problems have such a strong effect on you that spending time with them could interfere with getting well. Joe found this was the case with his older brother Matt. Matt's alcohol abuse was very distressing to Joe. He found that his anxiety level went up any time he spent time with Matt. During weight restoration, Joe decided not to see his brother. It was a hard decision to make but a healthy one for Joe. Joe felt he could cope either with his anxiety about gaining weight or with the anxiety he felt when he watched his brother drink—but not both at the same time. After Joe gained weight and his weight was stable, he was able to see his brother occasionally without putting his own recovery at risk.

The fourth and last factor is if you have a friend or family member who also has an eating disorder and is not working on getting well; if so, you may need to limit your contact with that person. Spending time with someone who is too thin and trying to lose more weight, for example, would be too difficult for most people with a starvation eating disorder. It would be like an alcoholic spending time with a friend who is drinking. This is different than being in eating disorder group therapy with others. In group therapy, you are there to encourage each other to get well. If someone is having a bad week, the group and the psycho-therapist can deal with the situation. But going to lunch with a friend who insists on counting every calorie and encourages you to do the same will not help you get well. It can be painful to decide not to see someone while you are getting well, but sometimes it's the right decision.

to sum up

Getting well involves a team. Even if that team is just you and one or two others, that can really help; you shouldn't try to get well alone. Picking a PCP you can have a good relationship with is essential because your PCP will need to monitor your health as you gain weight and get well. Nonprofessional coaches can help you stay on track by reminding you why you are choosing health, giving you ideas for new foods to try, or helping you analyze your food log. Eating disorder specialists and other professionals can also help you get well. Putting a team together and asking for help is a commitment to getting well that will prepare you for the challenges you'll face on the road to recovery. The next chapter looks at additional components of a treatment plan.

CHAPTER 8

treatment components

Successful treatment requires having a plan with components that address the multiple aspects of a starvation eating disorder. One of the challenges in treating a disorder like anorexia is that we know a lot more about what doesn't work than we know about what does. For children, we can be confident that the family-based treatment model is an effective treatment, but for older teens and adults, the research is less helpful (Lock and Le Grange 2005). We do know that the longer you have had a starvation eating disorder, the more difficult it is to gain weight and keep a stable healthy weight (Fichter, Quadflieg, and Hedlund 2006). In this chapter, the discussion starts with what we know doesn't work very well and then goes on to what does work, giving an overview of the different components of a treatment plan.

what doesn't work well

Sometimes starvation eating disorder treatments that seem intuitively helpful don't actually work very well—traditional treatments like nutritional education and talk therapy seem like good ideas but often don't lead to a successful treatment outcome. Let's look at these and other traditional treatments to understand their limitations.

Nutritional Education and Counting Calories

Often delivered by a registered dietitian, nutritional education is helpful for many kinds of problems. People with diabetes, for example, often benefit from nutritional education about what foods are best for management of glucose levels in the blood. Many people with starvation eating disorders find themselves working with a dietitian at some time in their lives. While a registered dietitian who is an eating disorder specialist can help you gain weight, many dietitians do not have specialized training in starvation eating disorders. Standard nutritional education focuses on calories and eating healthy foods, and it's easy to see how someone with diabetes would benefit from learning about the food pyramid and counting calories. But most people with a starvation eating disorder already know a lot about nutrition and can be quite adept at counting calories and staying away from high-fat or other "bad" foods. Both Amy and Grace reported using what they had learned about nutrition and weight loss to lose more weight. By following what both knew about a low-fat, low-carbohydrate diet (the diet most overweight Americans should follow), Amy and Grace restricted their intake of calories even more severely.

In chapter 10, you will learn how to gain weight by eating three meals a day with snacks. The goal of eating regular meals and snacks is to eat like people who maintain a healthy weight—not to be an expert in the caloric or nutritional content of foods. Eating three meals a day does not require a dietitian, but if you can find a registered dietitian who has experience treating self-imposed starvation, he can help you gain weight.

Medication

Many types of medications have been studied for treating people with starvation eating disorders. Unfortunately, most of these studies have shown little or no benefit from drug treatment, including treatment with antidepressant medications. In fact, people who have very low weight and are also depressed don't seem to respond to antidepressant medications in any way. Two medications have been shown to be of limited benefit for weight gain. Originally developed to treat psychosis, both of these medications are in a class called *second-generation antipsychotics* (so named because this group of medications was developed after the first-generation antipsychotic medications were developed in the 1940s). The two second-generation medications that have been shown to be beneficial in treating starvation eating disorders are Seroquel (quetiapine) and Zyprexa (olanzapine). Unfortunately, the benefits are limited, and the medications may be more effective in decreasing obsessive thinking about food and weight than in promoting long-term weight gain (Bissada et al. 2008; Dunican and DelDotto 2007; Powers et al. 2007). We have more data on Zyprexa than Seroquel, but more research on both drugs is needed to determine the long-term benefit for people with starvation eating disorders.

If you decide to try quetiapine, olanzapine, or another medication, make sure you consult with a prescriber who has expertise in eating disorders and can help you balance the risk of side effects with any potential benefit. And if you do start taking medication, remember that it is only a tool and should not be the major focus of your treatment.

Traditional Talk Therapies

When we think about treatment for psychological disorders, many of us think of insight-oriented talk psychotherapy. Most of the adult patients I see for treatment have had this kind of psychotherapy at some time in the past. Traditional *talk therapy* usually involves talking about your feelings and problems, sometimes exploring childhood issues, with someone who is nonjudgmental and caring, and in this way developing insight about those problems and about yourself. The process is intended to allow you to change your behavior based on your insights, which should lead you to feel better about yourself and your life. This kind of therapy is beneficial for some problems. For example, if you are going through a difficult situation in your life—say, you're getting a divorce—talking about your feelings and developing insight about your problems can be very helpful. Similarly, some people find that talking about problems from their past (such as an abusive childhood) is also helpful. But this talk therapy doesn't work for all problems. You may have had talk therapy in the past, and while it is possible that you got some positive things out of your therapy, it's probable that you did not gain weight or stop purging as a result of talking about your feelings or developing insight. In fact, if insight about how your starvation eating disorder was affecting your life was enough to cure your disorder, this book could have ended after the first five chapters.

The types of psychotherapies that are effective in starvation eating disorders are different from traditional talk therapy in that they are very active treatments that include homework and activities that challenge anxiety and distorted thoughts. There are two types of psychotherapy that do this for starvation eating disorders: cognitive behavioral therapy and specialist supportive clinical management. Many of the self-help strategies and exercises in this book are derived from these two therapies and will be discussed in the next section "What Does Work Well."

While insight-oriented talk therapy is unlikely to be helpful for recovering from your starvation eating disorder, once you gain weight, you can see a psychotherapist for other problems that may or may not be associated with your starvation eating disorder. Remember Amy's fear of becoming like her mother? After Amy gained weight and got her purging under control, she still experienced a lot of unresolved issues about her mother. Amy was healthy enough to become pregnant, but she decided to address the issues she had with her mother before having a child. I sent Amy to a colleague who wasn't an eating disorder specialist but who did more traditional talk therapy so Amy could talk with someone about her relationship with her mother while she and I worked on decreasing her anxiety about becoming fat like her mother, and this was very helpful in her weight gain. I could have worked with her on the other issues she wanted to address (such as the feeling of being abandoned by her mother), but Amy and I decided that it was more important that she and I concentrate on keeping her weight healthy as she went through her pregnancy. Amy was no longer starving her brain, so she was able to use insight to work with her psychotherapist, a marriage and family therapist, to resolve her feelings about her mother.

Residential Treatment Programs

Many people (including Amy) have tried residential treatment. There are many such programs throughout the United States, and they treat both children and adults. While people like Amy often gain weight in residential treatment, many lose weight again when they leave the program. If you have tried this kind of treatment, you know that while you're in treatment, you have little opportunity to restrict your eating and the staff watches you so closely that purging is also very difficult, if not impossible. But after you leave the structure of the residential program, it's very easy to go back to your old behaviors, and in my clinical experience, I've found that's what most people do. Amy and others have told me that they gained weight while in a residential program because that was the only way to be allowed to go home.

Unfortunately, residential treatment rarely means a lasting change in behavior *unless* you commit yourself to learning how to eat after you leave the program. Even residential treatment patients who want to get well and who feel committed to the program while in its sheltered environment can find it difficult to continue new, healthy behaviors after getting back to the "real" world. So if you choose residential treatment, make sure to choose a program that will help you transition to the real world. You will need a plan to maintain what you have achieved in the residential program, and good programs will build in a transition plan. Even with success during such a program, most people will have additional weight to gain after residential treatment. This book can help you gain the additional weight you may need to be healthy and, most important, can help you maintain the weight you gained during your stay in a residential program.

what does work well

The treatment methods that seem to be the most helpful for adults with a starvation eating disorder are those that focus on food, weight, and shape by doing things like keeping a food log and working on changing obsessive thinking about weight by writing down thoughts. Just talking about how you feel about these things or why you have an eating disorder is not effective in part because until you gain weight, your brain is starving, so it is difficult to have insight. As described in chapter 3, when your brain is starving, your emotions and thoughts are distorted. That's why gaining weight is always the first step.

Treating Eating, Weight, and Shape Concerns

Studies of starvation eating disorders focus on anorexia, not low-weight EDNOS, and most studies of anorexia have been of children, not adults, so there are too few studies of the treatment of adults with starvation eating disorders other than anorexia. Of the few studies that have been done, *specialist supportive clinical management* (SSCM) and *cognitive behavioral therapy* (CBT) have proven beneficial for initial weight gain in adults with anorexia (McIntosh et al. 2006; Bower and Ansher 2008). Both SSCM and CBT differ from traditional talk therapy in that both focus on eating, weight, and shape concerns, monitoring progress, and keeping food logs and less on insight. These are active treatments; they require you to do the kinds of things you have already started doing as you have worked through this book, like developing compelling reasons to get well. In addition, both treatments involve changing your thinking about food and weight. Let's look at SSCM and CBT to see how you can capitalize on some of the components of these two treatment modalities.

Specialist Supportive Clinical Management (SSCM)

The core feature of SSCM is to work with an eating disorder specialist who helps you focus on getting well through education, advice about what to eat, and treatment of specific symptoms such as purging. This book opens with a strong focus on education in part because the SSCM research indicates that education is an important part of getting well (McIntosh et al. 2006). SSCM is less structured than CBT, but, as with CBT, the focus is on keeping food logs, setting weight goals, and eating new foods while decreasing purging. It's unclear exactly how and why SSCM works, but it may be that having someone who is helping you stay focused on your goals and encouraging you to eat is what makes the difference.

There are not enough eating disorder specialists to work with everyone who has an eating disorder, but a nonprofessional coach can do many of the things a specialist does in SSCM. If you have decided to use a nonprofessional coach, your coach can help you stay focused on weight restoration.

Cognitive Behavioral Therapy (CBT)

CBT makes use of behavioral techniques like opposite action and cognitive therapy to change your thinking. Versions of CBT have been tailored to treat all kinds of psychological disorders including depression, anxiety, and eating disorders. One of the hallmarks of this kind of treatment is data collection and homework. Data collection (like logging your level of anxiety throughout the day or keeping track of how many times you purge) is common to all versions of CBT. Anxiety-reduction CBT techniques are widely used to treat all kinds of anxiety.

Reducing anxiety is an important part of recovering from a starvation eating disorder. We know a lot about how to reduce anxiety in people who have anxiety disorders such as panic disorder or obsessive-compulsive disorder. Distress-tolerance skills (Linehan 1993) are common anxiety-reduction skills used in CBT. These skills, which include self-soothing to reduce anxiety, can be very helpful for dealing with anxiety about gaining weight. You will learn distress-tolerance skills in chapter 9. Another behavioral anxiety treatment used in CBT is called *exposure and response prevention*. You will learn about this CBT technique in chapter 13. Both distress tolerance and exposure and response prevention will help you deal with your anxiety about gaining.

In addition to being used to treat anxiety, CBT has a well-established history of helping people improve their relationships and body image, both of which are helpful to people with starvation eating disorders.

Primary Treatment Components

There are some treatment components that are a must. For example, it's very hard to get well if you're not keeping track of what you eat. If you don't keep food logs, it's just too easy to restrict yourself to low-calorie foods or to not eat at all. Similarly, if you can't reduce your anxiety about gaining weight, your treatment will be hampered. The following sections look at the treatment components common to both CBT and SSCM that should be part of any treatment plan.

SELF-HARM REDUCTION

Harm reduction is an important part of both CBT and SSCM. Decreasing purging and other self-harm behaviors such as drinking alcohol will allow you to gain weight. Continuing to engage in self-harm while trying to gain weight will derail your plan. Reducing harm means reducing anxiety; self-harm is almost always an attempt to feel better by reducing anxiety. There are two major strategies for safely reducing anxiety: distress tolerance and exposure and response prevention.

- *Distress tolerance:* Gaining weight, keeping your weight at a healthy BMI, and eliminating purging create distress for someone with a starvation eating disorder. Distress-tolerance skills can decrease the distress everyone feels during treatment (Linehan 1993). Self-soothing and the other distress-tolerance skills you learn in chapter 9 will help you decrease your purging as well as tolerate weight restoration. Distress tolerance is a must for all treatment plans, and you can use it in all stages of treatment.

- *Exposure and response prevention:* Unlike distress-tolerance skills, exposure and response prevention methods challenge anxiety in a direct way by deliberately triggering anxiety. Doing this permits the natural physical response of *habituation* to allow your body to adapt to the anxiety trigger, thereby decreasing anxiety. The use of exposure and response prevention for reducing anxiety in eating disorders is new—it's typically been a CBT treatment for anxiety disorders—but there is growing interest in using these powerful techniques in this way. You will learn more about habituation and how to use exposure and response prevention to treat your anxiety in chapter 13.

In the beginning of weight restoration, you will focus on reducing anxiety with distress-tolerance skills. The goal will be to lower your anxiety enough to be able to eat and to keep the purging at bay until you can gain enough weight to be able to address your core anxiety with exposure and response prevention. But these anxiety-reduction strategies don't challenge your anxiety directly; you'll use exposure and response prevention for that. Once you have started to gain weight, you will need to add exposure and response prevention skills to your plan to address both your anxiety about leaving your starvation eating disorder behind and the anxiety you will probably have about doing new things like going back to school, getting a new job, or starting new relationships. In other words, you'll need to address the anxiety you have about the life activities that your starvation eating disorder has forced you to put on hold.

WEIGHT RESTORATION AND FOOD LOGS

It may seem silly to say the real treatment for a starvation eating disorder is food, but, in fact, food is the best medicine for your eating disorder. In chapter 10, you will learn how to set up your weight restoration plan, based on eating three meals and three snacks and called Three Plus Three. Keeping track of what and how much you eat is key. *The bottom line is this:* if you don't eat enough, you won't get well, and food logs can help you eat enough to gain weight.

Most people with a starvation eating disorder overestimate the amount they eat (in the same way that people with obesity will often underestimate the amount they eat). Keeping a food log will allow you to make sure you are eating enough. You will also use your food logs to identify triggers for purging as well as stressors that might be causing you to restrict your intake. Finally these food logs will help you to identify problems you will need to troubleshoot, like skipping breakfast or eating only a few types of food.

COGNITIVE THERAPY

Cognitive therapy is an important part of CBT. Cognitions are thoughts; cognitive therapy focuses on changing distorted thoughts into useful or helpful thoughts. The process of changing thoughts is often called *cognitive restructuring* because you are restructuring the thoughts that don't help you, making them useful thoughts. Starvation eating disorder thinking is very distorted. As you learned in chapter 5, distorted starvation eating disorder thoughts become obsessive, and they drive compulsive behaviors (like doing five hundred sit-ups a day). Psychologists know the kinds of distortions that are most common for people with starvation eating disorders, and in chapter 12 you will get to explore which of the common distortions you tend to make. After you have learned to identify the kind of distortions you are making, you will learn to restructure your distorted thoughts into nondistorted thoughts that can help you beat your eating disorder. Unlike CBT, SSCM does not directly teach you how to change your thinking, but having someone help you refocus your energies on gaining weight each time you get off track can change your thinking about weight and food over time.

Cognitive therapy is not specific to the treatment of starvation eating disorders. But learning how to restructure distorted thoughts is helpful for treating any type of eating disorder and has been shown to be very helpful in the treatment of depression and anxiety as well. The cognitive therapy skills you learn in chapter 12 will help you gain weight, keep it on, and cope with the depressive symptoms and anxiety that are commonly experienced by people with starvation eating disorders. You will continue to use cognitive therapy strategies when you move into weight maintenance in chapter 14. In fact, cognitive therapy skills are skills you can use for the rest of your life.

WORKING WITH A COACH

One of the reasons SSCM works appears to be support. In SSCM, an eating disorder specialist helps you stay focused on eating. A coach can support you in a similar manner. While not absolutely necessary, if you are not working with an eating disorder specialist, you should seriously consider using a coach. And even if you are working with an eating disorder specialist, a coach can add to the support you get from your eating disorder specialist. If you haven't decided yet if you want to use a coach, you may want to review the role a coach can play in helping you get well (see chapter 7).

Supplemental Treatment Options

In addition to the essential treatment components previously discussed, there are supplemental treatment components you can consider. Even some of the things that don't work very well alone, such as medication, can supplement what you do in this book. Let's look at these components, some of which will be familiar to you because they were discussed in the beginning of this chapter.

ZINC SUPPLEMENTATION

Zinc is an essential micronutrient that is found in the brain as well as other parts of the body. The idea that zinc might be a possible treatment component for starvation eating disorders came from a theory that zinc deficiency could be a causal factor in anorexia. Zinc is found in foods like milk and beef that many people with a starvation eating disorder avoid eating, so it's more likely that rather than being a *cause* of starvation eating disorders, zinc deficiency is a *result* of starvation. Research suggests that 14 mg of zinc each day can benefit people with anorexia during weight restoration (Birmingham and Gritzner 2006). Because low zinc levels adversely affect brain neurotransmitters, it's theorized that restoring zinc levels to normal can help a starving brain. As mentioned, neurotransmitters are chemicals in the brain that allow brain cells to communicate with each other. Most medications for mental disorders, like antidepressants, also target neurotransmitters. If you decide to try zinc supplementation, talk to your doctor to make sure there are no reasons you shouldn't take zinc. Also note that it has been studied for weight restoration but not for weight maintenance, so it's not known if its continued use after you are at a healthy weight is helpful.

PSYCHOTROPIC MEDICATION

As described in the beginning of this chapter, psychotropic medications have limited use prior to weight restoration, but there is some evidence that you can get a modest amount of reduction in obsessive thinking about weight and food with drugs like Zyprexa (olanzapine), and in a recent study, patients who took it gained weight faster than patients who took a placebo (Bissada et al. 2008). If you want to consider medication before you gain weight, try to find a psychiatrist or prescribing psychologist who has experience in treating starvation eating disorders. Remember that the benefit of these medications for weight gain is quite limited and depression does not respond to medication if your weight is very low. After you are weight restored, if you are still struggling with depression and anxiety, medication can be a more effective choice.

WORKING WITH A REGISTERED DIETITIAN

If you do choose to supplement your treatment by working with a dietitian, the focus should be on developing a weight-gain food plan rather than on the food pyramid or counting calories. During weight restoration, consulting a dietitian for assistance in choosing high-calorie food can help if you have been restricting for so long that you're not sure what to eat to increase your calories. After you are at a healthy weight, you can ask your dietitian to help you try new foods and you can even work with the dietitian on eating anxiety-provoking foods. If you find a dietitian who specializes in treating starvation eating disorder, that dietitian can be an important member of your treatment team.

RESIDENTIAL TREATMENT PROGRAM

If you decide to go to a residential treatment program, make sure you pick a program that has a good after-care plan, and consider using this book to continue your treatment. Residential programs are expensive and largely unregulated (Frisch, Herzog, and Franko 2006), so it's important to carefully check out the program you are considering to make sure a particular residential treatment program is a good choice for you. Most people leave residential programs still needing to gain additional weight. Even if you are lucky enough to leave the program at a healthy weight, you will need to maintain your healthy weight and not slip back into your self-harm behaviors. Cognitive therapy skills covered in chapter 12 and the anxiety exposure and response prevention skills in chapter 13 will be helpful for you. It can be very frightening to leave the sheltered environment of the residential program, so dealing with your anxiety will be essential to your success after you leave the program.

Supplemental Components of Your Treatment

Check off the supplemental treatment components you are going to consider:

- ☐ Zinc supplements

- ☐ Psychotropic medication

- ☐ Working with a registered dietitian

- ☐ Residential treatment program

---

treatment plan: component overview

Thus far we've discussed stage III treatment components. Starting with self-harm reduction, these components are meant to get you to a healthy weight. But relapse is a common problem in starvation eating disorders, so in stage IV you will learn about how to maintain a healthy weight, improve your body image, and, finally, move beyond your eating disorder.

Treatment Component Overview

Stage III—Getting Well

- Addressing self-harm (chapter 9)
    - Self-harm-reduction plan
    - Personal distress-tolerance plan
- Restoring health (chapter 10)
    - Weight restoration plan
    - Working with a coach
- Changing your thinking (chapter 12)
- Challenging anxiety (chapter 13)
    - Taking control of your anxiety

Stage IV—Living

- Maintaining a healthy weight (chapter 14)
    - Relapse prevention plan
- Building a life (chapter 15)
    - Improving body image
    - Taking your life back

to sum up

One of the challenges of treating starvation eating disorders is that we know more about what doesn't work than about what does work. Two treatment approaches have been shown to be effective in adults with starvation eating disorders: specialist supportive clinical management (SSCM) and cognitive behavioral therapy (CBT). Stages III and IV make use of some of the components of these approaches. Your treatment plan will include components such as self-harm reduction, weight restoration, changing your thinking, reducing anxiety, maintaining a healthy weight, improving body image, and developing a life beyond your eating disorder. There are also supplemental components (such as zinc) that you can add to your treatment plan. You will begin your treatment with self-harm reduction in the next chapter.

STAGE III

getting well—weight restoration

each part of stage III is designed to take you, step by step, to a healthy weight. The first step is self-harm reduction (chapter 9). Purging is a common type of self-harm, but it's not the only self-harm behavior that people with starvation eating disorders engage in. Other types of self-harm include restricting, diet pill abuse, and extreme exercise as well as self-harm not specific to an eating disorder, such as alcohol abuse. Eliminating self-harm is difficult because it serves a purpose—to decrease distress. If self-harm is not replaced with something else that can decrease distress, you will probably continue to engage in self-harm. So in stage III you will learn distress-tolerance skills to help with the distress that can come along with gaining weight.

Unless your BMI is now at 19, at a minimum, you will need weight restoration. Regardless of your BMI, if you are a woman in your childbearing years and not having regular periods, you will also need weight restoration. Chapters 10 and 11 cover the six phases of weight restoration. The first four phases set the foundation for eating enough to gain weight (chapter 10). During phase 5 and 6 you will start to gain weight by eating at regular times as well as consuming enough calories to gain weight (chapter 11). Once you have gained some weight, you will be ready to learn how to change your thinking with cognitive therapy (chapter 12) and work on challenging your anxiety with exposure and response prevention (chapter 13). At the end of stage III you will be prepared to move on to stage IV of your treatment and to develop a life beyond your starvation eating disorder.

CHAPTER 9

eating disorders and self-harm: minimizing health risks

anxiety about gaining weight (or just thinking about gaining weight), feeling fat, or hearing comments from others about weight are common triggers of self-harm behavior for someone with a starvation eating disorder. Self-harm isn't just a problem for those with eating disorders; self-harm is also seen in other psychological disorders, including personality disorders and mood disorders. Self-harm in starvation eating disorders is usually expressed in purging (including extreme exercise), diet pill abuse, and restricting; other kinds of self-harm (like cutting, drinking, or using street drugs) are common in other disorders but are also sometimes seen in people with starvation eating disorders. Regardless of the type of self-harm a person is relying on, it is almost always an attempt to escape anxiety.

See if you can relate to Grace's experience. Every time Grace thought about gaining weight, she felt panicky. Sometimes Grace had so much anxiety, her chest hurt and she felt like she was going crazy. Whenever Grace ate enough food to gain weight, didn't do her normal exercise routine, or felt too full, her anxiety triggered strong urges to get rid of the food by purging. Almost every time she felt that strong urge, Grace did purge. She purged because she knew from experience that she would feel better afterward. Grace's anxiety triggered a self-harm cycle that reinforced her starvation eating disorder by reducing her anxiety. Grace's self-harm cycle kept her from getting well for many years.

the self-harm cycle

The anxiety associated with starvation eating disorders, and the relief that behaviors like vomiting, extreme exercise, and restricting brings, sets up a self-harm cycle. Self-harm cycles are completely logical. All of us are drawn to behaviors that reduce anxiety. It's only natural to want anxiety to go away. Relief from anxiety is very reinforcing to all mammals. The problem is that if you use self-harm to decrease anxiety, the relief never lasts very long, and, invariably, a second anxiety trigger occurs and the cycle starts again. *The bottom line is this:* the more you use self-harm to cope with anxiety, the more anxiety you will have in the long term.

In chapter 10 you will start the process of weight restoration, but gaining weight while you are stuck in a self-harm cycle is very difficult. Even if you manage to gain a little weight, if you continue to purge, you will probably lose the weight again. Check off the reactions you have had in the past when you've tried to gain weight or thought about gaining weight:

☐ Felt a strong desire to purge

☐ Felt panicky and had physical symptoms of panic such as chest pain or palpitations

☐ Felt like you were going crazy

☐ Felt very anxious and checked your weight on the scale or checked yourself in the mirror over and over

☐ Weren't able to sleep because you ruminated about gaining weight

☐ Felt so anxious you felt like you couldn't sit still

☐ Weren't able to concentrate because all you could think about was being fat

How many reactions did you check off? These are the reactions that can start a self-harm cycle for you when you start to gain weight. In order to successfully gain weight, you will need to learn to deal with anxiety without having to resort to your self-harm behaviors. The next section explores the different kinds of self-harm behaviors that people with starvation eating disorders engage in.

Self-Harm Behaviors

There are several self-harm behaviors commonly associated with starvation eating disorders: purging (which includes extreme exercise), diet pill abuse, and restricting. Even if you don't purge, everyone with a starvation eating disorder severely restricts the amount of food they eat, and restricting is self-harm. People with starvation eating disorders sometimes engage in other self-harm behavior such as abusing alcohol or street drugs like methamphetamine. Alcohol abuse is particularly alarming in someone with a starvation eating disorder. One of the reasons drinking is so problematic is that low body weight can quickly lead to alcohol dependence and even alcohol toxicity. As with abuse of alcohol, stimulant abuse can be dangerous. Stimulants increase heart rate. A starving heart may have difficulty coping with the increase in heart rate that the stimulants in diet pills can cause. Cutting and burning, which are behaviors more common in people with bulimia, are sometimes seen in people with starvation eating disorders.

If you engage in any of these other self-harm behaviors, you should add them to your Self-Harm-Reduction Plan (at the end of this chapter). *If you are abusing alcohol or stimulants, you need to stop now.* If you need help to stop abusing these substances, you can go to a psychotherapist who is experienced in treating alcohol or drug abuse, you can go a 12-step program like Alcoholics Anonymous or Narcotics Anonymous, or you can do both.

Starvation Eating Disorder Self-Harm Behaviors

Check off any self-harm behaviors you engage in:

- ☐ **Purging**
  - ☐ Vomiting
  - ☐ Using laxatives
  - ☐ Using ipecac
  - ☐ Extreme exercising
- ☐ **Diet pill abuse**
- ☐ **Restricting**
- ☐ **Other self-harm behaviors**
  - ☐ Abusing alcohol or street drugs
  - ☐ Cutting or burning
  - ☐ Other: _____

Self-Harm Cycle Triggers

Not surprisingly, triggers for the self-harm cycle almost always have to do with things like thinking you are too fat, seeing an increase in weight, or feeling too fat—a common trigger that many of my patients describe as a physical sensation (akin to the way that pain is a physical sensation). Each trigger leads to anxiety, which leads to self-harm. When you self-harm, there is initial relief from anxiety, which is reinforcing of the self-harm behavior, but the more you engage in self-harm, the less it works. Most people experience a rebound of anxiety shortly after the self-harm behavior. So, in the end, your self-harm leads to more anxiety and then, of course, to more self-harm. And triggers don't just happen once—people with starvation eating disorders can experience triggers all day long. Let's look at the self-harm cycle in figure 2 to see how this works.

The self-harm cycle always starts with an anxiety trigger. For Grace, the anxiety trigger was usually feeling fat. This was a physical feeling for Grace that she described as her body feeling bloated and obese.

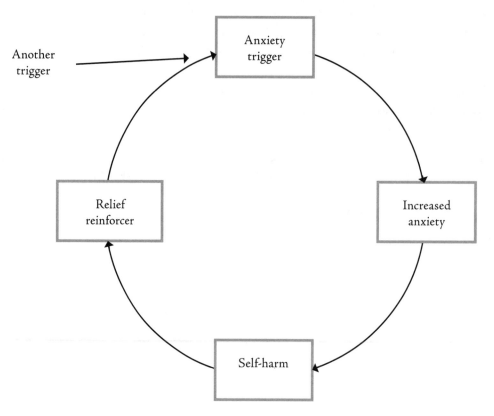

FIGURE 2: The self-harm cycle

Even if the scale didn't indicate a weight gain, Grace's feeling that she had gained weight was usually a powerful trigger for thoughts like, "The scale is wrong—I know I gained weight" and "If I gain weight, I won't be able to control it and I'll just keep gaining and gaining until I'm morbidly obese." These thoughts became additional triggers. Each thought increased her level of anxiety until it became overwhelming. Laxative abuse and exercising followed by restricting almost always decreased Grace's anxiety, so, understandably, she used these self-harm behaviors to cope with her anxiety. Because Grace's self-harm behaviors led to relief, her self-harm behavior was reinforced and strengthened. The reinforcement meant that the next time Grace experienced anxiety about her weight, she naturally went back to the behavior she knew would relieve her anxiety.

An anxiety trigger can be a thought, an emotion, a physical feeling, an experience, a stressor, or a behavior. Often more than one trigger will be involved in a self-harm cycle. Because emotions usually lead to thoughts, an emotional trigger or physical feeling will often lead to a thought trigger. Grace's example shows how her physical feeling of being fat led to thought triggers.

THOUGHTS

Our thoughts are powerful forces that trigger all kinds of behavior. We all have thoughts that are well practiced. These repetitive thoughts become triggers. For people with starvation eating disorders, "fat thoughts" are common triggers for self-harm. Thoughts can trigger an emotion or an emotion can trigger a thought. It doesn't really matter which comes first—the result is the same: self-harm. In the following list, check off any of the common thought triggers you experience:

☐ I'm so fat.

☐ I gained weight.

☐ If I eat, I won't be able to stop.

☐ My eating is out of control.

☐ If I gain weight, I'll be just like my mother.

☐ Other thoughts you have: _____

_____

EMOTIONS

Emotional triggers are often things like guilt and shame. These kinds of emotions trigger strong thoughts like, "I'm not good enough" or "I deserve the bad things that have happened to me." Joe experienced a lot of shame, and this shame often led to thoughts that he was unworthy because he wasn't perfect. When his weight became very low and his thoughts got more distorted, Joe had shame about eating even the smallest amount of food.

PHYSICAL FEELINGS

Physical feelings, like the feeling of being too full or fat, are common triggers. Grace, who abused laxatives, learned that her "feeling of fatness" was associated with constipation. Using laxatives set up a physical cycle for Grace that triggered a "fat feeling," which revved up her self-harm cycle. Constipation and feeling bloated are common triggers for people with starvation eating disorders.

Tips for Dealing with Constipation

If you experience constipation, the first thing to do is to stop using laxatives. Regular use makes your body dependent on laxatives. The only way to teach your body to function without the help of a laxative is to stop using them. Increasing dietary fiber with whole-grain bread and cereal can help. You can also try a wheat-bran supplement. Make sure to drink plenty of water when you use bran. If you absolutely cannot stop the laxatives, then cut down on laxative use—first to every other day, then every three days, and so on until you are no longer using laxatives.

EXPERIENCES

Like thoughts, experiences can be powerful triggers. The experience can be something someone else did that affected you or something that happened to you. Here are some examples of experience triggers:

- Someone commenting on your weight

- Getting in an argument with someone

- Going to the gym to find someone is using the machine you usually use

Comments from others about weight are common triggers for people with starvation eating disorders. Even comments about being "too thin," which you might think would decrease anxiety about being fat, can trigger anxiety. Many of my patients feel anxious whenever any kind of comment is made about their physical appearance. They tell me that comments like, "How do you stay so thin?" or "I wish I had your problem" are common triggers. Joe found that he became very anxious anytime someone commented about his weight. It didn't matter if the comment was positive or negative—the mere fact that someone noticed his weight was enough to make him exercise and restrict his eating more. Amy found that the comments that produced the most anxiety were from people she considered overweight. Any kind of comment from someone who was overweight made Amy think that she wasn't thin enough and might become obese. As a result, Amy's response to comments from people who were overweight was to engage in self-harm behavior like not eating for an entire day. Write down the comments that you find increase your anxiety.

Anxiety-Producing Comments from Other People
1. _____
_____
2. _____
_____
3. _____
_____

Does your anxiety increase even more if the comment is from one of the following?

Someone who is overweight	Yes	No
Someone who is underweight	Yes	No
A family member	Yes	No
Someone of the opposite sex	Yes	No
Do comments from others trigger self-harm?	Yes	No

STRESSORS

Some triggers have nothing to do with weight, shape, or food. Lorrie found that work stress was a trigger for her self-harm. Lorrie, who had a job as a middle manager for a large company, found that the more stressed she was at work, the more she wanted to purge to relieve the stress. Lorrie had practiced self-harm so many times to relieve anxiety associated with her eating disorder that self-harm had become her first choice for coping with any kind of distress. The stress of her job and the self-harm cycle became so difficult for Lorrie to handle that she left her job. Work stress, relationship difficulties, or money worries are all common stressors that can lead to anxiety. In the next list, check off any stressors that you find lead you to self-harm:

☐ Work stress

☐ Relationship stress

☐ Money problems

☐ School pressure

☐ Problems with children

☐ Other: _____

BEHAVIOR

Your behavior can be a powerful trigger for anxiety, which can then lead to self-harm. Amy found that eating out at a restaurant almost always triggered purging. This became such a problem for her that she stopped eating in restaurants. Unfortunately Amy found that her restaurant trigger was just replaced by other triggers, and she continued to purge. In the following list, check off behaviors that trigger anxiety for you:

☐ Eating a food that you consider to be an "unsafe" food

☐ Eating more than you planned or going over your calorie allotment for the day

☐ Putting on tight clothing

☐ Looking at yourself in a mirror

☐ Eating at a restaurant

☐ Missing your regular workout or exercising less than you planned

☐ Getting on the scale to check your weight

☐ Other: _____

Binge Eating

Binge eating can play such an important role in the self-harm cycle that it's worth looking at this behavior in more detail. Binge eating can be a trigger for self-harm, and for people with some kinds of eating disorders, binge eating itself can be a self-harm behavior. But for someone with a *starvation* eating disorder, binge eating is *not* self-harm. As described in stage I, binge eating is a normal behavior for someone who is starving; it is the result of the starving brain sending out strong "Feed me" messages, with chronic starvation leading to a "Feed me and don't stop" message. Many people get confused about binge eating and think that it is only associated with bulimia or binge-eating disorder, but bingeing is a common behavior in starvation eating disorders.

Joe's experience with binge eating is typical of the problem. Joe, who spent a lot of time and energy trying to ignore his brain's "Feed me" message, sometimes gave in and binged on cereal. When he binged on cereal, Joe's anxiety would increase so he usually planned his purging while he ate. After his binge episode, Joe would feel guilty and would think that he was a "bad person" for eating. These thoughts just intensified his anxiety and his desire to purge. Joe's anxiety would climb so high that he felt that the only way out was

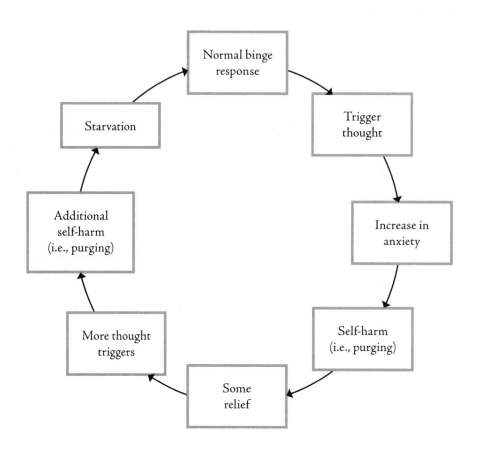

FIGURE 3: Joe's self-harm cycle

to purge. After he vomited, he felt some relief. But the relief never lasted very long, and soon Joe would start to worry that he hadn't purged all that he'd eaten or that some of the calories had been absorbed before he purged. This set up another wave of anxiety, and he would go to the gym to work out. Joe's purging, which extended to burning calories at the gym, starved his brain even more, and his brain sent out more "Feed me" messages. This trapped him in a vicious cycle of self-harm. While Joe's bingeing might look like a behavior trigger, the trigger that really started Joe's self-harm cycle was the fact that he didn't eat. Bingeing was just a biological response to starvation. Restricting was the trigger for Joe's self-harm. Figure 3 shows Joe's typical binge-and-purge experience.

your personal self-harm pattern

Everyone's self-harm pattern is a little different. Understanding your pattern means understanding the anxiety triggers you most often experience and learning how often you use self-harm, how much anxiety reduction you experience, and how long the relief from anxiety lasts before you start the cycle again. To learn about your self-harm pattern, complete the Self-Harm Log that follows.

Instructions for Your Self-Harm Log: You should log your self-harm behavior for at least two days and for at least five self-harm examples. These are minimums—the more you log the better. If you engage in self-harm frequently, it might take only two days to get five examples. If you don't engage in self-harm very often, it might take a week or more to log five examples. It's important that you log the self-harm episodes consecutively so that you can see how long your relief lasts before your anxiety returns and you engage in self-harm again. The more data you collect, the easier it will be for you to see patterns. If after logging the minimum you find your pattern of self-harm is not clear, try logging more than five episodes of self-harm to see if a pattern emerges. On your self-harm log, rate your anxiety from 0–5 with 5 being the most extreme anxiety you have ever experienced. Often more than one trigger is involved, so there is room for two triggers on your log. If you experienced more than two triggers, write down the two triggers you think had the most powerful influence on your self-harm behavior.

Self-Harm Log					
Date/time	Anxiety trigger 1	Anxiety trigger 2	Anxiety rating before (0–5)	Self-harm behavior	Anxiety rating after (0–5)

Learning from Your Log

Answer these questions to see what you learned from your self-harm log:

■ What triggers did you notice?

_____

_____

■ Did your triggers tend to be emotions, thoughts, stressors, behaviors, or experiences?

_____

_____

■ In general, how long did your relief last?

■ In general, how much anxiety relief did you experience from your self-harm behavior (that is, by how many points did your anxiety go down)? _____

your self-harm-reduction plan

Now that you have a picture of your self-harm pattern, it's time to look at how to reduce self-harm with a goal of eventually eliminating it. It's important that you develop a self-harm-reduction plan because if you continue to engage in self-harm behaviors like purging, you will sabotage your weight restoration. It is possible to gain weight while purging or engaging in other self-harm, but continuing to use self-harm to deal with anxiety will make it easier for you to limit your weight gain and make it more likely you will lose the weight again and be right back where you started. If you can't stop purging all at once, then reduce your self-harm as much as you can with the goal of stopping as soon as you are able.

The key to reducing self-harm is to find a way to interrupt your self-harm cycle. You can interrupt the cycle anywhere along the cycle's chain. You can even prevent the cycle by interrupting or preventing an anxiety trigger. Let's look at the basic self-harm cycle again to see how the cycle can be stopped. Look over your log and find a good example of your self-harm cycle. In figure 4, fill in the triggers and the type of self-harm you engaged in. If one trigger led to another trigger, write in the trigger that started the cycle first and then write the next trigger below it. If you experienced additional triggers shortly after engaging in self-harm, write those on the left side of the cycle.

Now that you have a good idea of what your typical self-harm cycle looks like, you can learn to interrupt or even avoid it. You can start by addressing an anxiety trigger and then learning how to tolerate the anxiety, once it is triggered, without using self-harm.

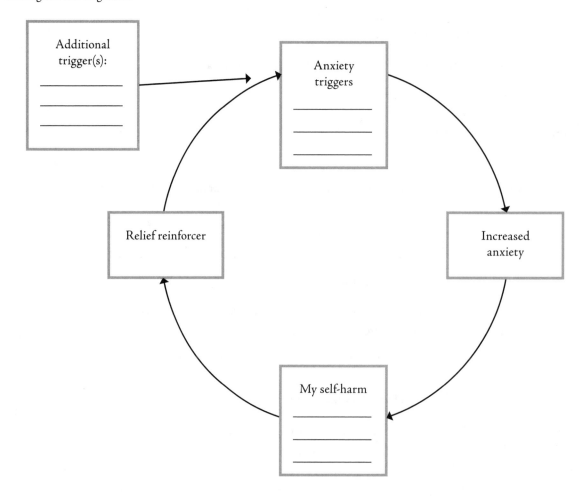

FIGURE 4: My self-harm cycle

avoiding or interrupting the anxiety trigger

Some triggers can be avoided. Restricting provides the best example. The starvation that comes from restricting is the ultimate trigger. Starvation leads to binge eating, which in turn triggers an anxiety-provoking thought like, "I shouldn't have eaten that." That thought is a trigger for self-harm, such as more restricting or purging. You avoid the trigger of restricting simply by eating: during weight restoration, eating three meals a day with regular snacks will be your most powerful strategy for keeping your self-harm cycle at bay.

Other anxiety triggers can also be avoided while you are gaining weight. For example, if eating in a restaurant is a trigger for you, it's okay to avoid that trigger until you gain weight. But after your weight is at least in the low normal BMI range, you should work on being able to go to a restaurant. In chapter 13 you will learn how to decrease the power of triggers so that you can engage in this normal behavior without triggering a self-harm cycle.

Some triggers can be interrupted. For example, thought triggers are susceptible to interruption. As you learn to change your thinking, you will be able to take a trigger thought like, "I'm fat" and change it to a useful thought like, "I feel fat, but feelings are not facts, and my weight is too low to be healthy." You already have some basic tools for changing your thinking. Your motivational cards can be used to interrupt trigger thoughts. By keeping your cards close by, you can use them when you have a trigger thought. Amy used her motivational cards in this way. When she started to have trigger thoughts, she got her cards out and reviewed her reasons for gaining weight. This interrupted her trigger thinking by reminding her of her compelling reasons for gaining weight. You will learn additional strategies for changing your thinking in chapter 12.

tolerating anxiety

Being able to tolerate anxiety so that it doesn't become overwhelming is a very useful way to interrupt the self-harm cycle. There are three basic ways to do this: (1) distress tolerance, (2) acceptance, and (3) exposure. You will start using the first two strategies before you gain and while you are gaining weight. Exposure is a strategy that involves challenging your anxiety, and it is covered in chapter 13.

Distress Tolerance

As discussed in chapter 5, the anxiety associated with starvation eating disorders can be overwhelming. Distress tolerance is a concept from dialectical behavior therapy (DBT). First developed by Marcia Linehan, Ph.D., at the University of Washington (Linehan 1993), DBT has been shown to be helpful in dealing with overwhelming emotions. Two DBT skills, *self-soothing* and *distracting*, are very helpful in coping with anxiety. These skills are part of a group of skills called *distress-tolerance skills*. Because starvation eating disorders tend to isolate you from others, I have added *social support* as a separate distress-tolerance skill. Distracting, self-soothing, and social support can prevent self-harm by allowing you to tolerate anxiety or stop self-harm once it has started. Let's look at each distress-tolerance skill to see how you can use distress tolerance to change your self-harm cycle.

DISTRACTING

Distracting yourself from self-harm works because self-harm urges come in waves. If you are able to wait and therefore not engage in self-harm right away, you will probably be less likely to engage in the self-harm later. You can also use distraction after you have started a self-harm behavior. When Amy was first reducing her self-harm, she used distraction several times to stop self-harm after she was already engaged in it. This minimized the amount of self-harm she engaged in. For example, before she started to work on her self-harm-reduction plan, Amy always followed vomiting with laxative abuse. Amy found that she could use distraction in the form of crossword puzzles or gardening to prevent the laxative abuse even if she had already vomited. Each time Amy did this, she got closer to using distraction to avoid vomiting as well and, in this way, to reducing both types of self-harm. Look over the following list of distracting ideas and check off distracting activities you can use. At the end of the list, add at least two ideas of your own.

Ideas for Distracting from Self-Harm Behaviors

- ☐ Read a book.
- ☐ Watch a favorite movie.
- ☐ Give yourself a manicure or pedicure.
- ☐ Sew or do some other kind of craft.
- ☐ Clean out a closet or drawer.
- ☐ Wash and fold laundry.
- ☐ Do volunteer work.
- ☐ Plant flowers.
- ☐ Do crossword or jigsaw puzzles.
- ☐ Take care of your house plants.
- ☐ Play solitaire or video games.
- ☐ _____
- ☐ _____
- ☐ _____
- ☐ _____

SELF-SOOTHING

Self-soothing reduces anxiety by soothing your mind and body. Many people with starvation eating disorders feel soothed after purging; binge eating can be soothing, too, for some people (although this is more typical for people with binge-eating disorder or bulimia than for those with a starvation eating disorder). Self-soothing can be used in a harmful way or a useful way. Purging, cutting, or drinking too much alcohol are all examples of destructive self-soothing. Because it's possible to self-soothe in a way that makes your eating disorder worse, make sure that you are using self-soothing behaviors, like the ones listed next, that decrease the strength of your starvation eating disorder. In the beginning, useful self-soothing activities won't be as powerful as your self-harm, but over time, as you decrease your self-harm, you will find these useful activities work better and better for soothing your anxiety.

Review the ideas for self-soothing. Check off the activities you think would work and add at least two self-soothing activities of your own to the list.

Ideas for Self-Soothing
☐ Take a warm bath and use some soothing lotion on your body afterward.
☐ Sit in the sun and listen to music.
☐ Listen to a relaxation recording.
☐ Look at pictures that prompt happy memories.
☐ Pet a cat or dog.
☐ Get a massage.
☐ Light scented candles.
☐ Listen to music.
☐ _____
☐ _____
☐ _____
☐ _____

Note: For more ideas for distress tolerance, see *The Dialectical Behavior Therapy Skills Workbook* by McKay, Wood, and Brantley (New Harbinger, 2007).

SOCIAL SUPPORT

Social support in the form of 12-step groups and other support groups has a long tradition of helping people decrease self-harm. Eating disorder support groups can be found online, and there are a growing number of in-person eating disorder support groups around the country. Many of these groups welcome people with all eating disorders, but some are specific to starvation eating disorders. See the Helpful Resources appendix for support-group resources.

In addition to group social support, your friends and family can provide you with support. Calling a friend just to chat about life or hear how she is doing is social support. The great thing about this kind of support is that you don't even have to talk about your eating disorder. In fact, it's often a good idea to focus on unrelated topics and take a break from your eating disorder. Using social support to reduce self-harm can be as simple as e-mailing a friend in your support group or calling your best friend to talk about his life. If you have decided to use a coach, your coach can be a good source of social support.

Joe called or e-mailed his coach when his anxiety over bingeing prompted strong urges to purge. Joe and his coach would review Joe's reasons for getting well. Talking to his coach served several purposes.

Their conversation distracted Joe from his self-harm urges, reinforced his motivation, and provided Joe (who had isolated himself from others) with the social contact he needed. Similarly, when her anxiety triggered thoughts about purging, Grace sometimes talked online to a childhood friend. Although Grace hadn't seen her friend in years, the friend was able to provide Grace with the support she needed. Because Grace's friend had been clean and sober from alcohol for five years, she understood what Grace was going through in a way Grace's other friends couldn't. If you know someone like Grace's friend who has gotten clean and sober through a 12-step group or other community program, she might be a good source of support for you. Many people use alcohol or other drugs to cope with anxiety. Using purging to cope with anxiety is a similar behavior. As Grace's friend put it, "I understood what Grace was feeling and how badly she wanted to purge because that's how I felt about alcohol."

Social support can come from many different places. Review following the social support activities. Check off the social support you plan to use and add at least two to the list.

Ideas for Using Social Support to Prevent Self-Harm

☐ Call a friend or family member.

☐ Go online to chat or send an e-mail.

☐ Meet a friend for coffee or shopping.

☐ Go to a church meeting.

☐ Go to a support-group meeting.

☐ Visit a neighbor and talk about things that have nothing to do with your eating disorder.

☐ Talk to someone who has recovered from alcohol or other addiction.

☐ _____

☐ _____

☐ _____

☐ _____

Your Distress-Tolerance Plan

Not every distress-tolerance skill works for everyone. Grace found music very soothing, while Joe didn't find that music worked at all for him. It's important to make a list of distress-tolerance activities that work for you. You can use your strategies for any kind of distress, but the most important use of your distress-tolerance activities is to deal with the anxiety of gaining weight. Your list should be a work in progress. You should add to the list as you find more things that work for you, and you may have to delete an item if you find that it just doesn't work for you. Let's look at Grace's list to see how an initial list might look.

Grace's Distress-Tolerance Plan for Weight Restoration		
Distraction	Self-soothing	Social support
Reading	Taking a warm bath	Talking to my best friend
Gardening	Listening to country music	Calling my sister
Knitting	Getting a manicure	Talking online to my friends
Scrapbooking	Praying	Visiting with my goddaughter
Watching TV	Sitting in my garden	Talking to my coach
Going to a movie	Petting my cat	Going to church
Cleaning out a drawer or closet	Writing in my journal	E-mailing my best friend

Notice that Grace put enough strategies on her list that she would be able to find one that worked for her even if the first thing she tried didn't decrease her anxiety. Look over the distracting, self-soothing, and social-support activities you checked off and transfer them to your distress-tolerance plan here. Remember, you need as many activities on your list as possible because in any given situation, some strategies will work better than others.

Distress-Tolerance Plan for Weight Restoration		
Distraction	Self-soothing	Social support

distress-tolerance card: By now you should have several motivational cards to help you remember why you need to gain weight. You can now start making distress-tolerance cards to use when you need to interrupt your self-harm cycle. Take several 3 by 5 cards and write down self-soothing, distracting, or social-support activities on the cards. As with your motivational system, the idea is to keep the cards handy so you can use them whenever the need arises. Add your distress-tolerance cards to your motivational cards.

Acceptance

Using acceptance as a way to manage distress has received attention in recent years. Several cognitive behavioral therapies, including DBT, use acceptance as a strategy to deal with anxiety and other difficult emotional states. Acceptance and commitment therapy (ACT), a type of cognitive behavioral therapy, has even been adapted for the treatment of eating disorders (Heffner and Eifert 2004). *Acceptance* means that we acknowledge that experiencing distress is common to all human beings *and* that there will be times when we cannot get rid of our distress. If we can't lower our distress in a healthy way, we need to accept the distress. If we refuse to accept the distress at these times, we are likely to engage in unhealthy behaviors like purging that may lower distress in the short term but will make our lives worse in the long term. Acceptance as a strategy is not unlike the Serenity Prayer that is used in 12-step programs. Some things we just can't change. If we try to avoid all distress, we will drink, take drugs, purge, or do other self-harm behaviors, which in the end will just lead to more distress.

Acceptance that you have to gain weight to be healthy and that gaining weight will cause a lot of anxiety is probably the hardest kind of acceptance that you will ever have to face. Distracting, self-soothing, and social support can help decrease the anxiety about weight gain, but these strategies will not take away all the anxiety you feel when you start to gain weight. You will have to accept a certain amount of anxiety to get well. Grace explained how she got to acceptance this way:

> I had to accept that I had to gain weight to have a life with my children. I had to accept the anxiety that I experienced as I gained weight and stopped purging. I didn't want to gain weight, but if I didn't, my life would have continued to be unmanageable and I know I wouldn't be able to be the kind of mom for my kids that I wanted to be. My starvation eating disorder had already hurt my children, and it was clear that not gaining weight would hurt them even more. It took a while, but I finally accepted that doing the opposite of what I wanted to do and accepting the anxiety was the only way out of the pain my eating disorder was causing for me and my children.

ACCEPTANCE STATEMENT

Acceptance is not something you do once. You will have to accept many times over that getting well will involve tolerating anxiety. An acceptance statement is one that you can reaffirm when you feel like giving in to your anxiety. Anxiety comes in waves, so if you can accept your anxiety without acting on it, your anxiety will recede over time. An acceptance statement should include why it's best to accept feeling anxious without resorting to self-harm as well as a reminder that you can sit with your anxiety without acting on it. Let's look at Amy's acceptance statement to see how to write an acceptance statement.

Amy's Acceptance Statement
Anxiety is part of life. Anxiety can be tolerated. By giving in to my anxiety in the past and purging, I have actually increased my anxiety about my weight. I can tolerate anxiety even though it is difficult. I am choosing to feel the anxiety rather than purge, which would reinforce my starvation eating disorder. I will tolerate my anxiety because I want to have children, and continuing to starve and purge will take the opportunity to become a mother away from me.

Now it's time to write your own acceptance statement. Reviewing your motivational cards can help you get in touch with why you are going to gain weight and stop purging. Write your acceptance statement here.

Your Acceptance Statement
Anxiety is part of life. Anxiety can be tolerated. By giving in to my anxiety in the past and _____,
(whatever self-harm behaviors have kept your starvation eating disorder going)
I have actually increased my anxiety about my weight. I can tolerate anxiety even though it is difficult. I am choosing to feel the anxiety rather than _____,
(self-harm)
which would reinforce my starvation eating disorder. I will tolerate my anxiety because _____
_____
_____
_____
_____
(your reasons for getting well)

acceptance card: Put your acceptance statement on a 3 by 5 card.

pulling together your plan

You now have cards for motivation, distress tolerance, and acceptance. Review them. Put a stack of cards together that you can carry with you throughout the day. Together, these are now your *self-harm-reduction cards*. Refer to the cards when you feel like engaging in self-harm.

Here are some things to remember about self-harm:

- Eating regularly is the key to preventing a binge that can trigger self-harm.

- Each time you tolerate anxiety and don't engage in self-harm behavior, you are taking control of your starvation eating disorder. If you engage in self-harm behavior, your starvation eating disorder is taking control of you.

- It's often possible to stop self-harm even after you have started to engage in a self-harm behavior. So if you slip, don't beat yourself up—just stop as soon as possible and recommit to reducing self-harm.

- Your self-harm-reduction cards won't help you if you don't use them. Commit to getting the cards out and reading them even if you think you're not going to use distress tolerance or acceptance. Just the act of reviewing your cards will often take you to the next step of using the strategies on the cards.

- If you can't stop all your self-harm behaviors yet, focus on reducing your self-harm as much as possible. Commit to continuing to reduce self-harm until you no longer engage in self-harm behaviors.

- If you engage in frequent self-harm behaviors (once a day or more often), spend the next two weeks practicing your self-harm reduction before going on to weight restoration.

Now fill in your self-harm-reduction plan.

Self-Harm-Reduction Plan
- List the self-harm triggers that you can avoid: _____   _____   _____   _____   _____

Check off the strategies you plan to use to tolerate anxiety:

☐ Distracting

☐ Self-soothing

☐ Social support

☐ Distress-tolerance card

☐ Acceptance card

☐ Review motivational cards (including your compelling reasons to get well)

to sum up

Self-harm will interfere with weight gain and weight maintenance. Self-harm such as purging also reinforces your starvation eating disorder. The reinforcing nature of self-harm comes from the way self-harm can temporarily reduce your anxiety.

There are a number of self-harm triggers, including thoughts, emotions, physical feelings, things others say to you, and stressors such as money worries. Triggers work by increasing your anxiety about your weight and shape. You can interrupt the self-harm cycle by using self-soothing or other strategies to decrease your anxiety. Binge eating is sometimes thought of as a self-harm behavior, but for someone with a starvation eating disorder, it is really a natural response to starvation. The self-harm trigger is the starvation itself, not the binge eating. By understanding your triggers and developing strategies to interrupt the self-harm cycle, you can avoid self-harm.

Acceptance is as valuable a strategy as practicing distress tolerance and eating regularly. Accepting that you need to gain weight, even though you don't want to, will allow you to get well and have a life beyond your eating disorder. Your self-harm-reduction cards can help, but only if you use them.

Few people are able to stop every form of self-harm all at once. The important thing to remember is that every time you decrease self-harm, you are increasing the chance that your weight restoration plan will be successful *and* you are decreasing your risk for medical complications associated with self-harm. Once you have started to decrease your self-harm, you will be ready to move on to weight restoration in the next chapter.

CHAPTER 10

restoring health with food:
the first four phases

getting healthy means gaining weight and maintaining a healthy weight. In order to gain weight, you will need to develop a weight restoration plan. Without a plan, your starvation eating disorder will take control. Your weight restoration plan will take the control away from your starvation eating disorder and put that control back in your hands. Gaining weight will be hard and you will probably experience increased anxiety as you work on your plan. Use the distress-tolerance skills you learned in chapter 9 to help you tolerate the anxiety.

There are six phases to a weight restoration plan. In this chapter you will work through phases 1–4, which will set the foundation for weight gain. In chapter 11 you will work through phases 5 and 6, which will focus on the specifics of eating enough to gain weight. While you work through the phases of weight restoration, you must continue to work to decrease purging by using distress tolerance and the other strategies you learned in chapter 9. The more you are able to get your purging under control, the better chance you have of gaining enough weight to be healthy.

If you are like most people with a starvation eating disorder, you have tried to gain weight before. That's okay—weight restoration can take several tries to be successful. Remember, the only way your eating disorder can win is if you quit trying to get healthy.

weight restoration plan—overview

Each phase of weight restoration is intended to move you successfully to the next phase. Jumping in and starting to eat normally with little preparation (especially after years of struggling with a starvation eating disorder) is overwhelming. Breaking weight restoration into phases can make the process of gaining weight manageable. In phase 1 you will gather the tools you need to be successful. In phase 2 you will collect data about your current eating, and in phase 3 you will set goals for your weight restoration. Phase 4, which involves setting a schedule for eating three meals and three snacks, is the last phase covered in this chapter. In phases 5 and 6 (chapter 11) you will learn how to implement your plan and troubleshoot any problems that arise. Check off each phase on the following list as you complete it.

Weight Restoration Phase Checklist
☐ Phase 1: Gathering Your Tools (in chapter 10)
☐ Phase 2: Collecting Data (in chapter 10)
☐ Phase 3: Setting Your Goals (in chapter 10)
☐ Phase 4: Setting Up an Eating Schedule—Three Plus Three (in chapter 10)
☐ Phase 5: Implementing Your Plan (in chapter 11)
☐ Phase 6: Troubleshooting (in chapter 11)

phase 1: gathering your tools

Phase 1 is about getting ready by gathering the tools you will need to be successful in gaining weight. Because you need to see your doctor or primary care provider (PCP) before you begin your plan, this phase can take several weeks. If you decided in chapter 7 to use a coach, you should also meet with your coach during phase 1. In addition to seeing your PCP and coach, you should review your distress-tolerance plan for weight restoration (in chapter 9), stop exercising, reduce daily activities, and review your reasons for gaining weight. Let's examine each of the steps in phase 1 to see what needs to be done.

Checklist for Phase 1

- ☐ I saw my primary care provider and discussed my weight restoration plan.
- ☐ I met with my coach or eating disorder specialist (if applicable).
- ☐ I reviewed my Distress-Tolerance Plan for Weight Restoration and my Self-Harm-Reduction Plan (chapter 9).
- ☐ I stopped exercising and decreased my physical activities.
- ☐ I reviewed why I need to gain weight.
- ☐ I planned ahead and set my target date for starting phase 3: _____

(*Date*)

Seeing Your Primary Care Provider (PCP)

Taking time to visit your PCP and discuss your weight restoration plan and weight goals with her is an important step in preparing to gain weight. If you are interested in taking zinc supplements, discuss this option with your PCP when you see her. When you see your doctor, consider asking for the following information:

- ☐ What health problems am I at risk for if I don't gain weight?

- ☐ What health issues should I be aware of as I gain weight?

- ☐ What do you think would be a healthy BMI (and weight) for me?

- ☐ Are there any blood tests or other lab tests I should do before I start my weight restoration plan?

- ☐ Do you want to do any lab tests periodically during my weight restoration?

- ☐ How much should I restrict my physical activity until I have gained weight?

- ☐ Should I take a multivitamins or any supplements (including zinc)?

Write a summary of your conversation with your PCP in your notebook. This will help you later when you set your weight restoration goals. Regular lab tests are particularly important if your BMI is very low or if you have had abnormal test results in the past. Be sure to follow through with any lab work your PCP wants you to do.

Meeting with Your Coach or Eating Disorder Specialist

Chapter 7 explored how to use the services of a nonprofessional coach or an eating disorder specialist. If you have a coach or are working with an eating disorder specialist, you should share chapters 1, 10 and 11 with your coach or specialist. Either team member can help you develop your weight restoration plan by doing the following:

- Helping you analyze your eating to determine eating problems, such as using caffeine to avoid eating

- Giving you ideas for foods to eat

- Helping you keep on track by reviewing your food logs and encouraging you to eat new foods

- Acting as a cheerleader

If you are working with both an eating disorder specialist and a nonprofessional coach, you should make sure that your eating disorder specialist knows about your coach. It's a good idea for your coach and specialist to meet. Ask your eating disorder specialist about bringing your coach to one of your treatment sessions.

COACHES

Remember, no one can tell you what to eat or make you eat. You have to do that for yourself, but a coach can support and encourage you. To make sure you and your coach are on the same page, it's a good idea to review the Advice for the Nonprofessional Coach in chapter 7 with your coach (especially if it's been a while since you worked through that chapter).

You and your coach need to agree on what you want him to do for you during weight restoration. This means agreeing on how often you will meet, talk, or e-mail while you are gaining weight and whether you want him to review your food logs. If your coach is not going to review your food logs, think about other ways he can support you (perhaps by reminding you, when you feel like giving up, why you are doing such a hard thing as weight restoration). If your coach is at a distance, you and he can use e-mail for support and food log review. Or if you would like your coach to help you stop purging, you can call or e-mail him when you feel like purging. Use the coach agreement that follows to make sure you and your coach agree on the coach's role.

Coach Agreement

My coach will do the following:

Coach activities

- ☐ Review my baseline food log with me and help me analyze what I need to change.
- ☐ Review my weekly food logs with me:
    - ☐ Make suggestions for new foods *or*
    - ☐ Act only as a cheerleader without making suggestions for new foods.
- ☐ Help me make changes in my thinking by working with me on chapter 12 (which involves making suggestions for new thoughts about food and weight).

Coach support

- ☐ Help me stop purging by supporting me when I call or e-mail when I'm feeling like purging.
- ☐ Help me keep on track by being a sounding board.
- ☐ Help me keep on track by reminding me why I need to gain weight to be healthy.

Frequency of contact with my coach

- ☐ My coach and I will use e-mail for food log review or support:
    - ☐ Daily
    - ☐ Every _____ days
    - ☐ Every week
    - ☐ Other: _____
- ☐ My coach and I will connect (meet or talk on the phone):
    - ☐ Once a week
    - ☐ Every other week
    - ☐ Once a month
    - ☐ Other: _____

EATING DISORDER SPECIALISTS

If you are working with an eating disorder specialist, you should discuss how often you are going to meet during weight restoration. Some eating disorder specialists will meet with patients more than once a week during weight restoration. Your specialist will probably want to see food logs when you meet, and sometimes you may even eat during your sessions. Like many eating disorder specialists, I often have patients eat in my office. Your eating disorder specialist may also offer group treatment. If you have this opportunity, take advantage of it. Group treatment can be very helpful during weight restoration. Eating with others who are having the same struggles that you are experiencing, and supporting others while you are being supported, are both powerful experiences.

Reviewing Distress-Tolerance and Self-Harm-Reduction Plans

Gaining weight is always anxiety provoking for someone with a starvation eating disorder. Now is the time to review the distress-tolerance strategies you have been using to decrease your purging. How have the strategies been working for you? Do you need to add to your Distress-Tolerance Plan for Weight Restoration list (in chapter 9)? It's not uncommon to need to update it every so often. You should also review your Self-Harm-Reduction Plan (in chapter 9) to see if you need to look at any additional self-harm triggers. If you haven't already done so, make 3 by 5 cards listing the distracting, self-soothing, and social-support skills you listed in chapter 9. Hopefully you have been practicing these skills as you have decreased your purging.

Stopping Exercise and Decreasing Physical Activity

While you are gaining weight, you need to stop exercising. If your BMI is under 15, you should not only stop exercising, but avoid physical activity as much as possible until your BMI is at least 15 or your PCP says it is safe for you to resume normal activities. Restricting physical activity means avoiding calorie-burning activities like housework, gardening, or shopping. If you enjoy exercise, you can use the ability to return to exercise as a reward for gaining weight. Joe, who loved to go to the gym, started to go back three days a week when his BMI reached 18. He restricted himself to twenty to thirty minutes of strength-building exercises until his BMI reached 20. When his BMI was stable at 20, he rewarded himself with one hour of exercise, four to five times a week. This exercise schedule allowed Joe to keep his weight stable and healthy.

In deciding how much physical activity you should do, consider the following guidelines:

- *BMI under 15:* Restrict all physical activity as much as possible. Again, this means no housework or other calorie-burning daily activities.

- *BMI 15–16:* No exercise but you can do limited, regular daily activities such as moderate housework (for example, washing the dishes) as long as you continue to gain weight.

- *BMI 16–18:* No exercise but you can engage in most regular daily activities as long as you continue to gain weight and avoid activities that consume a great deal of calories such as vigorous housework.

LIMITING ENERGY-BURNING ACTIVITIES

See the following list of common activities and the range of energy you would use if you did any of these activities for one hour. The energy ranges are based on a person with a BMI in the low normal range and are intended to give you an idea of which activities use more energy and which use less. Use the table as a guide only. Remember, if your BMI is under 15, you need to limit your activity as much as possible—that means staying seated or lying down most of the time, limiting your physical movement, and avoiding even light housework.

Energy Needed for Common Activities (Based on a BMI in the Low Normal Range)			
	Low	**Moderate**	**High**
Examples of activities	■ Reading in bed ■ Watching TV ■ Bathing ■ Putting on makeup ■ Cooking ■ Folding laundry	■ Bowling ■ Weight lifting ■ General housework ■ Child care ■ Walking (3.5 mph)	■ Gardening ■ Tennis ■ Aerobics—high impact ■ Calisthenics ■ Walking up stairs ■ Swimming

BED REST

Sometimes an eating disorder specialist or a PCP will put a person with a starvation eating disorder on bed rest. This means staying in bed except for using the toilet, bathing, or eating (although eating can be done in bed as well). If this has been suggested to you, talk to your doctor about why it's important to be on bed rest and how long you need to be on it. Usually bed rest can be stopped after a certain amount of weight is gained. If you are put on bed rest, this probably means your weight is so low that even low-energy activities like standing in the kitchen and cooking are not safe for you at your current weight. Bed rest at home can prevent a medical hospitalization. So if you need bed rest at the beginning of weight restoration, don't despair; it's better than being in the hospital with calories going in your veins and down a tube in your throat.

Follow the instructions you have been given for bed rest and you should be able to do low-energy activities as soon as you gain some weight. If you have a coach, ask your coach for support during bed rest. Being able to look forward to getting e-mail or a visit from your coach during this time can make bed rest easier.

Reviewing Why You Need to Gain Weight

Weight restoration is hard, so before you set your target BMI, you should review why you are going to gain weight. The anxiety and the distorted thoughts that accompany the fear of gaining weight can get you to side with your eating disorder. Reminding yourself why you are embarking on this hard task will help you stick with your weight restoration plan, even when your emotions are telling you to stop. Review your motivational cards, and particularly those you made in chapter 6, outlining your compelling reasons to get well. Make a list of why you are going to gain weight. Grace came up with the following reasons to gain weight:

Grace's Reasons for Gaining Weight

1. *Spending time with my daughters and not worrying about what I am eating when I'm with them*

2. *Keeping my bones healthy*

3. *Giving me a life outside of what I weigh and how my body looks so that I can enjoy activities like sewing again without thinking about the size of the dress I'm making*

4. *Going to Thanksgiving dinner with my family and focusing on the conversation—not the calories*

5. *Being able to socialize with my friends at a restaurant without worrying about eating in public*

6. *Being able to exercise at the gym three to four times a week in a healthy way*

Notice that Grace's reasons are very specific. She could have listed reason 5 as simply "Being able to socialize," but that would have been too general and not as effective a reason. By specifying that she wanted to be able to go to restaurants with her friends, Grace states exactly what she will achieve by getting well. The more specific you are, the more effective your reasons will be. *Effective reasons* are those that will lead to weight gain and maintenance of your weight gain. *Ineffective reasons* are ones that you come up with just because you have to or just because someone else gives you the reason. An example would be "Gaining weight to get my doctor off my back." Grace's reasons are effective because they are reasons that are compelling *for her*. Review your compelling reasons from chapter 6 to see if they still resonate for you now and add to those reasons if you can. *The bottom line is this:* the more effective the reasons you come up with, the easier it will be for you to get well.

Your Reasons for Gaining Weight
1. _____ _____
2. _____ _____
3. _____ _____
4. _____ _____
5. _____ _____
6. _____ _____

reasons-to-gain-weight card: Make a card to add to your collection of cards, detailing your reasons to gain weight. Keep your cards in your pocket or purse so that you can review them whenever you might feel like abandoning your weight restoration plan.

Planning Ahead and Setting a Target Date for Starting Phase 3

During phase 2 you will collect the data you need to understand how to change your eating. You can go on to phase 2 before you see your PCP, but you will need your PCP's input to set your goals during phase 3. Set a target date for starting phase 3 that gives you enough time to meet with your PCP and finish any lab or other tests your PCP wants you to take; without a target date, it will be too easy to procrastinate and not move on to phase 3.

You also need time to meet with your coach or eating disorder specialist, if you have one, during phase 1. Most people will need at least two weeks to complete phase 1, but it may take longer if you can't get an appointment with your PCP right away. If there is a delay in meeting with your PCP, you can still move on and start phase 2 (and you can make good use of the time by working on decreasing your purging) but you will need your PCP's input for goal setting in phase 3.

phase 2: collecting data

In order to change behavior, you need to know what needs to change. This requires collecting data. A baseline food log will give you the data you need to plan your weight restoration. A *baseline food log* is a record of what you are eating now, before you make any changes. The data in your baseline food log will give you valuable information that will help you gain weight. Your baseline food log will include the following:

- Exactly what you ate

- Approximate amounts (you don't need the exact weight or measurements)

- How anxious you felt before and after you ate

- Whether or not you purged

- How you felt during and after eating

- Everything you ate or drank even if it had no calories

Let's look closely at days 2 and 7 of Amy's food log, which follows, to see how to complete and analyze a baseline food log.

When Amy and her coach sat down and studied Amy's baseline food logs, Amy realized that her cereal binge was triggered by hunger. Not eating in the morning set Amy up for bingeing. Amy's binge pattern was fairly straightforward. While some people will purge in the absence of a binge, Amy only purged after a binge. Amy's coach noticed that Amy's anxiety went down in the mornings if she didn't eat. This meant that to get well, Amy would have to tolerate morning anxiety. This gave Amy and her coach the idea to make a distress-tolerance card with things Amy could do in the morning to deal with the anxiety of eating. Amy put "Taking a warm bath and listening to soothing music after eating breakfast" on her new card. In addition to the information about bingeing and hunger, Amy and her coach noticed that Amy used coffee and caffeine to avoid eating. Using caffeine is a common way for people with a starvation eating disorder to avoid eating, because caffeine can dull hunger pains. Amy realized that going off caffeine might help her gain weight, so she set up a caffeine-withdrawal plan. If you're like Amy and use caffeine to avoid eating, be sure to go off caffeine slowly to avoid a caffeine-withdrawal headache (one of the most frequent side effects of caffeine withdrawal). The easiest way to do this is to cut your caffeine by one-third each week until you are caffeine-free.

Now it's time for you to collect your data. If you are using a coach and she is going to help you with your food log, you should meet with her before starting the baseline log so that she understands what you are doing. Let your coach know for which week you will be collecting data, and set up a time to go over your data. A week of food logs should give you the data you need to move toward weight restoration. You can copy the blank food log or use a journal or notebook to keep your data. As long as you include all the information in the baseline food log in this book, you can use any data collection method you prefer.

Amy's Baseline Food Log

Day: 2

Time	Food	Amount	Anxiety (0–5)	Purged?	Analysis
8 A.M.	Coffee—black with artificial sweetener	2 cups	Before: 3 After: 1	No	Hungry, but didn't want to give in to the hunger. My anxiety went down when I didn't eat.
2 P.M.	Cereal with nonfat milk	About 4 cups	Before: 2 After: 5	Yes	I was very hungry. Had one cup of cereal and couldn't stop. I had to get rid of all that food and purged.
3 P.M.	Diet soda	2 cans	Before: 5 After: 1	No	Soda and purging helped me feel better—my anxiety decreased.
6 P.M.	Small potato with salt and pepper and mixed vegetables (broccoli, carrots, and peas) Coffee—black with artificial sweetener	About 2 cups of food, 2 cups of coffee	Before: 2 After: 3	No	Ate what I planned to eat. Had some anxiety but because I stuck with my plan, I didn't purge.
8 P.M.	Coffee—black with artificial sweetener	1 cup	Before: 3 After: 1	No	Thought about having more food but drank coffee instead.
10 P.M.	Sugar-free ice cream	1/3 cup	Before: 2 After: 2	No	Had a little ice cream in the freezer. Might have binged if I had had more. Hungry. Went to bed so I won't eat more.

Amy's Baseline Food Log

Day: 7

Time	Food	Amount	Anxiety (0–5)	Purged?	Analysis
7:30 A.M.	Coffee—black with artificial sweetener	2 cups	Before: 4 After: 2	No	Very hungry. My anxiety went down when I didn't eat.
1 P.M.	Cereal with nonfat milk	About 3 cups	Before: 3 After: 5	Yes	I was very hungry. Just like last week, I had one cup of cereal and couldn't stop.
1:30 P.M.	Diet soda	1 can	Before: 5 After: 1	No	Soda and purging helped me feel better again—my anxiety decreased.
7 P.M.	Salad with nonfat dressing and mixed vegetables (broccoli, carrots, and peas) Coffee—black with artificial sweetener	About 2 cups of food, 2 cups of coffee	Before: 1 After: 2	No	Ate less than I planned to eat. Had some anxiety but less than last night.
8 P.M.	Coffee—black with artificial sweetener	1 cup	Before: 2 After: 1	No	Thought about having more food but drank coffee instead.
10 P.M.	Carrots	4 small	Before: 2 After: 2	No	Still felt hungry.

Your Baseline Food Log

Day: _____

Time	Food	Amount	Anxiety (0–5)	Purged?	Analysis
			Before: ___ After: ___		
			Before: ___ After: ___		
			Before: ___ After: ___		
			Before: ___ After: ___		
			Before: ___ After: ___		
			Before: ___ After: ___		

Learning from Your Baseline Food Log

You (and maybe your coach, if you have one) probably have collected some valuable insights from your baseline log. Read over these common patterns for starvation eating disorder and check off any patterns you found in your logs:

☐ Bingeing after longer periods of restricting

☐ Purging after bingeing

☐ Exercising after eating

☐ Eating only a small range of foods or eating the same thing for each meal

☐ Eating only one meal a day

☐ Planning all eating

☐ Eating alone

☐ Dealing with the fatigue associated with starvation by drinking caffeine instead of eating

☐ Drinking a lot of water or some other zero-calorie drink to feel full and fend off hunger

☐ Cutting food into small pieces and eating very slowly

☐ Using sleep to keep from eating (for example, going to bed early)

Answering the following questions will help you analyze the data in your logs. If you have a coach, it will be helpful to answer these questions with your coach. If you are working with an eating disorder specialist, take your food logs to your appointment and go over the logs with the specialist.

■ Which common patterns showed up in your food logs the most often?

_____

_____

■ Did you find any patterns that were not on the list? (List these patterns.)

_____

_____

■ Did you eat in the mornings on any day? If you did, how did you feel later in the day?

_____

_____

■ Did you notice anything else about your food logs that you think will help you get well?

_____

_____

EFFECTIVE USE OF INFORMATION

As you analyze your food logs, focus on how you can use the information you learned in an effective way that will lead to being healthy. Effective use of the information from your food logs means using what you learned to gain weight and get well. Occasionally I have had patients who use the information in their food logs to gain insights that serve to reinforce their starvation eating disorder. For example, if Amy used the information she got from her food log about caffeine to increase her caffeine use and decrease her calorie intake, that would be an ineffective use of information. If you find yourself wanting to use what you learned in an ineffective manner, take out your motivational cards and review your reasons for getting well. In the following log, write down how you can use your insights from your food logs in an effective, healthy way. Review these statements with your coach or eating disorder specialist to see if they can come up with any other ideas for you.

Insights from Your Baseline Food Log	
What you learned	**How you can use this insight**
Example 1: *I use coffee and caffeine to avoid eating.* **Example 2:** *I go to bed early every night rather than listen to my hunger and eat something—as a result, I wake up feeling very hungry.*	**Example 1:** *I will slowly go off coffee and all caffeine over the next two weeks.* **Example 2:** *I can plan on a healthy snack after dinner and not go to bed hungry. This might make me feel better in the mornings. Feeling better in the mornings shouldn't lead to not eating, or I will start the pattern all over again.*
1.	1.
2.	2.
3.	3.
4.	4.
5.	5.
6.	6.

phase 3: setting your goals

You will need to set several goals for weight restoration. Goal setting can be difficult when the goals address gaining weight. You may have been in a treatment program in the past where the goals were set for you. In some ways this is easier; if someone else tells you how much weight you need to gain or how much food you need to eat, you're off the hook—you don't need to ask yourself why gaining weight is important to you or to commit to a goal of your own. In the past, your target weight may not even have been shared with you. This is what happened when Amy went into a residential program. The food was given to her, and no one told her how much she weighed or what her target weight was. This meant that while Amy could tell she was gaining weight by the way her clothes fit, she didn't know how much she weighed or how much she had gained.

The problem is that when someone else sets your goals, you don't have to take ownership of those goals and the control is in someone else's hands. *The bottom line is this*: if it is *their* goal and not *your* goal, it's easier to ignore. For your weight restoration plan, you will take control by assuming ownership of your goals. Ownership can be anxiety provoking when the distorted thinking of your disorder is telling you that you shouldn't eat or shouldn't gain weight. Strong fear will keep pushing you not to eat and not to gain weight. Setting your goals is pushing back against that fear and taking control.

Weight Restoration Goals

Now you're ready to set your goals—for how much to gain each week as well as for a target weight that will get you to a target BMI. The target BMI should be a *soft target*, meaning a target you know you might need to change. This is particularly true for women. If you are a woman in your childbearing years, you will need to gain enough weight to have regular periods. If you find after you reach your target BMI that you are still not having periods, you will need to increase your target BMI. It's a good idea to consult with your PCP or eating disorder specialist about your target BMI. Plan on gaining ½–2 pounds a week, knowing that speed is not as important as moving steadily toward your target BMI. There is one exception to this rule: if you are in a medically supervised weight restoration program, you should follow the recommendations of your doctor.

Several pieces of information can help you set your target BMI:

- Your PCP's recommendation for your healthy weight, which you got at your most recent visit

- The lowest weight in the past that allowed you to have regular periods without taking birth control (if you are a woman in your childbearing years)

- A weight that would give you a BMI of at least 19 (see chapter 1 to review how to calculate your BMI)

RAISING YOUR TARGET BMI

Remember that target BMIs rarely need to be lowered, but sometimes the target BMI does need to be raised. Reasons for raising your target BMI include not having regular periods and needing to gain additional weight to have enough energy to do sports. As mentioned earlier, after Joe maintained a weight in the low healthy range for one year, he decided to increase his time at the gym. In order to do more weight lifting and gain muscle, Joe raised his target BMI and gained additional weight.

HOW MUCH WEIGHT SHOULD YOU GAIN EACH WEEK?

You should plan on gaining ½–2 pounds a week. If your BMI is under 16, you should gain at least 1 pound a week. Although you need to set a goal for how much weight you will gain each week, your main focus should be on simply gaining weight rather than on how fast you gain it. If you gain more slowly but are still making progress each week, you will be on your way to improving your health.

MEDICALLY SUPERVISED WEIGHT GAIN

If your PCP has told you that you need medically supervised weight gain (also called *refeeding*), you should follow the guidelines your health care providers have set for you. It's very important that you get regular lab tests and show up for all of your refeeding appointments so that your medical status can be monitored. Medically supervised refeeding is usually only done when someone's weight is extremely low or they have life-threatening medical complications from starvation. So if this is the case for you, make sure you are following your medical treatment plan and let your doctor know if you are having any problems following this plan or if you have new symptoms.

Now write down your goals for weight restoration.

Goals
Weight to gain per week: _____
Target BMI: _____
Target weight: _____

phase 4: setting up an eating schedule—three plus three

In order to gain weight and stay at a healthy weight, you will need to set up an eating schedule with three snacks in addition to three regular meals. After reaching a healthy weight, most people can drop one or two snacks and can be a little more flexible about when to eat.

The first step in the process is to establish times to eat, following the rules for Three Plus Three:

- Eat breakfast, lunch, and dinner.

- Eat three snacks.

- Eat at predetermined times no more than three hours apart.

This is *scheduled eating*, which means you need to eat whether or not you feel hungry. In fact, in the beginning you can assume you will not feel hungry before most of your meals or snacks. For most people with a starvation eating disorder, this means opposite-action eating. It's very important that you don't miss any meals or snacks, so consider your work and family's schedule when planning when to eat. After you have achieved a healthy weight, you will do appetite training (chapter 14) and then you will be able to pay attention to when you are hungry or full, but for now stick to your schedule.

Why Do You Need Three Plus Three?

The idea of having three meals and three snacks can be frightening for someone with a starvation eating disorder. But there are important reasons why Three Plus Three will help you get well. Review the reasons for eating this way:

Reasons for Three Plus Three

- Eating regularly will keep you from becoming overly hungry and decrease the chances you will binge.

- The extra calories you need in order to gain weight can later be decreased by dropping a snack once your weight is healthy. This way you can maintain a healthy weight without gaining too much weight.

- Your health will improve when you eat regularly.

- Three Plus Three will give you control by taking control away from your starvation eating disorder.

Establishing Your Schedule

Now it's time for you to plan your schedule. Look at your Food Schedule, which follows. Put in the times for your meals and snacks. This schedule is set up with snacks between meals, but you can change the order of your snacks and meals as long as you follow the rules for Three Plus Three. In the beginning, it's best to keep the same schedule seven days a week. After you have gained a little weight and are feeling more comfortable with eating on a schedule, you may want to have separate schedules for weekends and for weekdays. This is okay as long as both schedules follow the rules for Three Plus Three.

Food Schedule	
Meal or snack	Time
Breakfast	
Snack	
Lunch	
Snack	
Dinner	
Snack	

to sum up

Weight restoration will be one of the hardest things you will ever do. But as is often the case, doing difficult things can lead to great rewards. Phases 1–4 set the foundation for the next two phases. It's important to meet with your PCP before starting your weight restoration. Using a coach and gathering data are powerful tools that can help you get ready to gain weight. Gaining weight will require that you eat three meals and three snacks per day (Three Plus Three). Updating your distress-tolerance skills is a strategy that will help you deal with the anxiety that you will feel when you start eating Three Plus Three. In this chapter you have set up your eating schedule and have the information you need to start eating by the rules for Three Plus Three. Now it's time to move on to the next chapter to implement your weight restoration plan in the next two phases.

CHAPTER 11

restoring health with food: phases 5 and 6

now that you have laid the foundation for weight gain, it's time for you to move on to phases 5 and 6 of your weight restoration plan. It has probably been two to three weeks since you started decreasing your purging (if purging or other self-harm behaviors are still significant problems for you, review your Self-Harm-Reduction Plan from chapter 9). Now it's time to eat enough to gain weight. At this point, it's normal to get cold feet. Few people start out perfectly. It's a common experience, for example, to start off doing well and then get scared, and then restrict or purge. Don't get discouraged; you'll likely get off track at least once or twice. Because everyone gets off track sometimes, the last phase of weight restoration is troubleshooting.

phase 5: implementing your plan

When you start to eat Three Plus Three, you will probably experience a few problems right away. One of these problems is delayed gastric emptying. It's important to know about this because it will affect you as soon as you start to eat normally. Luckily you can learn how to deal with this common problem.

Delayed Gastric Emptying

Most people with a starvation eating disorder will experience delayed gastric emptying. This symptom creates the feeling of being overly full if you eat even a small amount of food (see chapter 2). This is problematic; if you aren't aware that restricting only makes delayed gastric emptying worse, the feeling of being overly full after eating only a few bites will derail Three Plus Three. The good news is that delayed gastric emptying isn't dangerous, and it will resolve over time. But the only way it will resolve is to put food in your stomach even though you feel full. Until it does resolve, the following tips can make it easier to tolerate.

Tips for Dealing with Delayed Gastric Emptying

- *Try eating more often during the first week or two of phase 5.* You can eat eight times a day instead of six times a day by cutting your lunch and dinner into two meals, each meal one hour apart.

- *Eat dense food.* Dense foods are those, like nuts or cheese, that have a lot of calories and nutritional value for the portion size. Eating dense food will make you feel less full while giving you the same or more nutrition than eating other foods. Amy used this strategy by eating cream soups, peanut butter, cheese, and regular cottage cheese. These four foods gave her good nutrition but allowed her to eat less bulk so that she felt less full. You will find a table of suggested dense foods later in this chapter.

- *Drink some of your nutrition.* Juice, whole milk, and liquid supplements for weight gain can all help. Liquids don't cause the same overly full feeling as solid food. For the first week, drink your snacks. Make sure you are drinking enough—drink at least two cups of something that has calories. Fruit smoothies made with yogurt are good because they have a reasonable amount of calories.

While these ideas can help, it's likely you will experience some uncomfortably full feelings as your body gets used to eating Three Plus Three. Like constipation, delayed gastric emptying won't disappear right away, but it will resolve as your stomach gets used to normal amounts of food. There is no set timetable for how long it will take for someone's stomach to adjust. Everyone will be a little different. Accept that it will take a little time for your body to adjust. You can also use your self-soothing and distraction skills to help you get through the discomfort.

Tracking Your Success and Increasing Calories

Simply eating Three Plus Three will not be enough to help you gain weight if you're not eating enough food. The amount of food or calories that you will need in order to gain weight will be individual to you. The only way to know how much you need to eat is to track your weight gain (Herrin 2003). If you're not gaining ½–2 pounds a week, you're not eating enough. People who have very low weight actually need to eat more calories to gain weight than a person who weighs a normal amount (Sunday and Halmi 2003).

It would be very unusual for someone with a starvation eating disorder to gain weight on less than 2,000 calories a day, and most people will have to eat more than that. In fact it's not unusual to need 3,000 calories or more to gain weight (Herrin 2003). Your Weight Chart will help you track your weight gain. If you are seeing your PCP or an eating disorder specialist, you will probably also be weighed when you see him. You may be tempted to weigh yourself more than once a week, but, in general, it's a good idea to stick to weekly weigh-ins. The exception to this is if you are in an intensive weight restoration program, where you might be weighed more often.

Instructions for Filling Out Your Weight Chart: Each week you'll record the weight you've gained. For each pound you gain, fill in a box. If you gain less than a pound, fill in the amount of the box that represents your weight gain. So, for example, if you gain half a pound, fill in half that box. Ideally, you want to be able to fill in an entire box representing a gain of 1 pound. As you can see from Grace's chart, the chart shows cumulative weight gain: Grace gained 1.5 pounds the first week, 1.5 pounds the second week, and then 1 pound a week for the next ten weeks for a total of 13 pounds in twelve weeks.

Grace's Weight Chart

Starting weight: _____ 105 _____   Starting BMI: _____ 18 _____

Target weight : _____ 118 _____   Target BMI : _____ 20 _____

Pounds \ Weeks	1	2	3	4	5	6	7	8	9	10	11	12
1	■	■	■	■	■	■	■	■	■	■	■	■
2	■	■	■	■	■	■	■	■	■	■	■	■
3		■	■	■	■	■	■	■	■	■	■	■
4		■	■	■	■	■	■	■	■	■	■	■
5			■	■	■	■	■	■	■	■	■	■
6				■	■	■	■	■	■	■	■	■
7					■	■	■	■	■	■	■	■
8						■	■	■	■	■	■	■
9							■	■	■	■	■	■
10								■	■	■	■	■
11									■	■	■	■
12										■	■	■
13											■	■

Your Weight Chart

Starting weight: _____   Starting BMI : _____

Target weight : _____   Target BMI : _____

	Weeks											
Pounds	1	2	3	4	5	6	7	8	9	10	11	12
1												
2												
3												
4												
5												
6												
7												
8												
9												
10												
11												
12												
13												
14												
15												
16												
17												
18												
19												
20												
21												
22												
23												
24												
25												
26												
27												
28												
29												
30												
	1	2	3	4	5	6	7	8	9	10	11	12
	Weeks											

what to eat

Now that you have established when to eat and have a way to track your progress, you need to figure out what to eat. It's common for someone with a starvation eating disorder to have difficulties figuring this out. If you have been restricting your food intake for a long time, you may have lost touch with how much food or what kind of food goes into a normal meal. From Amy's Baseline Food Log in chapter 10, you can see that she had a small dry potato with a few vegetables for dinner. This was not enough for dinner, but it could have been a snack if she'd added a little butter. A reasonable dinner would have been the potato with butter, a chicken breast, salad with regular dressing, and hot chocolate or a glass of juice.

When Grace first started on weight restoration, she had difficulty deciding what to eat. Grace and her coach sat down together and did some meal planning. In addition to asking your coach to work with you to figure out what to eat, the general rules that follow can help you make sure your meals are actual meals and not just snacks.

- Make sure your portion sizes are reasonable (for example, a fourth of a cup of cereal is not a reasonable breakfast). You will find portion suggestions in the Serving Sizes table (see the "Adding Calories" section); if you are working with an eating disorder specialist or a dietitian, these professionals can also give you ideas about portion sizes.

- Use the website MyPyramid.gov (at www.mypyramid.gov) for ideas about what and how much to eat. The government's website has a calculator that can help you determine how much to eat to gain weight. Go to MyPyramid Plan and put in your weight and how active you are, and the website will give you an idea of how many cups of carbohydrates, protein, fruits, and vegetables you need to eat to gain weight. Some of the MyPyramid website and other related sites are geared toward losing weight, so make sure to put your current (low) weight into the MyPyramid Plan calculator or you might be looking at tips for people who are overweight.

- Avoid diet foods (for example, low- or nonfat foods or foods with artificial sweeteners).

- Use real sugar, 2 percent or whole milk, and real butter or margarine.

- Focus on nutritional value and calories.

- Add liquid supplementation if you aren't gaining enough weight.

- Keep a food log.

- Include a carbohydrate (for example, bread or cereal), some protein, and a vegetable or fruit in each meal.

- Make sure to include fat in your diet every day.

- Consult with a dietitian to get food ideas.

- If you're not drinking a liquid supplement with your meal, drink milk, juice, or some other drink with at least 200 calories (see "Drinking Calories: Liquid Supplementation" later in this chapter).

In addition to following these rules, you will probably want to start out with the foods you are more comfortable eating. This will make your first weeks of weight restoration less anxiety provoking. We sometimes call foods that trigger less anxiety *safe foods*. Dense foods, which, as described previously, are nutritionally concentrated, can also help you gain weight in the beginning. Let's look at how safe foods and dense foods can help you gain weight.

Safe Foods to Start

Safe foods are those foods you can eat without feeling panicky. Not all safe foods will work for weight gain. Let's look at a few foods from Lorrie's list of safe foods to see what kind of foods can help with gaining weight and which foods are not appropriate for eating Three Plus Three.

Here's Lorrie's list of safe foods:

- Sugarless Jell-O

- Lettuce salad with nonfat dressing

- Apples

- Cereal with skim milk

- Hard-boiled egg

- Dry, whole-wheat toast

The first two items on Lorrie's list are not appropriate for a weight restoration plan. Both the foods break the no-diet-food rule, and both have little or no nutritional value. Lorrie should not make these foods part of her Three Plus Three. The other foods can be part of Lorrie's first week but with a few modifications. Lorrie needs to have her cereal with at least 2 percent milk, and she should add butter or, better yet, peanut butter to her toast. The foods on Lorrie's safe food list will not be enough for her to gain weight—she will have to add other foods, but these items can get her started. If you are like Lorrie and have a lot of anxiety about starting your Three Plus Three, you can start out with safe foods and then add other foods each week.

The rules for safe foods that can be used for weight restoration are simple:

1. The food must have some nutritional value.

2. The food should have 50 or more calories per serving (foods with at least 100 calories are best).

3. Avoid foods with artificial sweeteners.

4. Foods with some fat (like peanut butter) are ideal.

5. Foods with complex carbohydrates, like whole-wheat breads, are good choices.

Now make a list of *your* safe foods. Next to each food, indicate if that food is a good choice for your Three Plus Three.

Your Safe Food List	
Safe food	Follows the rules?
1. _____	_____
2. _____	_____
3. _____	_____
4. _____	_____
5. _____	_____
6. _____	_____
7. _____	_____
8. _____	_____
9. _____	_____
10. _____	_____

Eating Dense Foods

Dense foods are foods that pack a lot of calories into small amounts. Many dense foods also have the healthy fat that many people with starvation eating disorders need in their diet. The next list cites some healthy dense foods that you can use to boost your calories. If you aren't gaining weight, add some of these foods to your diet.

Dense Food Ideas		
Peanut butter	Ice cream	Nuts
Regular cottage cheese	Refried beans	Cheese
Muffins	Cornbread	Avocado
French fries	Corn	Cream sauce

Your First Week

The first week of weight restoration is often the hardest. Your list of safe foods can help and so can planning ahead of time what you are going to eat during your first week of Three Plus Three. By planning in this way, you will eliminate the distress of deciding each day what to eat. Let's explore two days of Joe's food schedule logs to see how he planned his first week of Three Plus Three.

Joe's First-Week Food Schedule		
Time	**Food for day 1**	**Food for day 2**
Breakfast Time: 7 A.M.	*2 eggs* *Whole-wheat toast with jam* *1 cup of orange juice*	*2 cups of cereal with 2 percent milk and sugar* *1 cup of orange juice*
Snack #1 Time: 10 A.M.	*1 apple—medium sized* *1½ cups of 2 percent milk*	*1 apple—medium sized* *1½ cups of 2 percent milk*
Lunch Time: Noon	*Turkey sandwich with two slices of whole-wheat bread and mayo* *2 cups of fruit smoothie with yogurt*	*Turkey sandwich with two slices of whole-wheat bread and mayo* *1 cup of orange juice*
Snack #2 Time: 2:30 P.M.	*1 slice of wheat bread with peanut butter* *1½ cups of 2 percent milk*	*2 cups of fruit smoothie with yogurt*
Dinner Time: 6 P.M.	*2 eggs* *1 cup of rice* *1 cup of green vegetables* *1 cup of orange juice*	*2 turkey slices* *1 cup of rice* *Green salad with regular dressing* *1½ cups of 2 percent milk*
Snack #3 Time: 9 P.M.	*1 apple—medium sized* *1½ cups of 2 percent milk*	*2 cups of fruit smoothie with yogurt*

Notice that Joe did not start his weight restoration with lots of variety. He stuck with food he considered pretty safe. Joe did make good use of drinking calories. By drinking calories, he was able to add nutrition without overfilling his stomach, which might have triggered purging.

Keeping a Food Log

Once you have established an eating schedule, you need to start keeping food logs. This should not be a new skill for you because you kept food logs for your harm-reduction plan. As you did for your baseline food log in chapter 10, you will also want to keep track of purging behaviors and anxiety levels along with recording what you are eating. You should make copies of your food schedule and log, on the following page, so that you can continue to keep track of what and how much you are eating. It's a good idea to keep all your food schedules together in a binder because you will need to keep a food log not only until you are at your target BMI but until you've stayed stable at your target BMI for at least three months.

Your food schedule is a helpful tool for the following:

- Making sure you are eating enough

- Tracking anxiety

- Keeping a record of how much you are purging

- Troubleshooting problems like skipping meals (see Missing or Being Late for a Meal or Snack in the "Phase 6: Troubleshooting" section in this chapter)

- Recording the introduction of new foods

- Consulting with your PCP or a dietitian if you need to work on problems such as anemia

Typically, I review food schedules every time I see someone, and I think it's a good idea for you to review your food schedule with others including your coach, PCP, and eating disorder specialist each time you see them also. You can use the food schedule and log that follows or write down what you eat in your notebook, but if you don't use the food log, be sure to note in your notebook your anxiety levels before and after you eat.

adding calories

Few people will start out eating Three Plus Three with enough calories to gain much weight. The only way to learn how many calories you need in order to gain weight is simply to add calories, incrementally, until you start gaining. So plan on adding 200–500 calories to your daily calorie intake each week, during the first few weeks of eating Three Plus Three, until you are gaining ½–2 pounds a week. This is not about counting *every* calorie, so once you have an idea of about how much you need to add, concentrate on trying new foods and becoming aware of the nutritional value of foods.

Some people will gain a few pounds at first and then stop after two to three weeks. If this happens to you, the only answer is—add calories until you start gaining weight again. Use the Serving Sizes table as a guide for how much to eat in each serving; this and the food log are important resources for you to use in your weight restoration.

Time	Food	Amount	Anxiety (0–5)*	Purged?
Your Food Schedule and Log **Day:** _____				
Breakfast Time: _____			Before: ____ After: ____	
Snack #1 Time: _____			Before: ____ After: ____	
Lunch Time: _____			Before: ____ After: ____	
Snack #2 Time: _____			Before: ____ After: ____	
Dinner Time: _____			Before: ____ After: ____	
Snack #3 Time: _____			Before: ____ After: ____	
Extra snack Time: _____			Before: ____ After: ____	

*A rating of 5 is the most extreme anxiety you have ever had.

Serving Sizes

Serving and portion sizes can be confusing. Most people in the United States eat portions that are too large. But if you have a starvation eating disorder, you have been eating portions that are too small. The serving-size guide here will give you some idea of how much to eat at each meal or snack. The suggested serving sizes are intended to support weight gain.

Proteins

- Meat: 3–5 ounces

- Eggs: 2 (*Note:* This is a good serving size for gaining weight. Eat the whole egg, not just egg whites.)

- Beans: ½–1 cup

- Nuts and seeds: ½ cup

Carbohydrates (breads, cereal, rice, and pasta)

- Bread: 2 slices

- Cereals: 1–2 cups

- Rice or pasta: 1 cup

- Pancakes: 2–3 pancakes (4" diameter)

- Potato: medium, with butter

Milk, yogurt, and cheese

- Milk or yogurt: 1 cup regular yogurt or 2 percent milk

- Cheese: 2–3 ounces

Fruit

- Whole fruit: medium-sized apple, banana, or orange

- Chopped, cooked, or canned fruit: ½–1 cup

- Fruit juice: 1 cup

Vegetables

- Leafy vegetables: 1 cup

- Other vegetables: ½–1 cup

- Vegetable juice: 1 cup

My patients are often surprised at how much food they need to add to gain weight. Remember, your feelings about how many calories you need to consume will not be an accurate measure of whether you need to add more or not—the bathroom scale is your best measuring device: your weekly weight will let you know if you need to eat more. Sometimes people worry about adding calories too fast. This is rarely a problem if you are eating food orally. Even if you are drinking liquid supplementation (described below) along with regular food, it's very difficult to trigger what's called refeeding syndrome when taking in all your nutrition orally.

Refeeding Syndrome

If you are being fed by a tube or IV, follow the instructions your doctor gives you about how many calories to consume. This is because non-oral feeding can cause *refeeding syndrome*, which occurs when calories are added too quickly.

Refeeding Syndrome
Refeeding syndrome is a medical condition that occurs when a body that has been starving is given a large number of easily metabolized calories too quickly for the body to adjust. This can occur if someone is fed too quickly through tube feeding or total parenteral nutrition (a type of IV feeding). Refeeding results in an imbalance of potassium, magnesium, phosphate, and other important nutrients and can lead to serious metabolic complications. Talk to your PCP about refeeding syndrome if you are being fed by a tube or IV. Regular lab tests can monitor your levels of these important nutrients (Birmingham and Beumont 2004).

Drinking Calories: Liquid Supplementation

One way to make sure you are getting enough calories to gain weight is to add liquid supplementation to your diet. You can drink calories with your meals or drink a supplement in between your meals and snacks. Another option is to make one of your snacks a liquid snack. You can use as much liquid supplementation as you need as long as you are *also* eating calories. *The bottom line is this:* liquid supplementation is not meant to be your major source of calories.

Here are the basic rules for liquid supplementation:

- You can choose from a variety of liquid supplements that are on the market. (Liquid supplements are readily available at major supermarkets or health food stores.)

- Make sure to use a supplement with at least 200 calories per serving.

- Don't use liquid supplementation by itself for more than one snack per day, but you can add the supplement to solid snacks as many times as you want. For example, you could have a piece of fruit and a liquid supplement or a piece of bread and a liquid supplement.

- You can drink a liquid supplement with your meals instead of drinking milk or water.

- Pick something that tastes good!

You can also drink a fruit smoothie with yogurt. A smoothie packed with fruit and yogurt or ice cream is as good as most liquid supplements. The advantage to commercial liquid supplements is convenience; they usually come in a can that you take with you or keep in your desk at work.

starting

The only way to start is to start! Review your motivational cards to remind yourself why you have committed to gaining weight. If you have a coach, this is the time to remind that person of what you need. Although you may plan to meet weekly with your coach or eating disorder specialist, it can be helpful to check in with your coach or specialist at the end of the first day. If you are not working with a coach or specialist, ask your PCP if you can call or e-mail her at the end of the first day to let her know you have started your weight restoration. Even a friend who is not acting as a coach can help. Make plans to meet your friend for breakfast on the second day of Three Plus Three. Just knowing you will report to someone about how your first day went may be enough to get you started.

You should expect to spend two to three weeks adding calories to your Three Plus Three before seeing a steady weight gain of ½–2 pounds a week. And remember, during weight restoration, everyone runs into roadblocks. With the support of your coach, you can work through the roadblocks and get back on track with your plan. Phase 6 of weight restoration is about solving these problems.

Opposite Action

One of the most important techniques you have acquired is opposite action. You learned about opposite action in chapter 6; now you will use opposite action to gain weight. There is no way to get around it—you can't wait until you want to eat more, because that will probably never happen. Check off the actions you will need to do in order to start your weight restoration:

- ☐ Eat three meals a day

- ☐ Eat foods that cause you anxiety, such as high-fat foods

- ☐ Add calories if you don't gain weight

- ☐ Not purge when you want to purge

- ☐ Meet with your coach or eating disorder specialist

- ☐ Get the lab tests your PCP wants you to get, even when you feel fine

- ☐ Keep food logs

☐ Not weigh yourself every day

Opposite action is hard to practice but necessary for gaining weight. Keep in mind that your emotions about your weight, shape, and food are distorted by your starvation eating disorder. Gaining weight—and everything that goes into it—is always an opposite action for someone with a starvation eating disorder.

phase 6: troubleshooting

If you're like most people, you'll have run into a few problems by the time you've been following your Three Plus Three for a week or two. If you have been increasing your intake each week but haven't gained weight yet, you may just not have reached the amount of calories you need in order to gain weight. Review the "Adding Calories" section earlier in this chapter, and keep adding until you gain.

If you think you've been increasing calories but it's been more than four weeks and you still haven't seen any weight gain, you will need to troubleshoot the problem. The common problems that people with starvation eating disorders run into during weight restoration are as follows:

- Not gaining weight or not gaining enough weight

- Missing a meal or snack

- Eating very few types of foods

- Changing your mind about gaining weight

- Conflict with your coach or eating disorder specialist

- Increased purging

Let's look at these problems to see how each can be solved.

Not Gaining Weight or Not Gaining Enough Weight

If you think you have been adding calories but you're still not gaining or you are gaining very little, sit down with someone and go over your food logs. This may be the time to consult with a dietitian. Common problems include the following:

- Serving sizes that are too small

- Eating food with little nutritional value (such as lettuce)

- Needing to add a fourth snack

- Not keeping a food log (it's easier to fool yourself if you're not writing down what you eat)

Check off the solutions that you will try:

☐ Double your portion sizes.

☐ Follow the Serving Sizes table (in the "Adding Calories" section of this chapter).

☐ Go out to eat twice a week—portions in restaurants tend to be bigger.

☐ Start keeping a food log.

☐ Look at Dense Food Ideas above and pick a few foods from this list to add to your plan.

☐ Add a liquid supplement.

Missing a Meal or Snack

Missing scheduled meals or snacks is a common problem, and it can make the difference between success and failure. Review the following suggestions for what to do if you are late with a meal or snack or miss one altogether.

Missing or Being Late for a Meal or Snack

If you are late for or miss a meal or snack, you can do the following:

- Eat as soon as you can eat.

- Don't skip the next meal or snack even if it means you are eating one hour (or less) later than your late meal or snack.

- If you miss a meal or snack altogether, use liquid calories in the form of a liquid supplement. Add the liquid supplement at the end of the day or add it to the next meal or snack to boost the calories for the day.

- If you find you are chronically missing meals or snacks, sit down with your coach or eating disorder specialist to see if there is some kind of pattern (like always missing breakfast). Troubleshoot the problem. Here are some solutions for missed meals or snacks:

  - Prepare the food for the meal or snack ahead of time.

  - E-mail your coach at the end of the day with data on what you ate. For some people, just knowing they will have to make a report helps to keep them on track.

  - Plan to have the meals you tend to miss with others (for example, breakfast with your children, lunch with a friend).

  - Keep high-calorie energy bars or a can of liquid supplement with you so that you can eat a bar or drink the supplement as soon as you realize you have missed a meal or snack.

Eating Very Few Types of Foods

Eating from your safe food list is fine, but you need to eat more than one or two things. If you are only eating cereal and oranges, that is not enough. You need to have at least as much variety as was listed on Joe's First-Week Food Schedule (earlier in this chapter). If you can't come up with some additional food choices on your own, you can ask your coach for some ideas or use the services of a dietitian. Check off the solutions that you are willing to try:

☐ Eat at least four foods from Dense Food Ideas in this chapter.

☐ Ask your coach for ideas.

☐ See a dietitian.

☐ Eat at least two things from each food group each day (see the website www.mypyramid.gov for a description of the basic food groups and food-choice ideas).

Changing Your Mind About Gaining Weight

It's normal to get cold feet (no pun intended). Often when people are not doing what they need to do to gain weight, it's because their reasons for gaining are not compelling enough. Review your motivational cards or make new cards with reasons to get well that you find more compelling. Check off the solutions you are willing to try:

☐ Review your reasons for getting well with someone else. This person could be your coach, a friend, or your eating disorder specialist.

☐ Review chapters 2 and 3 to remind yourself of what starvation is doing to your body and mind.

☐ Practice opposite action.

Conflict with Your Coach or Eating Disorder Specialist

Conflict with coaches and eating disorder specialists is not common, but such conflicts can happen. If the conflict cannot be worked out and the stress it generates is interfering with getting well, you may need to consider a change. Before you do that, make sure that the conflict is not just an excuse to quit. Talk to your coach or eating disorder specialist about the conflict. Review what you need from them in terms of support. If you feel your coach is pushing too hard, review the Coach Agreement in chapter 10 and make sure you are both on the same page. Change coaches or eating disorder specialists if you need to but don't quit.

Increased Purging

It's not unusual for someone with a starvation eating disorder to increase their purging at times during weight restoration. This is often related to anxiety about weight gain. Here are some strategies you can use to decrease your purging; check off the ones that you plan to use to deal with increased purging and add any additional strategies you think of at the bottom.

- ☐ Review your Self-Harm-Reduction Plan (chapter 9) with your coach or eating disorder specialist. Make modifications like adding additional self-soothing activities to the plan to improve its effectiveness.

- ☐ Review your purging triggers to make sure you have a plan to deal with strong triggers.

- ☐ Make a plan to eat as many meals as you can in places where purging is difficult, like at a restaurant or friend's house.

- ☐ Leave the house after eating. Try sitting outside if the weather is nice or going to a coffee shop after dinner.

- ☐ Arrange to call your coach after eating.

- ☐ Review the medical complications of purging to remind yourself how purging is affecting your health.

- ☐ Other strategies:

_____

_____

_____

to sum up

Eating enough to gain weight takes some trial and error. You need to take in enough nutrition to gain ½–2 pounds a week. You will probably need to add food each week to find out how much food you actually need in order to gain weight. Liquid supplementation and dense foods (like peanut butter) can help. Most people will have to troubleshoot one or two problems as they work on eating Three Plus Three. In the next chapter you will learn how to change your distorted thoughts into useful ones that will help you continue to gain weight and maintain a healthy weight.

CHAPTER 12

cognitive therapy: changing your thinking

*C*ognitions are thoughts, and *cognitive therapy* is aimed at changing distorted thoughts that don't work very well into thoughts that are useful. Useful thoughts are those that move us toward good health and a full life. We have known for a long time that how we feel is connected to what we are thinking. Change your thinking and you change how you feel. Changing habitual thoughts that have been practiced over and over can be difficult, but it is possible. It's like changing any habit—changing a habitual distorted thought takes time and effort.

Cognitive distortions are sometimes called *automatic thoughts*. They are automatic in that the distorted thought comes to us without effort. They are the first thoughts that come to mind. Distortions are generated in a variety of ways. For example, a distorted thought can be generated by *all-or-nothing thinking* ("all dietary fats are bad") or by *intolerance of uncertainty*—that is, our natural tendency to avoid uncertainty ("I need to know how many calories are in everything I eat"). Often the most powerful distorted thoughts are generated by faulty beliefs that support *emotional reasoning*. For example, you might associate being fat with being lazy. Being lazy has strong emotional meaning. Most of us believe we shouldn't be lazy. If you believe that being fat and being lazy are the same thing, this belief will generate distorted thoughts. This chapter will examine all-or-nothing thinking, intolerance of uncertainty, emotional reasoning, and other sources of distorted thinking.

Changing your thoughts is a multistep process. The first step is to become aware of your thoughts. The best way to do this is to write them down. The next step is to identify the type of cognitive distortions you are making. The last two steps involve "rewriting" your distorted thoughts into useful thoughts and then practicing the new thoughts until they become *useful* automatic thoughts.

Cognitive Therapy Steps

1. Write down the thought.

2. Identify the distortions.

3. Restructure thoughts into useful, nondistorted thoughts.

4. Practice the nondistorted thought.

By the end of this chapter you will have had the opportunity to practice all four steps of cognitive therapy. *The bottom line is this:* by practicing these steps, you will weaken the hold your starvation eating disorder has over you by depriving your disorder of the distorted thoughts that sustain it, making weight restoration and maintenance easier.

step 1: write down the thought

Everyone has distorted thoughts. Because distorted thoughts are so prevalent, psychologists and other behavioral scientists have been able to identify the most common types of thought distortions—ones we all make as well as types of distorted thoughts that are more commonly made by people with a starvation eating disorder. "Step 2: Identify the Distortions" will explore these types of distortions, but first, you will need to collect data about your thoughts.

Collecting Data

It's hard to change something you aren't aware of, and cognitive distortions are so much a part of our thinking that most of us are unaware of all of them. The best way to discover the distorted thoughts your starvation eating disorder is generating is to record your thoughts. Your thought record will give you the data that can help you identify the thoughts you need to address. You are probably working on weight restoration or maintenance at this point. The good news is that both activities will give you lots of opportunity to look at and collect rich data on your distorted thoughts. For example, if you have already gained enough to be at a healthy weight, you are probably finding that your distorted starvation eating disorder thinking is telling you to lose the weight you have worked so hard to gain. Grace's Basic Thought Record shows other distorted thoughts that might happen at this time and demonstrates how a thought record works.

Grace's Basic Thought Record	
Situation	**Thoughts**
I'm eating breakfast.	*I shouldn't be eating this. I'm fat. I am weak. Eating is weak. I hate being like this!*
My daughter is angry with me.	*I'm a bad mother. I am making my daughter have an eating disorder. I should go away by myself so I don't hurt my children.*
I got on the scale at my doctor's office and found I gained 2 pounds.	*I have to lose this weight. I'm fat. No one will want to be around me. I can't do this anymore. I need to purge now. My doctor thinks I need to gain, but I felt better when I was thin.*
My clothes are tight.	*The only thing I have is my eating disorder. This is who I am, and I can't give who I am up. What if I can't stop gaining weight, and I keep getting fatter and fatter?*

All of the thoughts Grace recorded are distorted. Like most people with a starvation eating disorder, she associates eating with being bad or weak and she makes the assumption that everything is about her eating disorder. For example, it didn't occur to Grace that her daughter might be upset about something else. When Grace and I went over her thought record, we discovered that her daughter was upset about something that had nothing to do with Grace's eating disorder.

Before going on to look at the type of distortions Grace and others with starvation eating disorders tend to make, use the thought record that follows. The data you record will give you useful examples to refer to as you learn about types of distortion in "Step 2: Identify the Distortions."

Instructions for Your Basic Thought Record: Record your thoughts when you become distressed about gaining weight or not being able to purge. In addition to recording thoughts that you think are related to your eating disorder, record your thoughts whenever you feel upset. This will give you more data to work with. Record each thought as close to the time when you had the thought as possible. Don't worry about complete sentences or grammar; thoughts rarely follow the rules of grammar. Record your thoughts for at least two days. The more thoughts you record, the better. For now, leave the new "Distortion type" column blank. You will come back to this Basic Thought Record and fill in this last column after you have learned about the different types of distortions.

Basic Thought Record		
Situation	Thoughts	Distortion type

step 2: identify the distortions

As I've worked with patients with starvation eating disorders, I've noticed that certain types of cognitive distortions come up more often than others. As you read through these common types of distortions, think about the kind of thoughts you recorded in the Basic Thought Record. We all make cognitive distortions, and most of us tend to make certain distortions more than we do others. Understanding which distortions you have a tendency to make will help you to be on the lookout for them and to target them for change. After you read about each of the distortion types, you should do two things:

1. *Complete the distortion scale for each distortion described.* The scale is intended to show you how much of a problem that distortion is for you. If you score 5 or more on a scale, that means you make that distortion often.

2. *Look over your thoughts from the Basic Thought Record and find examples of that distortion.* It's possible for a thought to have more than one kind of distortion, so don't worry if a thought fits more than one distortion type. For each thought, write down the distortion type(s) in the last column of the Basic Thought Record.

Here are the distortion types:

- Emotional reasoning

- All-or-nothing thinking

- Body image distortion

- Body misinterpretation

- "Should" distortion

- Intolerance of uncertainty

- "What if" distortion

Emotional Reasoning

Emotional reasoning is treating a feeling or emotion as a fact. Feeling that you are fat is a good example of this type of distortion—as, for example, in Grace's food log, when she thought, "I'm fat," after she ate breakfast, even though her weight was still very low. The fact was, she was *not* fat—she was too thin, but Grace feared that she was fat and she distorted her fear into a fact. *Emotional reasoning* is probably the number one kind of distorted thinking people with starvation eating disorders engage in. As shown in chapter 3, a starving brain generates strongly distorted emotions. This is a biological effect of starvation, and it doesn't matter whether you have an eating disorder or not: if your brain doesn't get enough fuel to function, you will have problems with *emotional reasoning*.

Let's look at the strength of your tendency to engage in *emotional reasoning*.

Emotional Reasoning Scale

Indicate how strongly you agree with the following statements:

I can tell if I'm fat by how I feel.

Strongly disagree   Strongly agree

    1   2   3   4   5

Gaining weight means I'm weak.

Strongly disagree   Strongly agree

    1   2   3   4   5

I can keep purging and gain a little weight and be in control.

Strongly disagree   Strongly agree

    1   2   3   4   5

Add up your points. If you scored 5 or more points, you have a strong tendency toward emotional reasoning.

Score: _____

Look over your Basic Thought Record. How many examples of *emotional reasoning* can you find?

All-or-Nothing Thinking

All-or-nothing thinking is a rigid type of thinking in which we categorize things into all right or all wrong, for example, "Eating fat is always bad" or "I need to eat in the perfect way." Joe experienced this distortion when he went to the gym. You may recall that going to the gym was very important to Joe. After he gained weight with his weight restoration plan, he and I agreed that he could start going to the gym for twenty to thirty minutes of strength building three times a week. But when Joe went to the gym, he had powerful all-or-nothing thoughts that if he was going to go to the gym, he had to do a full four-hour workout. It was either no workout or a four-hour workout—that's all-or-nothing thinking.

Along with emotional reasoning, all-or-nothing thinking is a very common starvation eating disorder distortion. You may recall that being a perfectionist is a common personality trait for someone with a starvation eating disorder. Perfectionist thinking tends to be all-or-nothing thinking: "I need to do this perfectly or I shouldn't attempt this at all." In addition, as learned from the World War II starvation study, even people who don't start out being rigid in their thinking get more rigid when their brain is starving (Tucker 2006). So, like emotional reasoning, all-or-nothing thinking can be a result of starvation. And if you started out with a tendency in this direction, it's easy to see how starving your brain will just make your thinking even more all-or-nothing.

All-or-Nothing Thinking Scale

Indicate how strongly you agree with the following statements:

Eating even a little amount of fat is bad.

Strongly disagree				Strongly agree
1	2	3	4	5

If I don't stay very thin, I will be obese.

Strongly disagree				Strongly agree
1	2	3	4	5

I need to follow all my rules for what to eat and what not to eat. If I break one rule, I will break them all.

Strongly disagree				Strongly agree
1	2	3	4	5

Add up your points. If you scored 5 or more points, you have a strong tendency toward all-or-nothing thinking.

Score: _____

Now review your Basic Thought Record. As you did for emotional reasoning, mark the thoughts that represent all-or-nothing thinking.

Body Image Distortion

A distorted body image is one of the hallmarks of a starvation eating disorder and results from *body image distortion thinking*. A common distortion is looking at your body in the mirror and thinking a body part looks fat. Another is comparing your body to someone who is thin and thinking you need to lose weight to look like that person, when, in fact, you are thinner than the person to whom you are comparing yourself. Lorrie experienced this kind of distorted thinking when she was walking into a restaurant. As she came into the restaurant, a woman was coming out. The woman was a little overweight and said to Lorrie, "I wish I was thin." This prompted Lorrie to compare herself to the woman and to think that she was close to the same size as the woman. Lorrie couldn't shake the thought that she was overweight like this woman, and she left the restaurant without ordering. At the time, Lorrie's BMI was below 16, and it was clear to everyone except Lorrie that her weight was very low. Body image distortions often confuse those around you because your family and friends look at your body and see someone who is too thin and needs to gain weight, but, at the same time is trying to lose weight. Fill in the Body Image Distortion Scale to see how strong your tendency is to have body image distortions.

Body Image Distortion Scale

Indicate how strongly you agree with the following statements:

I need to lose weight to be attractive.

Strongly disagree				Strongly agree
1	2	3	4	5

Other people may not see it, but when I look in the mirror, I see the fat.

Strongly disagree				Strongly agree
1	2	3	4	5

When I look at other people, I realize just how fat I am.

Strongly disagree				Strongly agree
1	2	3	4	5

Add up your points. If you scored 5 or more points, you have a strong tendency to have body image distortions.

Score: _____

How many examples of distorted body image do you find in your Basic Thought Record? If you tend to make this distortion frequently, you will want to pay particular attention to the body image exercises in chapter 15. You may also want to use a workbook like *The Body Image Workbook: An Eight-Step Program for Learning to Like Your Looks* (Cash 1997).

Body Misinterpretation

Body misinterpretation distortions result from being out of touch with your body. For example, you might ignore the signals your body is giving you about starvation and think "I feel fine" when, in fact, you are very tired. Another example of this kind of distortion is thinking, "I'm full, so that means I ate enough" after you've eaten only a few bites. Grace's Basic Thought Record contains a common distortion of this type. Grace had a thought that she felt physically better when she was thinner. She persisted in believing this despite the fact that her doctor had put her on bed rest at one point because her weight was so low she was having difficulty with dizziness. During that time, Grace was in poor shape physically, but she ignored that fact as well as the messages her body was trying to give her.

Body Misinterpretation Scale

Indicate how strongly you agree with the following statements:

I feel fine, so that means my starvation is not hurting my body.

Strongly disagree				Strongly agree
1	2	3	4	5

I know I have eaten enough when I feel full even if I have only eaten a few bites.

Strongly disagree				Strongly agree
1	2	3	4	5

I don't need to be in touch with my body to get well.

Strongly disagree				Strongly agree
1	2	3	4	5

Add up your points. If you scored 5 or more points, you have a strong tendency to misinterpret or ignore your body.

Score: _____

Did you score high on this scale? How many of your thoughts on the Basic Thought Record seem unconnected to the actual state of your body? In addition to changing your thinking about your body, see chapter 15 to learn other ways to get reconnected to your body.

"Should" Distortion

While many of your *"should" distortions* are probably about weight, food, or shape, "should" distortions in general are common in people with and without eating disorders. In fact it would be difficult to find a human being who doesn't experience "should" distortions, which are simply thinking that things should or shouldn't be a certain way or that we should or shouldn't do something (for example, "I should exercise more" or "I shouldn't eat after 4 p.m."). "Should" distortions get us in trouble even if the thoughts seem positive on the surface. For example, you might think, "I shouldn't purge." This seems like a useful thought, but in fact this thought often leads to emotions like shame and guilt that will likely lead to more purging, not less. "Should" distortions are easy to identify. If the thought includes a "should," "shouldn't," "have to," or "need to," it's a "should" distortion. Look at Grace's Basic Thought Record and count the number of "should" distortions you can find. Here they are:

- I shouldn't be eating this.

- I should go away …

- I have to lose weight.

- I need to purge now.

"Should" Distortion Scale

Indicate how strongly you agree with the following statements:

I should be able to control my starvation eating disorder.

Strongly disagree				Strongly agree
1	2	3	4	5

I shouldn't eat anything I didn't plan to eat.

Strongly disagree				Strongly agree
1	2	3	4	5

I shouldn't purge.

Strongly disagree				Strongly agree
1	2	3	4	5

Add up your points. If you scored 5 or more points, you have a strong tendency toward "should" distortions.

Score: _____

How many "should" distortions did you find in your Basic Thought Record? Did you make any "should" distortions that were unconnected to your eating disorder? Changing "should" distortions into useful thoughts will help you in all parts of your life.

Intolerance of Uncertainty

In the same way that people with starvation eating disorders tend to be perfectionistic, it's common for people with such disorders to be very uncomfortable with uncertainty. An example of *intolerance of uncertainty* is thinking, "I have to know how much I weigh every day" or "I have to know ahead of time exactly what I'm going to eat." A common distortion for women with starvation eating disorders to have is to want to know how much weight gain it will take for their periods to start, but it's very difficult to determine this specifically because every woman is different. Amy, who had great difficulty with uncertainty, was very distressed when I couldn't tell her exactly how many pounds she needed to gain to get her period back. We often can't know ahead of time exactly what is going to happen, so if you're like Amy, you may have to work on changing your intolerance-of-uncertainty thinking into more useful thinking, like, "I may not know how much I need to gain for my periods to start again, but I can learn to trust that my body will tell me when I have gained enough."

Intolerance-of-Uncertainty Scale

Indicate how strongly you agree with the following statements:

I have to weigh myself several times a day or check myself in the mirror so I know if I've gained weight.

Strongly disagree				Strongly agree
1	2	3	4	5

I can't stand not knowing what I'm going to do for the day. I can't tolerate a disruption of my normal routine.

Strongly disagree				Strongly agree
1	2	3	4	5

If I don't plan everything, I can't function.

Strongly disagree				Strongly agree
1	2	3	4	5

Add up your points. If you scored 5 or more points, you have a strong tendency toward intolerance for uncertainty.

Score: _____

Did you find frequent intolerance-of-uncertainty thoughts in your Basic Thought Record? As with "should" distortions, you may find that these thoughts also affect your life outside of your eating disorder, making them important to target for multiple reasons.

"What If" Distortion

"What if" distortions (also called *catastrophizing thoughts*) are thoughts that anticipate some kind of disaster even if you don't have any evidence that a disaster is about to happen. An example of this kind of thinking is, "What if I have to take time off work for my eating disorder treatment and I lose my job?" Grace has a common "what if" thought in her Basic Thought Record: "What if I can't stop gaining weight, and I keep getting fatter and fatter?"

"What If" Distortion Scale

Indicate how strongly you agree with the following statements:

What if I can't stop purging and I never get well?

Strongly disagree   Strongly agree
    1   2   3   4   5

What if I start to eat and can't stop?

Strongly disagree   Strongly agree
    1   2   3   4   5

What if my family doesn't like me when I gain weight?

Strongly disagree   Strongly agree
    1   2   3   4   5

Add up your points. If you scored 5 or more points, you have a strong tendency to have "what if" distortions.

Score: _____

Did you find "what if" distortions in your Basic Thought Record? "What if" distortions are particularly identified with anxiety. If this is a common type of distortion for you, in addition to learning how to change these thoughts into useful thoughts, you will be able to address these anxiety-producing thoughts with the worry exposure techniques in chapter 13.

Identifying Your Distortions

Overall, what did you learn about the kind of distortions you tend to make? Look over all of your distortion scales. On how many scales did you score 5 or higher? Consider the information from both your distortion scales and Basic Thought Record. Write down the distortions in the tables that follow. Put them in order based on how likely you are to make each distortion, from your most common distortion at the top of the first list to your least common in the second list. If you think two or three distortions are equal in frequency, put them on the same line.

Your Most Common Distortion(s)
_____
_____
_____
_____
_____
_____
_____

Your Least Common Distortion
_____
_____
_____

Now that you have some idea which distortions you are most likely to make and have some experience identifying your distortions on your Basic Thought Record, it's time to move on to cognitive therapy step 3 to learn how to change your distorted thoughts into useful thoughts.

step 3: restructure thoughts into useful, nondistorted thoughts

Cognitive restructuring is the process of taking distorted thoughts and, by restructuring, changing them into useful, nondistorted thoughts. The best way to learn this skill is to do the rewriting on paper; actually writing the useful thought down is more powerful than just thinking it. To do this, you will need to switch from the Basic Thought Record to the more detailed format that follows, which you should use from now on.

As you can see, the new record includes additional columns. Two of the new columns are for *prompted emotions*—emotions that thoughts have triggered. For example, when Grace thought, "I shouldn't be eating this," that thought prompted anxiety, so "anxiety" would be listed in the "Prompted emotion 1" column. Prompted emotions can come from distorted thoughts or useful thoughts. You'll record your distorted trigger thought in the second column of the table—preceded by the situation you are in (in the first column) and the prompted emotion (in the third column). Then you'll rewrite that distorted thought as a useful one (in the fifth column) and you'll add its prompted emotion (in the sixth column). "Prompted emotion 2" can help you determine if a thought is truly useful or not: if a thought improves your emotional state, it is useful; if you feel distressed, the trigger thought is still a distorted one and you'll need to try again to come up with a useful thought.

The seventh column—also new to this thought record—is a check on how the new thought affects the strength of your starvation eating disorder. If the new thought makes your eating disorder weaker, then the thought is a useful one. If, on the other hand, you feel better but your eating disorder has been reinforced, the thought is distorted. For example, say you change a distorted "should" thought from "I shouldn't purge" to "I can purge and I will feel better." This new thought probably prompts a decrease in anxiety but it also reinforces your starvation eating disorder and makes it more likely that you will purge; therefore, it can't be a useful thought. Instead, a useful thought might be "If I purge, I will feel better in the short term but will hurt my health and reinforce my eating disorder." This thought may not decrease your anxiety as much as the first one, but it's not distorted because it doesn't make your starvation eating disorder stronger. *The bottom line is this*: make sure that your new thought *both* improves the prompted emotion and weakens the hold your starvation eating disorder has on your life.

Let's look at some examples from Grace's Basic Thought Record and put them in this new thought record to see how this works.

Grace's Thought Record						
Situation	Distorted thought	Prompted emotion 1	Distortion type	Useful thought	Prompted emotion 2	Eating disorder strength? ↑↓
1. Eating breakfast at home	1. I shouldn't be eating this.	Anxiety	"Should" distortion	I have to eat or I will get sick*	Anxiety and anger	No change
2. Eating breakfast at home	2. I shouldn't be eating this.	Anxiety	No distortion	It makes me anxious to eat, but I have committed myself to a plan to eat breakfast.	Slightly less anxiety	No change
3. Eating breakfast at home	3. I shouldn't be eating this.	Anxiety	No distortion	It makes me anxious to eat, but I have committed myself to a plan to eat breakfast because I want to have a life with my girls that doesn't revolve around being thin.	Anxiety cut in half and increased feelings of competence	↓

Analysis of Grace's Rewrites: Grace's thought, "I have to eat or I will get sick," was not a useful thought. You may have noticed that Grace substituted one "should" distortion for another, resulting in more negative emotions. Grace's second try was better. She got rid of the "should" distortion but she still had more anxiety than was useful. On Grace's third try, she took the nondistorted thought and added to it to make it more useful. By adding one of her compelling reasons for getting well, Grace was able to cut her anxiety in half. In addition to decreasing her anxiety, Grace, who came into treatment doubting that she could get well, gained a sense of competency. Like many useful thoughts, this new thought decreased the strength of her eating disorder and was one that Grace would be able to use more than once.

Instructions for the Thought Record: Now it's time for you to restructure your distorted thoughts. Fill out the following Thought Record (first making copies of it so you can use a new one each day). As with the Basic Thought Record you filled out earlier, the sooner you can record your distorted thought, the better. If you are working with an eating disorder specialist or coach, you can ask for help with ideas for useful thoughts, but the ones you write in should be thoughts that are meaningful *for you*. In general, you want to try for a decrease in negative prompted emotions as well as the development of a positive emotion, like hopefulness. Remember to fill in the final column too: if you find that a new thought strengthens your eating disorder, then that thought is distorted and you will need to come up with a replacement useful thought that doesn't reinforce your eating disorder. If you have problems coming up with useful thoughts that work, consult the Thought Record Troubleshooting Guide. See the table that follows for examples of distortion types.

Thought Record Troubleshooting Guide
■ Check to make sure you haven't substituted one distorted thought for another.
■ If you can't think of a useful thought, look at your motivational cards for ideas.
■ Ask others for ideas.
■ Don't expect to get rid of a negative emotion completely at first. It takes time to decrease emotions such as anxiety. Go for a significant reduction.
■ Make sure you write out the thought.
■ If the new thought strengthens your eating disorder, it is distorted—get rid of it.
■ Sometimes it may take several tries to get a useful thought that really works for you. Don't give up—just try again with a new thought, or try expanding on a thought that works a little to see if you can improve it.

Distortion categories	Examples
Emotional reasoning	*I'm weak because I ate.* *I feel fat so I have to lose weight.*
All-or-nothing thinking	*Any fat on my body is bad.*
Body image distortion	*My legs are fat.*
Body misinterpretation	*I felt better when I was thinner.*
"Should" distortion	*I shouldn't purge.*
Intolerance of uncertainty	*I can't stand not knowing my weight every day.*
"What if" distortion	*What if I can't stop gaining weight?*

Thought Record

Situation	Distorted thought	Prompted emotion 1	Distortion type	Useful thought	Prompted emotion 2	Eating disorder strength? ↓↑*
1.	1.					
2.	2.					
3.	3					
4.	4.					

* Does the new thought weaken or strengthen your starvation eating disorder?

step 4: practice the nondistorted thought

All of us have "practiced" some of our distorted thoughts over and over again, making a habit of them. So just rewriting a distorted thought to make it a useful thought is not enough to complete the substitution—you need to practice your new useful thoughts. One way to do this is to write useful thoughts that can be used more than once on a 3 by 5 card. This is what Grace did with the useful thought, "It makes me anxious to eat, but I have committed myself to a plan to eat breakfast because I want to have a life with my girls that doesn't revolve around being thin." Grace put that thought on a card and read it before breakfast each morning. After a few weeks, she found that she automatically thought of this useful thought as she was making her breakfast and didn't have to read the card anymore. As you do your thought records, look for thoughts that you can write on a card. And remember that the more thought records you complete, the better you will become at substituting useful thoughts for distorted ones.

beliefs about starvation

As described previously, emotional reasoning leads to distorted thoughts. While emotional reasoning can occur for many reasons, sometimes we are predisposed to it because of the beliefs we hold. If the beliefs we hold are faulty, they'll lead to emotional reasoning that, in turn, yields distorted thoughts.

Most people with starvation eating disorders hold beliefs about weight and food that are faulty, leading to emotional reasoning and thus to distorted thoughts. To understand how this works, let's first look at a non-eating-disorder example. Consider the thought, "I can't take care of myself." Sometimes the belief underlying a thought like "I can't take care of myself" is unimportant; at other times, the belief is very powerful. For example, if you get the flu, you might think, "I can't take care of myself when I have the flu." But it's probably not true that you can't take care of yourself. Most of us can take care of ourselves when we have the flu, so the thought is emotional reasoning. Happily, this thought won't have a big impact on you if you generally hold the belief that you are an independent person. But if you believe that you can't take care of yourself in general, the belief underlying the thought, "I can't take care of myself," is one of dependency. And this belief about your own dependency would likely be powerful enough for you that it would have an impact on you past just having the flu and would generate distorted thoughts, like "I can't do things alone; I need to depend on others to make decisions for me."

Put another way, if you think that something you believe is true, it will create an emotional response for you. For example, if you believe that being thin makes you a mentally strong person, the belief will generate certain thoughts, like "I have to be thin to be strong."

An investigation of beliefs about starvation found that there are eight common starvation themes for people with starvation eating disorders (Nordbo et al. 2006). Each theme or belief generates distorted thoughts. Examine the following themes and check off those that fit your thinking about starvation. After you have checked a theme that represents how you think, rate how strong that theme is for you on a 0–5 scale (with 5 being very strong).

Distorted Beliefs About Starvation

☐ **Security:** Feeling that you are safe and secure when you starve; feeling secure when you follow starvation eating disorder rules, like only eating safe foods; wanting the structure your starvation brings to your life

Strength of this belief: _____

☐ **Avoidance of negative emotions:** Starvation eating disorder behaviors as distress tolerance; feeling that starvation and purging will keep negative emotions away or will reduce any negative feelings you are experiencing

Strength of this belief: _____

☐ **Mental strength:** Believing that starvation or very low weight is equivalent with being mentally strong and that eating or gaining weight means you are weak; feeling that your starvation eating disorder will give you inner strength

Strength of this belief: _____

☐ **Self-confidence:** Believing that you are worthy of compliments only when you are very thin and that you are not worthy if you gain weight

Strength of this belief: _____

☐ **Identity:** Wanting a new identity and feeling that by being very thin, you are achieving a new identity or becoming someone else

Strength of this belief: _____

☐ **Care:** Feeling that you need to be taken care of and that the only way you will be cared for is to be very thin

Strength of this belief: _____

☐ **Communication:** Using your body to communicate; feeling that being very thin will allow you to communicate something that is important to you; believing that the only way you can get people to understand the emotional pain you experience is to show your pain in your body

Strength of this belief: _____

☐ **Death**: Equating being very thin or purging with death*

Strength of this belief: _____

How many themes did you check off? _____

Which themes did you rate as a 4 or 5? _____

_____

*__Important note:__ If you are having thoughts about dying or killing yourself, please get help from a mental health professional as soon as possible.

Each of these themes represents a faulty belief that leads to emotional reasoning, which yields a thought distortion. Distorted thoughts based on faulty beliefs respond very well to facts. Let's look at how the theme of security can be challenged by looking at the facts.

We all need some security in our lives; wanting security is normal and healthy. Wanting it only becomes a problem when you think the only way you can have it is if you starve. If you checked off the theme of security in the table, you may think that the *emotional feeling of security* you have when you starve is a *fact*. But the fact is that starving makes you *less* secure, not more secure. Starving only gives you a feeling of security; it doesn't give you actual security. Here is how Grace disputed her distorted sense of security.

Grace's Examination of Security: *The security theme says I am safe and secure when I am very thin.* **Fact:** *Starvation and purging make me unsafe and at higher risk for many medical problems. The predictability and structure that comes with starvation is a sham. Starvation causes medical problems that can destroy my daily structure by sending me to the hospital.*

Instructions for Challenging Distorted Starvation Themes: Now it's time for you to dispute your beliefs about starvation for yourself. Use facts to dispute each theme in the next table. When you finish, write the themes that are the strongest for you on one side of a 3 by 5 card and write the challenges to the theme on the other side. Add the cards to those you've made of useful thoughts. Pull out the theme cards whenever you are struggling with beliefs about starvation to remind yourself that all the themes are based on distortions, not facts.

Facts to Challenge Distorted Starvation Themes

■ **Security:** This theme says I am safe and secure when I am very thin.

Fact: _____

_____

■ **Avoidance of negative emotions:** This theme says that I can keep from feeling bad if I starve and purge.

Fact: _____

_____

■ **Mental strength:** This theme says that I am strong because I don't need to eat like the rest of the world.

Fact: _____

_____

■ **Self-confidence:** This theme says that I'm worthy of compliments only when I'm very thin and that I'm not worthy if I gain weight.

Fact: _____

_____

■ **Identity:** This theme says I can be a different person or remake myself through starvation.

Fact: _____

_____

■ **Care:** This theme says I can't take care of myself and I will be taken care of if I am very thin.

Fact: _____

_____

■ **Communication:** This theme says people will only listen to me and understand my emotional pain if I starve.

Fact: _____

_____

■ **Death:** This theme associates starving with my death.*

Fact: _____

_____

*__Important note:__ If you find you have problems challenging this theme and are having thoughts about dying or killing yourself, please get help from a mental health professional as soon as possible.

to sum up

Cognitive therapy is a powerful tool for changing the distorted thoughts that reinforce your starvation eating disorder. The first step is to write down your thoughts. After you've collected data about your thinking, the second step is to identify the kinds of cognitive distortions you are making; there are a number of such distortions for people with starvation eating disorders, but two common ones are emotional reasoning and all-or-nothing thinking. The third step is to learn how to restructure your distorted thoughts into useful thoughts that weaken the hold your starvation eating disorder has on you. The fourth and final step in cognitive therapy is to practice your new useful thoughts.

Faulty beliefs about starvation generate distorted thoughts for people with starvation eating disorders. Using facts to challenge your beliefs about starvation is an effective way to change the distorted thinking associated with your beliefs into thoughts that can help you get well. The next chapter builds on this foundation by teaching you to challenge your anxiety about getting well and gaining weight.

CHAPTER 13

challenging core anxiety

Several strategies for decreasing anxiety have been covered: You learned how to use self-soothing and distracting skills to deal with anxiety in preparation for weight restoration in chapter 9. And in chapter 12, you learned how to change distorted thoughts that cause anxiety into useful thoughts that can reduce anxiety as well as how to tolerate anxiety through acceptance. In this chapter, you will learn how to address anxiety in a very direct way—by challenging it.

Much of what you will learn in this chapter has been taken from anxiety disorder research. Researchers who study anxiety disorders have learned that using special techniques to expose someone to anxiety in the short term actually produces a decrease in anxiety over time (Marks 1997). While it may seem counterintuitive to treat anxiety by triggering anxiety, challenging anxiety in this way has the potential for long-term anxiety reduction. People with anxiety disorders who have used this kind of treatment often report that their anxiety is under control years later (Marks 1997).

Over the last few years, I have used some of the anxiety-challenging techniques from treatment of anxiety in other disorders, such as panic disorder and obsessive-compulsive disorder, to treat starvation eating disorders. These techniques deliberately trigger anxiety and then allow the body to deal with that anxiety through a process called *habituation*. Habituation is a natural process that allows our bodies to adapt to the physical and emotional components of anxiety, making us unresponsive to anxiety triggers. But habituation only works if we don't try to escape the anxiety we are experiencing. In my grandmother's words, it's about "facing your fear head on and not running away." If you run away by giving in to the anxiety, habituation will not occur. For example, when you give in to your anxiety by purging or engaging in some other starvation eating disorder behavior (like only eating a few safe foods), you are, in fact, running away.

In this chapter you will learn to face your fear and not run away. But before you can learn to face your fear and allow your body to start the natural process of habituation, you need a good understanding of the fight-or-flight response, which is responsible for our physical and emotional response to fear.

Important note: Because some of the exercises in this chapter will increase your heart rate, you should make sure you are healthy enough to deliberately increase your heart rate. You should already have gone to your primary care physician, but if for some reason you skipped that step in chapter 10, make an appointment with your PCP now. ***If your doctor has you on bed rest, you should not attempt to do these exercises until you are off bed rest.*** You have probably gained some weight at this point, but if you haven't gained any weight or your BMI is under 16, you should talk to your doctor before doing these exercises. With the exception of food exposure (which is described later in this chapter), I usually start these exercises after my patients have had a physical and have gained 30–50 percent of the weight they need to gain to be healthy. If you're not sure if you are ready, take this book to your doctor, show her the exercises in this chapter, and ask her if you are healthy enough to do the work in this chapter.

the fight-or-flight response

The *fight-or-flight response* is a natural response that all mammals experience when faced with an emergency situation. While meant for situations where we have to take action to save ourselves from some threat, the fight-or-flight response can also be triggered when there is no true emergency. The response involves two possible emotional responses—fear (the desire for flight) and anger (the desire to fight). While these emotions seem different to us, most of the physical components of fear and anger are the same. For example, when we are very afraid or very angry, our heart rate increases and digestion stops or slows down. All the physical symptoms of the fight-or-flight response are designed to increase our ability to react appropriately to danger, to either run away or to fight. The fact that we can do both during fight-or-flight response makes it easy to switch back and forth between these two emotional components of the response. Fear is thought to be the core emotion of the fight-or-flight response, which is why the fear response is so much a part of any kind of anxiety. But fear is not enough to protect us in all emergency situations. In a life-or-death emergency, switching from anger to fear or fear to anger can save us. For example, if you are mugged, you might need to fight first and then run. If you talk to people who have had this experience, you may be surprised to find them say they felt anger at first and didn't feel fear until later. Whether you feel fear or anger depends on many factors, including the situation, your personality, and even your age. And it's even possible to feel both anger and fear at the same time.

The physical side of the fight-or-flight response plays an important part in dealing with life-or-death situations. Common physical responses include racing heart, breathing faster, feeling nauseated, and feeling like your hands are numb or tingling. Some of these responses are known to have an important function during an emergency. For example, increased heart rate and breathing moves blood to the large muscles as well as provides more oxygen to the brain. The nausea occurs because during an emergency the body needs to focus all of its energy into running or fighting rather than digesting lunch. The numbness and tingling in your hands and other places in the body (feet and face) is a side effect of the body moving blood to the large muscles, where the blood is needed to improve strength.

While the body's emotional and physical response to the fight-or-flight response is meant to be life saving, most of us don't have to respond to life-or-death emergencies very often. Perhaps in the past when people were living in caves there was more opportunity to use the fight-or-flight response, but for most of us, life-or-death situations just don't come up very often. What we may find instead is that our fight-or-flight response is being triggered in non-emergency situations—we feel anger at the driver who cuts us off on the highway or we feel anxious about paying our bills. For someone with a starvation eating disorder, the fight-or-flight response becomes associated with food and gaining weight.

Non-Emergencies and the Fight-or-Flight Response

As described in the last section, many of the physical symptoms of the fight-or-flight response have a purpose. During a true emergency, we don't notice the physical components of the response because we are too busy reacting to the emergency. But when the fight-or-flight response is triggered outside of a true emergency and we are experiencing the fear side of the response, we refer to the feelings we have as *panic*. If fear as well as most of the physical symptoms of the fight-or-flight response are triggered, we call this a *panic attack*. In addition to panic, the fight-or-flight response produces lower levels of anxiety and worry that also make us uncomfortable.

If our fight-or-flight response is triggered in a non-emergency, we tend to notice the uncomfortable symptoms of the response and may even become alarmed by the symptoms. This is what happens in panic disorder. People with panic disorder become afraid of the fight-or-flight response and avoid situations they think will trigger that response.

Although the anxiety part of the fight-or-flight response often gets the most attention, there are plenty of people who have problems with the anger part of the response. For example, people who experience road rage or other anger problems are also experiencing a fight-or-flight response to a non-emergency. You may have experienced this anger side of the fight-or-flight response with your starvation eating disorder when someone pushed you to gain weight. If you started out with fear, became angry, and then went back to fear again, you experienced a common reaction to needing to gain weight. You may even be feeling some anger now as you move through weight restoration. Grace described it this way, "I was angry at the thought of needing to gain weight—I didn't want to gain weight and then I became panicky about eating higher-calorie foods. Sometimes I felt anger and fear at the same time."

Triggers of the Fight-or-Flight Response in Non-Emergencies

In non-emergency situations, it is often a thought that triggers the fight-or-flight response. For someone with an anxiety disorder such as obsessive-compulsive disorder, a fight-or-flight response might be triggered by thoughts about germs. For someone with a starvation eating disorder, the trigger thoughts are usually about being fat or gaining weight. But things other than thoughts can trigger a fight-or-flight response, as, for example, when just looking at food makes you anxious.

The more practice your fight-or-flight response gets with a particular trigger, the easier it is for that trigger to elicit the response. A well-practiced trigger will often generalize (that is, extend) to triggers that are similar to the original trigger. This is part of what happens to people who experience war firsthand. If you talk to soldiers who have come back from war, they will often say that when they first got home, their fight-or-flight response was triggered by everything from a car backfiring to a child crying. For someone with a starvation eating disorder, the fight-or-flight response becomes conditioned over time to respond to triggers involving food and weight. The stronger the response, the more likely you will be to act on that response by restricting or purging (including exercising). To find out how strongly conditioned your fight-or-flight response is to gaining weight, complete the following Fight-or-Flight Response Test.

Instructions for the Fight-or-Flight Response Test: This test will help you determine how strong your fight-or-flight response is and which fight-or-flight symptoms you feel when your response is triggered. The first step in the test is to find a quiet place where you won't be disturbed. Next imagine gaining weight—a lot of weight. Imagine gaining so much weight that you become obese. When you notice your fear rising, check off the symptoms you are experiencing (the list contains the most common symptoms). For ten minutes, continue imagining being fat, unable to stop eating, and completely out of control. If your anxiety doesn't get very high, it's probably because you're trying to escape the anxiety by telling yourself you will not eat for the rest of the day or that you can go to the gym after this test. Those are escape thoughts that will lower your anxiety. But try to stay away from any thoughts that decrease your anxiety; this is not the time for useful thoughts. The idea is to get your anxiety as high as you can. It's helpful to use a numeric rating scale to rate the overall amount of anxiety you are experiencing. On a scale of 0–5 points (with 5 being the worst anxiety you have ever felt), try to get your anxiety to at least a 3. If you switch over to anger, that's okay—just rate the strength of your anger instead. The only wrong way to do this test is to escape the fight-or-flight response altogether.

Fight-or-Flight Response Test

Which of the following happens when you imagine yourself to be very fat?

- ☐ Your heart pounding or racing

- ☐ Tightness in your chest

- ☐ Feeling like you can't breathe or that you are breathing fast

- ☐ Nausea

- ☐ Dry mouth or feeling like you can't swallow

- ☐ Feeling like you have to move or get away

- ☐ Numbness in your hands or other parts of your body

- ☐ Feeling light-headed or even dizzy

- ☐ Feeling hot or very cold, or sweating

- ☐ Feeling very scared or angry

- ☐ Other symptoms: _____

Response rating:

Calm feeling				Worst anxiety ever
1	2	3	4	5

How many symptoms did you check? If you checked more than a couple of symptoms and the strength of your response was higher than 3 you may have experienced a panic attack. A panic attack occurs when the full fight-or-flight response is triggered. If you did experience a panic attack—congratulations! You get an A+ for this test. The idea was to get your anxiety as high as possible, and you did exactly that.

Most people will notice that one part of their response is stronger than other parts. For Joe, this was a tightening in his chest. He felt this uncomfortable feeling whenever he tried to eat. Not eating made the feeling go away. It was like his fight-or-flight response was telling him that eating was dangerous. In the next exercise, write down what you learned about your fight-or-flight response, including your strongest symptoms and how you think your fight-or-flight response is affecting your eating disorder.

What You Learned from Your Fight-or-Flight Response Test

Observations: _____

_____

My strongest symptom(s): _____

Effect on my eating disorder: _____

_____

_____

---

taking control of your fight-or-flight response

We all need a healthy fight-or-flight response so we can respond if we do encounter a true emergency. However, if our fight-or-flight response is going off in non-emergency situations and causes us to experience anxiety throughout the day, then we are being controlled by our anxiety. Luckily we can take control of our anxiety by taking control of the fight-or-flight response. One way to do this is to challenge our anxiety through *exposure and response prevention* (ERP).

Exposure is the process of exposing yourself to what you are afraid of. There are two kinds of exposure: *worry exposure* (also called *imaginative exposure*) and *in vivo exposure*. We can think of worry exposure as being exposure to a thought, for example, intentionally thinking about gaining weight, like you just did in the fight-or-flight test. *In vivo* means "in life," so in vivo exposure involves actually doing what you are afraid of, like eating a hamburger and fries.

Response prevention involves not doing what the anxiety is telling you to do. Think of this as opting not to run away or escape. For example, if you are afraid of germs, response prevention would involve *not* washing your hands when your fear is telling you to wash your hands. For someone with a starvation eating disorder, response prevention might be *not* vomiting after you eat when your anxiety is telling you to get rid of the food by vomiting, or *not* going to the gym to work out when your anxiety is pushing you to spend the afternoon at the gym to burn off calories.

Both worry and in vivo exposure use the process of habituation. Before exploring exposure further, it's important to understand what happens during habituation.

Habituation

Think of habituation as the process by which the body learns that something that seemed dangerous on the surface is not dangerous and then resets the fight-or-flight response. Think about modern car alarms. Sometimes something happens that sets off the alarm by mistake, say, a cat jumps on the car hood. The car is not in danger of being stolen by the cat, so the car alarm is not useful in this situation. When triggered in these situations, newer generations of alarms will stop after a few minutes and the alarm system will reset; in the first generation of car alarms, there was no reset, and the alarm would just keep going off until the battery died. Our bodies are smarter than that. If the full fight-or-flight response was going all the time, the body would use up all of its resources. But the body has a built-in habituation process; not only does the body reset the fight-or-flight response, but unlike a car alarm, it learns from experience not to "go off" at all in situations that aren't really emergencies.

In terms of exposure, habituation will occur whether exposure is imagined or real (for example, whether you are imagining an anxiety-provoking situation, such as being obese, or are doing something that is very anxiety provoking, such as eating candy). But habituation occurs only if anxiety is triggered. *The bottom line is this:* if you run away from your anxiety about gaining weight by doing things like purging or restricting, your fight-or-flight response will never habituate. Now let's look at how worry exposure first triggers anxiety so that you can teach your body, through habituation, not to trigger anxiety.

Worry Exposure

Worry exposure is a process of imagining your worst fear. You did this when you took the fight-or-flight test earlier in this chapter. When you do worry exposure, you need to think of the scariest scenarios you can imagine. Because the fear of being fat is such a strong fear for people with starvation eating disorders, most of the scenarios will involve gaining weight. Here are some examples of effective worry exposure scenarios:

- Becoming so fat you can't fit into an airline seat

- Gaining 10 pounds

- Not being able to stop eating

- Being told by someone you are fat

- Being laughed at because you are fat

- Being just like someone else who is fat

- Going shopping for clothes and finding you have to buy larger clothes or even shop at the "fat" store

The first step in worry exposure is to come up with your personal list of scenarios. Some anxiety is healthy, so you wouldn't want to decrease healthy anxiety, like being worried about the health problems caused by purging. So when you develop your Worry Exposure Scenarios list, make sure that you're choosing scenarios that will lead to getting well, not to staying sick. Worry exposures are written as if the scenario is acutely happening to you right now. So rather than write down, "I might become fat," you would write, "I am so fat that. . . ." You should also try to make your scenarios specific to you. Reviewing your core anxieties in the What Does It Mean If I Gain Weight? exercise in chapter 5 can help you come up with your personalized scenarios. When Amy reviewed her answers to that exercise, she added, "I am just like my mother" to her list. You may recall that when Amy did that exercise, she found that she was afraid she was like her mother. Her mother (who was obese) left the family when Amy was young, and Amy grew up hearing negative things about the mother she didn't really know. Amy was very close to her father, and the idea of being like her mother was very anxiety provoking for her. Amy associated gaining weight with being like her mother, so this was a good worry exposure scenario for Amy because it got at one of the fears that reinforced her starvation eating disorder.

In the next list, write down at least five worry exposure scenarios that are personal to you. The more scenarios you write down, the more material you will have to work with when doing your worry exposure.

Your Worry Exposure Scenarios
Write each scenario as if it is happening in the present. Then write down how much anxiety that scenario causes you on a scale of 1–5 (with 5 being the most anxiety you can imagine having and 2.5 being the middle point of your anxiety—moderate anxiety).
Scenario: Anxiety rating: _____
Scenario: Anxiety rating: _____
Scenario: Anxiety rating: _____
Scenario: Anxiety rating: _____
Scenario: Anxiety rating: _____
Scenario: Anxiety rating: _____
Scenario: Anxiety rating: _____

After you have written down your scenarios and ratings, the next step is to put the scenarios in a hierarchy. Your hierarchy should be based on how much anxiety each scenario causes you. Let's look at some of Grace's scenarios to see how this works.

Grace's Worry Exposure Scenarios
Scenario: *I have gained so much weight, I have to shop at the fat-lady shop.* Anxiety rating: 3.5
Scenario: *My daughters don't want to be seen with me because they are embarrassed by my obesity.* Anxiety rating: 5
Scenario: *My legs are so fat, I can't find pants that fit and I can hardly walk.* Anxiety rating: 4
Scenario: *I am eating cake and I can't stop until I have eaten the whole cake.* Anxiety rating: 3
Scenario: *I am so out of control that I can't do anything except stay home and eat all day.* Anxiety rating: 4.5

Based on Grace's scenario anxiety ratings, her hierarchy looks like this.

Grace's Worry Exposure Hierarchy	
Most anxiety	*My daughters don't want to be seen with me because they are embarrassed by my obesity.*
↓	*I am so out of control that I can't do anything except stay home and eat all day.*
	My legs are so fat, I can't find pants that fit and I can hardly walk.
	I have gained so much weight, I have to shop at the fat-lady shop.
Least anxiety	*I am eating cake and I can't stop until I have eaten the whole cake.*

Grace's least anxiety-provoking scenario is eating cake, and her most anxiety-provoking scenario is her children being embarrassed by her obesity. Grace could choose to do her first worry exposure using the most anxiety-provoking scenario, but that would be very difficult, and it's possible she wouldn't be able to get though the exposure. It's more effective for Grace to work through these exposures starting with the easiest scenario and moving up to the hardest.

Now put your scenarios in hierarchical order with the least anxiety-provoking scenario on the bottom.

Your Worry Exposure Hierarchy	
Most anxiety ↓	
Least anxiety	

WRITING YOUR WORRY EXPOSURE STORY

After you have made a hierarchy, it's time to take your least anxiety-provoking scenario and write a story behind the scenario. The task here is to scare yourself as much as you possibly can—so *no happy endings* to this story. You should catastrophize. This is not the place for nondistorted thinking, so go for it and use all the all-or-nothing thinking, "what if" thinking, and other distortions you can. If you have trouble making the story intensely anxiety provoking, you can ask your coach for suggestions. Let's look at the exposure stories that Grace and Joe wrote. When you read their stories, notice that in addition to catastrophizing, both Grace and Joe wrote their stories in the present tense as if these things were happening as they were writing.

Grace's Story: *I am eating a piece of cake. It's a big piece, and all I can think of, with each bite of cake I take, is eating the rest of the cake. I'm done now with the first piece. I am cutting another piece. Before I know it, I have eaten the entire cake and I'm now looking for other things to eat. I'm opening my refrigerator. I see leftover pizza. I eat all three pieces of the leftover pizza. I can feel, now, my body becoming more and more fat each minute. My pants are becoming very tight, but I don't care; all I can think about is eating more. I know I can't purge, so all this food is going to make me fat. I'm leaving the house because I've eaten everything I have in the kitchen. I'm going straight to my favorite fast-food restaurant. I'm at the restaurant and I'm ordering two big hamburgers and a large order of fries. I can feel my stomach and hips grow as I eat the hamburgers. I'm home and I get on the scale and see I have gained 25 pounds. I know this is just the beginning. I can't stop eating and I know that eating that first piece of cake is the reason I can never stop eating. I go back out to the store to buy more food.*

Joe's Story: *I am at a pool party with my friends. My bathing suit is under my clothes. I know I have to take my clothes off and get in the pool. I have gained so much weight, my stomach hangs over my bathing suit. I try to take off my clothes and get in the pool really fast so my friends don't see my gut hanging out. But now they are all laughing at me and pointing. Everyone can see I'm fat, and my stomach makes me look like a pregnant lady. I stay in the pool until it gets dark. Now I have to get out. I can't escape it—as soon as I get out, everyone will see my fat stomach again. I'm so embarrassed. Now I'm out of the pool trying to get my shirt on as fast as I can. I'm wet, and my shirt sticks to my stomach. I can't get the buttons buttoned because of my fat stomach. One of my friends brings me a big plate of food and says, "Here you go, fat boy." Everyone is laughing and pointing to my stomach as I try to get my shirt buttoned. I will never be able to go swimming again.*

When Grace and Joe finished writing their stories, both of them felt very anxious (above 3 on the anxiety scale). High anxiety is the sign of a good exposure story. Now it's time for you to write out a story for the scenario at the bottom of your hierarchy. You may use your notebook or the space below to write your first story. At the end of the story, rate your anxiety from 1–5. If the rating is 2 or less, rewrite the story until your anxiety is over 2.

Your Worry Exposure Story

_____

_____

_____

_____

_____

_____

_____

_____

_____

_____

Anxiety rating: _____

Instructions for Worry Exposure: Now that you have a story that evokes at least a 2 on the anxiety scale, it's time to do your first worry exposure exercise. You have several options. You can rewrite or reread the story over and over again or you can make an audio tape of yourself reading the story out loud four or five times and then listen to the tape repeatedly. As you can see, repetition is the key here. You have to repeat the story as many times as it takes for you to no longer feel high anxiety. Find a quiet place and make sure you have at least one hour for the first time you do a worry exposure. Read, write, or listen to your story. Each time you get to the end of the story, note your anxiety by rating it on a scale of 1–5 and then repeat the story. Keep repeating the story over and over until your anxiety level drops. Don't stop until your anxiety has reached half of the peak anxiety (the highest anxiety you have recorded for that scenario). For Grace, whose anxiety went to 5 the first time she did the worry exposure about eating the cake, that meant no stopping until her anxiety fell to 2.5. The first time she did the worry exposure, it took almost fifty minutes for her anxiety to get to 2.5. Use the chart at the end of this chapter to track your anxiety, recording your final anxiety rating there. Go on to the next scenario in your hierarchy when you can no longer generate a score of more than 1 on the scenario.

Worry Exposure Guidelines

- Start with a story at the bottom of your hierarchy and work up to higher levels.

- Make sure you have a quiet place to do worry exposure where you won't be interrupted or distracted.

- Plan to spend an hour on each of your first few worry exposure sessions. If it takes longer than an hour, that's okay.

- Read, write, or listen to a tape of your exposure story. You can also use a combination of these techniques if you wish.

- Don't stop the worry exposure session until your anxiety has dropped to half of the peak anxiety for that exposure.

- There should be no happy endings in your worry exposure stories.

- During a worry exposure, don't change the distorted starvation eating disorder thoughts into useful thoughts that could bring your anxiety down too soon.

- Avoid self-soothing during the worry exposure as that will also bring your anxiety down too quickly.

- Avoid distracting yourself. Stay with the story.

- Try to keep your anxiety up as long as you can.

- When you can't get your anxiety higher than 1 on the anxiety scale for a story, go on to the next story as you work your way up the hierarchy.

Sometimes people have problems doing worry exposure. Those problems can include not being willing or able to tolerate the anxiety and stopping the worry exposure session before it is finished, or not feeling very anxious during the worry exposure session. If you run into difficulty with worry exposure, use the Worry Exposure and ERP Troubleshooting Guide at the end of this chapter to help make your worry exposure sessions successful.

In Vivo Exposure and Response Prevention

In vivo exposure differs from worry exposure in that you are experiencing the situation rather than imagining it. Despite this difference, in vivo exposure is similar to worry exposure in many ways. The goal of in vivo exposure, as for worry exposure, is to become as anxious as you can and then continue the exposure until your anxiety decreases by 50 percent. In vivo exposure is used for all kinds of anxiety problems. Examples of in vivo exposure for phobias include exposing yourself to a live spider or going to the top of a very tall building and looking down. Basically, in vivo exposure is doing what you are afraid of. For someone with a starvation eating disorder, in vivo exposure might include eating food you are afraid to eat or taking a picture of your body and then staring at the body part you think is the fattest.

In vivo exposure is often paired with response prevention and this is what's most often meant when the term "exposure and response prevention" or "ERP" is referenced. Response prevention is like doing opposite action. So if you have a spider phobia, the ERP would be to find a spider and then deliberately *not* run from the room. A starvation eating disorder example of ERP is eating a food you consider very fattening (the exposure) and then *not* using laxatives or exercising (the response prevention). Consider this list of ERP examples:

- Eating a food that increases your anxiety and not purging or restricting at your next meal

- Eating something you think is fattening without checking the calories

- Sitting at the gym and watching others work out without exercising

- Standing in front of the mirror looking at the fat on your body and not checking your weight to see if you've gained weight

- Wearing tight clothes that make you feel fat and not checking your weight

You can get creative with ERP. The only requirements are that your ERP exercise has to cause anxiety and you have to keep your anxiety up as high as you can for as long as you can. As with worry exposure, your anxiety will habituate naturally unless you intervene to reduce your anxiety. Any time you try to escape the anxiety, ERP will be less effective. There are three natural ERPs for people with starvation eating disorders:

- *Food ERP*: Eating foods that are anxiety provoking and not purging or restricting

- *Mirror ERP*: Looking at yourself in the mirror and telling yourself how fat you look

- *Scale ERP*: Standing on the scale and scaring yourself with how much you weigh

FOOD ERP

Food ERP consists of eating anxiety provoking foods (exposure) and not purging (including exercising) or restricting at the next meal (response prevention). As you did with worry exposure, the first step is to make a hierarchy. In the following lists, write down as many "bad" foods as you can think of. Try to come up with at least ten foods. High-fat foods or those with lots of carbohydrates, like donuts, are examples of foods that most people with starvation eating disorders find difficult to eat. As you did with your worry exposure scenarios, next to each food, rate the level of anxiety you have using a scale of 1–5.

Your ERP Food List	
Food	**Anxiety rating : 1–5**
1.	
2.	
3.	
4.	
5.	
6.	
7.	
8.	
9.	
10.	
11.	
12.	
13.	
14.	
15.	

Now take the list and make a hierarchy. Put foods with the same rating on the same line.

Your Food Exposure Hierarchy	
Most anxiety ↓	
Least anxiety	

Instructions for Food ERP: You have several choices for how to do food ERP. You can spend a week or two doing food ERP for each meal and snack, or you can do food ERP once a day over a longer period of time. Regardless of the way you plan your food ERP, make sure to do food ERP often enough to be effective. Doing one food ERP a week is usually not frequent enough to make a difference. The more concentrated you make your food exposure plan, the better it will work. You will probably have to eat each food more than once before your anxiety related to that food decreases. After you are able to eat most of the foods on your list, you should continue to eat some of these foods at least once a week for maintenance. Where you start on your list is also your choice. You can start with the food that causes you the most anxiety or the least, or you can start somewhere in the middle. It's also a good idea to expand your food list over time as well. So if donuts were too scary to make your list the first time, try putting them on your list the second time around.

When you do food ERP, you will probably get strong urges to purge or to restrict at your next meal. Make sure you don't ignore the response prevention part of this treatment. While you shouldn't use distraction, self-soothing, social support, or change your distorted thoughts while you are eating (because these skills will interfere with getting your anxiety to a high level), you can use these skills to help you with response prevention. Joe, who got very strong urges to go to the gym when he did food exposure, sometimes made a date with his coach or his sister to go to the movies or to do some other kind of activity on the days he did food exposure. Lorrie scheduled her food exposures in the morning so she would have to go to work after the exposure, which helped her to stay away from the purging she felt like doing every time she ate food she found anxiety provoking.

MIRROR ERP

Mirror ERP (also called *mirror exposure* or *mirror confrontation*) is one of the few types of exposure or ERP that has been the subject of starvation eating disorder studies (Vocks, Wachter, and Kosfelder 2007; Key et al. 2002). Mirror ERP involves standing in front of the mirror and looking at all the areas of your body you think are fat while you tell yourself you are fat. Mirror ERP is different than checking behavior. Checking behavior is looking in the mirror to see if you have gained weight. Checking is reassuring. Exposure should be the opposite of reassuring.

While you are doing mirror ERP, you need to use response prevention to avoid all kinds of checking behavior including mirror checking, checking how tight your clothes are, pinching your skin to see how much fat you can pinch, or checking your weight. Checking will undo the mirror exposure by decreasing your anxiety before habituation develops. If you are someone who checks, make sure that your anxiety goes up during mirror ERP, not down. Ensuring that anxiety goes up usually involves three things:

- Looking in the mirror a long time rather than checking briefly many times during the day

- Telling yourself you are fat while you look in the mirror

- Looking at the parts of your body that you hate the most

Plan your mirror ERP like you plan worry exposure. You will probably need at least one hour of uninterrupted time the first few times you do a mirror exposure. After you have done a few exposures, the time it takes for your anxiety to drop by 50 percent will probably decrease. Grace found that it took fifty-five minutes for her anxiety to drop the first few times she did mirror ERP, but after the first few times, thirty-five minutes was enough. In the end, Grace couldn't get her anxiety over a rating of 1 even if she spent more than thirty minutes trying.

SCALE ERP

During weight restoration, the recommendation was to weigh yourself no more often than once a week. As with mirror ERP, checking your weight many times during the day is escaping, not scale ERP. Checking is quick and meant to reassure, while scale ERP is about standing on the scale while telling yourself you are fat. The response prevention part of scale ERP is to prevent yourself from purging or restricting before you practice ERP again by stepping on the scale. The idea is to stand on a scale for an extended period of time every day for as long as it takes for you to no longer feel anxious about your weight. One observation here—modern digital scales often turn off after a minute or two. If you can't find an old-fashioned scale that continues to show your weight, you will have to get off and then back on the scale repeatedly. This seems to work just as well.

Scale ERP is a great exposure to do when you reach your target weight. Often when people with a starvation eating disorder reach a healthy weight, they get strong urges to lose the weight they worked so hard to gain. Decreasing your anxiety about how much you weigh will help you maintain a healthy weight. As with mirror ERP, time is the key to practicing scale ERP. Also, doing a lot of scale ERP over a short period of time works better than doing this ERP every once in a while over a longer period of time. Follow the guidelines below for mirror and scale ERP.

Mirror and Scale ERP Guidelines

- Make sure you have given yourself enough time for each session (it's not unusual for the first few ERPs to take an hour each).
- Don't stop the exposure until your anxiety has dropped to at least half of your peak anxiety rating.
- Tell yourself how fat you are while you do the exposure.
- Stay away from any reassuring strategies.
- Try to get your anxiety as high as you can for as long as you can.
- Make sure to plan for the response prevention part of the ERP. That means make sure you don't do anything that will deliberately decrease your anxiety.
- Record your anxiety every few minutes to see whether it is going up or down.

OTHER ERP IDEAS

There are many other ways to do exposure and response prevention. You can personalize your ERP to problems that crop up for you as you are getting well. For example, Joe did a personalized gym ERP. After Joe was at a healthy weight, he had difficulty going to the gym for only thirty minutes at a time. Remember Joe's all-or-nothing attitude about exercise? For Joe it was either staying away from the gym or doing a four-hour workout. Joe developed a "going to the gym" ERP where he went but sat watching others work out without working out himself. This exposed Joe to the anxiety of the gym while he used response prevention to just watch. Here are some ideas for additional exposures:

- Going to a new restaurant every week
- Taking a picture of yourself looking as fat as you can and viewing the picture while telling yourself how fat you look
- Putting on clothes that you think make you look fat and going out in those clothes

Planning Your Exposure Exercises

Few people will be able to do all the different kinds of exposure in the same week. It's helpful to plan out your worry exposure exercises to make sure you are able to make time to do them. Worry exposure can be done any time. In order to get through all your worry exposure scenarios, you will probably need at least two months. One idea is to plan on doing a worry exposure every other day or so while you are working on weight restoration. Or, if you prefer, you can focus on cognitive therapy during weight restoration and then start worry exposure after you are at a healthy weight. If you wait to start worry exposure, review your worry exposure scenarios before you begin them because scenarios can change after you're at a healthy weight.

Food ERP is a great tool to use while you are still doing weight restoration because it will help you gain weight. Scale ERP can be done once you are at a healthy weight or during weight restoration. Scale exposure is also useful if you reach a plateau and have stopped gaining weight. Plateaus are common because as people gain weight, their anxiety about their healthy weight goal often increases. This is what happened to Amy. She got so anxious after gaining 10 pounds that she stopped gaining. Amy did three weeks of scale ERP before she was able to get back on track with her weight gain.

PLANNING WORRY EXPOSURE AND ERP

It is best to plan your worry exposures and ERP. Let's look at Lorrie's plan to see how she set up her worry exposures. At the end of the chapter you will find charts you can use to keep track of your anxiety for both worry exposure and ERP.

Lorrie's Worry Exposure and ERP Plan			
Type of intervention	**Early weight restoration— frequency**	**Mid-weight restoration— frequency**	**Weight maintenance— frequency**
Worry exposure	*Three times a week*	*Three times a week*	*As needed—when I start to feel very worried about my weight.*
Food ERP	*Daily*	*Daily*	*Once or twice a week*
Mirror ERP	*None*	*Weekly*	*Twice a week*
Scale ERP	*None*	*Once a week at my weekly weigh-in*	*Three times a week on days when I'm not doing mirror ERP*

Notice that Lorrie planned to practice exposure more frequently once she was weight restored. This worked well for Lorrie, who had gained weight many times only to lose it again, so she and I decided to put more emphasis on keeping weight on. Everyone is a little different, and there is no right or wrong way to plan your worry exposure and ERP. You can always change the plan, but starting out with a plan will help you ensure you do the worry exposure and ERPs.

Your Worry Exposure and ERP Plan			
Type of intervention	Early weight restoration—frequency	Mid-weight restoration—frequency	Weight maintenance—frequency
Worry exposure			
Food ERP			
Mirror ERP			
Scale ERP			

MAINTENANCE WORRY EXPOSURE AND ERP

Weight maintenance and long-term avoidance of purging can be difficult. As you will see in stage IV, worry exposure and ERP can be used as part of a relapse prevention plan to help you deal with your anxiety about maintaining a healthy weight.

to sum up

This chapter focused on directly addressing the anxiety associated with starvation eating disorders through worry exposure and exposure and response prevention (ERP). These techniques, which are used to treat anxiety disorders such as obsessive-compulsive disorder, take advantage of the body's ability to habituate. Habituation allows the body to learn not to respond with anxiety to a particular situation. Anxiety is part of the fight-or-flight response. The fight-or-flight response is the body's emergency response system. In a true emergency, the fight-or-flight response can save your life, but if your fight-or-flight response is associated with eating and gaining weight, this life-saving response can put your life in danger. Worry exposure and ERP can reset your fight-or-flight response through habituation. Exposure is about challenging yourself with what makes you anxious, and response prevention is about stopping yourself from escaping the resultant anxiety. Exposure and response prevention use the body's natural system of habituation to adapt to triggers such as new foods or weight gain. Worry exposure allows you to decrease your anxiety about your worst fear, which for people with starvation eating disorders is often getting fat. ERP that uses in vivo exposure includes eating new foods, looking at yourself in the mirror, and standing on the scale and confronting your weight without escaping by purging (including exercising) or restricting. Challenging your anxiety in a direct way with worry exposure and food, mirror, and scale ERP will increase your anxiety in the short term but decrease your anxiety in the long term.

Most people will have to repeat their worry exposure scenarios and ERPs many times over before seeing an anxiety reduction. The following forms will help you track your progress. It is not uncommon to run into roadblocks while doing worry exposure and ERPs. After the record forms, you will find a troubleshooting guide. Use this guide to make sure your worry exposures and ERPs are working for you. Remember, making yourself feel anxiety is a requirement for habituation to occur. If you find you are having difficulty challenging your anxiety (for example, your anxiety rating doesn't get high enough or you don't get around to doing your ERPs), consult the troubleshooting guide for solutions.

Anxiety Scale Record Form for Worry Exposure

Anxiety level	1	2	3	4	5	6	7	8	9	10	11	12	13	14	15	16	17	18	19	20	21	22	23	24	25	26	27	28	29	30
5																														
4																														
3																														
2																														
1																														

Exposure number

Anxiety Scale Record Form for ERP

Anxiety level	1	2	3	4	5	6	7	8	9	10	11	12	13	14	15	16	17	18	19	20	21	22	23	24	25	26	27	28	29	30
5																														
4																														
3																														
2																														
1																														

Exposure number

Worry Exposure and ERP Troubleshooting Guide	
Problem	**Solution**
You ended the session before reaching half of your peak anxiety.	■ Most people stop early because the anxiety becomes intolerable. If this happens to you, try a worry exposure story that's lower in your hierarchy. If you are at the bottom of your hierarchy, come up with a few more scenarios. This time think of scenarios that create less anxiety. For Joe this meant adding a scenario where he gained just 5 pounds. This was the first scenario Joe was able to do. He then went to a scenario where he gained 10 pounds.
You can't get your anxiety up very high from the first session.	■ Move up to the next scenario in your hierarchy. ■ Develop additional scenarios. If the scenario doesn't make you anxious when you are developing the story, it's not going to be an effective scenario for you. ■ Make sure you haven't added a happy ending such as "My weight has stabilized." ■ Make sure you are not using self-soothing, cognitive restructuring, or distraction during the session.
You didn't get around to doing your worry exposure or ERP.	■ Schedule worry exposure and ERP time. Don't wait until you have a free hour—put worry exposure on your calendar. ■ If you are working with a coach, ask your coach for help. Make a commitment to review your worry exposure results with your coach and set up a time to do this. That way you will feel obligated to get the worry exposure done before you meet with your coach. ■ If you are avoiding doing worry exposure or ERP because you feel too anxious, make sure you have a worry exposure scenario or ERP activity that is low enough (a 3 or even a 2 on the anxiety scale) to start with. ■ Set up a reward for yourself if you do the worry exposure or ERP. For example, you could tell yourself that if you do the worry exposure, you can go out shopping. Assuming you like shopping, this could give you something to look forward to after the hard, anxiety provoking work of doing worry exposure.

STAGE IV

living—staying healthy and building a life beyond a starvation eating disorder

You should now be weight restored or close to your target weight. Congratulations—you have taken control of your life back. The final chapters of this book are concerned with staying healthy by maintaining a healthy weight, addressing body image issues, and learning to live without your starvation eating disorder. If you have been living with a starvation eating disorder for a long time, it will take time for you to adapt to a life that doesn't revolve around food and weight. It is normal to still struggle with anxiety and some occasional purging at this stage in treatment. As long as you continue to work on dealing with your anxiety about weight and on reducing self-harm, you can start to build a healthy life.

In chapter 14 you will develop a relapse prevention plan. This is a very important step because your starvation eating disorder will try to get control of your life again. Many of my patients experience small relapses before they are able to stay healthy long term. In chapter 15 you will have the opportunity to work on improving your body image and to develop life activities that don't revolve around having an eating disorder. Following the chapters, you will find an appendix of additional resources that can help you beat your starvation eating disorder for good.

At the end of chapter 15, I will tell you about one more patient. To date, she is the oldest patient I have ever treated. Her starvation eating disorder almost took her life several times over the more than thirty-five years she lived with self-imposed starvation and purging. Her courage continues to be an inspiration to me, and I hope she will inspire you as well.

relapse prevention: maintaining a healthy weight

for someone with a starvation eating disorder, becoming weight restored is a huge accomplishment. But gaining weight is not enough—keeping the weight on and not purging are just as important. If you haven't reached your target weight yet, you should continue to work on gaining weight. If you have reached the target weight you set in chapter 10, you are ready to move on to weight maintenance and to developing a relapse prevention plan. The first step is to notice how your health has changed.

improvements in health

One of the important parts of staying well is noticing what has changed since you have become weight restored. As described in chapter 2, many people with a starvation eating disorder ignore the signals their bodies are sending. Now that you are weight restored, it's important to get in touch with improvement and with resolution of the physical problems your starvation and purging have caused. Some symptoms of your starvation eating disorder may not have completely resolved. For example, if you damaged your esophagus from vomiting, you're probably still having problems with GERD. But many symptoms can resolve altogether. Feeling cold all the time or having edema in your feet usually completely resolves with weight gain.

Some symptoms, such as dental problems, take time to resolve. Complete the Improvement Checklist to see which symptoms have improved or have been resolved.

Improvement Checklist			
Starvation eating disorder symptoms	**Improved**	**Resolved**	**Never experienced**
Gastroesophageal reflux disorder (GERD)			
Constipation			
Delayed gastric emptying: feeling too full after eating a small amount of food			
Hypothermia: feeling cold all the time			
Having difficulty sleeping			
Dry skin			
Edema: swollen ankles and hands			
Feeling light-headed, particularly when you stand up too fast			
Feeling tired			
Bruising easily			
Muscle weakness			
Dental problems			
For women: not having a period or having erratic periods			
Fine-hair growth on your body			
Abnormal lab results: for example, low potassium			
Anemia			
Problems with concentration			

physical improvements card: Make a 3 by 5 card, or several, listing the improvements you have noticed. When you feel like restricting or purging, use the card(s) to remind yourself of the improvements in your health.

weight maintenance and relapse prevention plan

Relapse is a common problem for people with a starvation eating disorder. You may have experienced this problem yourself in the past. The longer you have struggled with a starvation eating disorder, the more likely it is that you will have a relapse. However, a relapse that is addressed quickly need not give your life back over to the starvation eating disorder. A good relapse prevention plan will be your safety net and will allow you to keep your weight within a safe zone as well as stop any purging behavior right away before it gets out of control. We know that both behavioral components (for example, continuing to get on the scale every day) and cognitive components (such as thinking you are fat) of a starvation eating disorder can cause relapse, so it's important that you address both in your relapse prevention plan.

Review Components of a Relapse Prevention Plan below. Each component is designed to help you stay healthy. The first eight components are covered in this chapter. The last two components are covered in chapter 15. You will start by setting a healthy weight range. Check off each step in this relapse prevention plan as you complete it.

Components of a Relapse Prevention Plan
☐   Determining a weight range (chapter 14)
☐   Following the rules for healthy eating and weight maintenance (chapter 14)
☐   Developing a plan for weight gain if you lose weight (chapter 14)
☐   Developing a safe plan for weight loss if you gain too much weight (chapter 14)
☐   Eliminating residual starvation eating disorder emotions, thoughts, and behaviors with cognitive therapy and ERP (chapter 14)
☐   Training appetite (chapter 14)
☐   Reintroducing exercise in a healthy way (chapter 14)
☐   Treating comorbid depression or anxiety (chapter 14)
☐   Improving your body image (chapter 15)
☐   Developing a life beyond your eating disorder (chapter 15)

Determining a Weight Range

A relapse prevention plan always starts with setting a weight range. The bottom end of the range is the weight that you should never go below. The top end of the range is considered by some of my patients to be their reassurance number. This is the number they know they can stay below. This healthy weight range can keep your starvation eating disorder at bay and reassure you that you won't become obese. We know that weight normally fluctuates within a 5-pound range. For a woman, this fluctuation often follows her menstrual cycle. Insisting on a weight that is exactly at a certain number each time you get on the scale is an example of starvation eating disorder thinking. *The bottom line is this:* setting a 5-pound weight range is a healthy behavior that will further weaken your starvation eating disorder. Follow these next steps to set your weight range.

Setting Your Weight Range

Rules for setting the low end of your 5-pound range:

- Determine the lowest weight that puts your BMI at 18.5 and add 2 pounds.

- For women who are still able to have periods: Determine the lowest weight at which your body will still have regular periods and add 2 pounds.

- Take the higher of these two weights as your low end of the range and then add 5 pounds to determine the top end of the range.

Example: For Grace's height, a BMI of 18.5 put her weight at 120. Grace didn't have periods until her weight was at least 122. So Grace took 122 and added 2 pounds for the low end and 5 pounds to that for the high end. This made Grace's range 124–129 pounds.

Now it's time for you to determine your range.

- Your lowest weight to be at a BMI of 18.5 plus 2 pounds: _____

- If you are female and still able to have periods, the lowest weight that allows you to have a regular period plus 2 pounds: _____

- Write down the higher number: _____. This is the low end of your range.

- Add 5 pounds to get the high end of your range: _____.

My weight range is _____ to _____ pounds.

Rules for Healthy Eating for Weight Maintenance

It's not uncommon for people with a starvation eating disorder to find that any change in eating triggers starvation eating disorder behavior. To ensure you don't give your starvation eating disorder a foothold when you change your eating from a weight restoration to a weight maintenance pattern, follow these rules for healthy eating:

Healthy Eating for Weight Maintenance
■ Eat three meals a day. No matter how much you want to, don't skip a meal.
■ Drop one snack.
■ You can drop your liquid supplements if you were using one. If you have been using a liquid supplement more than once a day, don't drop all liquid supplements at once.
■ As you did when you were working on weight restoration, stay away from "diet food."
■ Eat a small amount of fat every day.
■ Eat protein and carbohydrates at each meal.
Remember, everyone's body is different, so if you follow these rules and find that you lose weight, add calories by adding back a snack or a liquid supplement.

Weight Gain Plan

Staying in your range means having a plan for correcting your weight by either gaining or losing if your weight moves outside of your range. As you did during weight restoration, you will weigh yourself once a week. A once-a-week weigh-in is often enough to make any corrections in your weight. Weighing yourself more often than once a week is likely to trigger your starvation eating disorder. The most common problem for someone who has recovered from a starvation eating disorder is dropping too much weight. So you need a weight gain plan in the event your weight drops below the low end of your weight range. While weight loss is often the result of a person's eating disorder rearing its ugly head, you might also lose weight if you get the flu or some other kind of illness.

The bottom line is this: regardless of the reason, if your weight gets below the low end of your range, correction of this weight loss is necessary. There are two ways to gain weight: add calories and stop or reduce physical activity. Usually just adding calories will do the trick, but if you ever find you are more than 4 pounds below the low end of your weight range, you should also stop exercising until you are back in your range. If you find you are repeatedly below your weight range, work on keeping your weight at the high end of the range or consider increasing your range by 2 pounds. Let's look at how to add calories.

Adding Calories

There are several ways you can add calories. For many people, the easiest thing to do is to add a snack or add back your liquid supplement. Check off the strategies you plan to use if you need to gain weight:

- ☐   Eat an extra snack.
- ☐   Add a liquid supplement.
- ☐   Add high-calorie dense foods (for example, add extra cheese on your sandwich).
- ☐   Have ice cream or some other dessert.
- ☐   Use whole milk in your cereal and use real cream for coffee or tea, or over fruit.
- ☐   Drink a fruit smoothie or other high-calorie drink with or between your meals.

Safe Weight-Loss Plan

While gaining too much is rarely a problem for an adult with a starvation eating disorder, becoming obese is a common fear. Your weight range can help. The upper part of the range is the weight at which you can increase your exercise or decrease your calories in a safe way to make sure you don't gain too much weight. If at your weekly weigh-in you find you have gained weight and are over the upper end of your weight range, you can lose weight—but you need to do it in a way that doesn't trigger your starvation eating disorder. Because you are going to be weighing yourself each week, you can reassure yourself that you can take action before your weight goes too high. Follow the rules below for losing a pound or two to get you back into your weight range.

Safe Weight Loss

Follow these rules if you have to lose a little weight:

- ■   Never skip a meal to lose weight.
- ■   You can either
  - ■   Eliminate snacks **OR**
  - ■   Decrease your intake of calories by decreasing the calorie count of a meal, but don't decrease the amount of food you eat by too much. You should try to put about the same amount of bulk in your stomach regardless of the calorie count.
- ■   Increase your exercise time.

Eliminating Residual Starvation Eating Disorder Emotions, Thoughts, and Behaviors

If you are like most people who have finished weight restoration, you will still have some eating disorder emotions, thoughts, or behaviors. Complete the following questionnaire to see what residual problems you may have.

Residual Starvation Eating Disorder Emotions, Thoughts, and Behaviors		
Do you feel down or depressed about your weight gain?	Yes	No
Do you worry about food, your weight, or shape much of the day?	Yes	No
Do you weigh yourself every day or still carefully count calories?	Yes	No

If you answered yes to any of these questions, you have residual emotions, thoughts, and behaviors that can trigger your starvation eating disorder. Take action by following the next set of tips to rid yourself of the problem thinking and behaviors.

Problem Emotion, Thought, and Behavior Solutions	
Problem	Solution
You feel down or depressed about your weight gain.	If you are experiencing feelings of depression around your weight gain, this is probably not a symptom of a *comorbid depression* (which is a depression separate from your eating disorder) but rather your starvation eating disorder trying to take control again. Work on your thinking about your weight and focus on the body image exercises in chapter 15. Also, go back to chapter 12 and target the distorted thoughts that are leading you to feeling down about your weight. Reminding yourself of how many physical improvements you have made can also help—read your physical improvement card(s) at least once a day.
You worry about food, your weight, or your shape much of the day.	Thoughts about being fat are strongly associated with relapse, so if you are often thinking about being fat, you should work on changing those thoughts (Bachner-Melman, Zohar, and Ebstein 2006). Review chapter 12 and focus on changing these distorted "I'm fat" thoughts. Do additional worry exposures about being fat (review chapter 13).

Problem	Solution
You weigh yourself every day, check your weight in other ways, or still count calories.	While it's normal to still have some anxiety related to your starvation eating disorder after you are weight restored, if you are still engaging in starvation eating disorder behaviors like checking your weight and counting calories, you should go back to chapter 13 and do more exposure work. Limit your weigh-ins to once a week and do exposure and response prevention (ERP) around counting calories: Eat a high-calorie food each day without adding up the calories. Ask your coach to help with response prevention. Your coach may be able to give you some distraction ideas when you feel like checking or counting. Going to a restaurant to eat is a good way to do food exposure because it's harder to know the calorie count. Throw out any calorie-counting books you have.

Appetite Training

Up to this point, you should have been keeping a food log. Now that you are weight restored, you will switch to an appetite training log. Most people with an eating disorder lose touch with the normal feelings associated with hunger and satiation. Appetite training can help you notice those normal feelings. The idea of appetite training is to keep track of how you feel before and after you eat so that you can start to learn what hunger and satiation feel like. I suggest you start appetite training after you have been weight restored for at least six weeks. This will give your body enough time to start to resolve your delayed gastric emptying. If you start your appetite/satiation training before your delayed gastric emptying is completely resolved, you will notice that you are feeling full too fast. Let's look at a section of Joe's Appetite Training Log to see how the log works.

Joe's Appetite Training Log (Partial)

Hunger/satiation ratings	Aftereffect

☑ Snack ☐ Meal

Started	Not hungry				Very hungry
	1	2	3	4	(5)

Stopped	Hungry				Too full
	1	2	3	4	(5)

Important information: *I skipped breakfast.*

Aftereffect:
- ☑ Wanted to purge
- ☐ Purged
- ☐ Felt satisfied
- ☑ Felt too full
- ☑ Restricted later

☑ Snack ☐ Meal

Started	Not hungry				Very hungry
	(1)	2	3	4	5

Stopped	Hungry				Too full
	1	2	(3)	4	5

Important information: *Ate a snack before going to the gym; felt good after my workout.*

Aftereffect:
- ☐ Wanted to purge
- ☐ Purged
- ☑ Felt satisfied
- ☐ Felt too full
- ☐ Restricted later

☑ Snack ☐ Meal

Started	Not hungry				Very hungry
	1	2	3	(4)	5

Stopped	Hungry				Too full
	1	2	(3)	4	5

Important information: *Felt a little empty so I ate an extra snack. I felt satisfied after cheese and four crackers.*

Aftereffect:
- ☐ Wanted to purge
- ☐ Purged
- ☑ Felt satisfied
- ☐ Felt too full
- ☐ Restricted later

Analyzing Joe's Appetite Training Log: Analyzing Joe's log to see how he is attending to his body's signals and nutritional needs shows the following:

- The first time Joe ate for the day, he waited too long and was very hungry when he finally ate a snack. This meant that Joe ignored feelings of hunger until it was too late. As a result, Joe ate past the point of being full. The aftereffect was that Joe wanted to purge, felt uncomfortably full, and restricted later.

- The second time Joe ate, he didn't feel hungry but because he was going to the gym, he ate his planned exercise snack. This is a good strategy for someone like Joe who wants to exercise. Joe spent six months getting healthy enough to be able to work out six days a week, and he learned that a snack before each workout was essential. Joe's workout plan called for a high-carbohydrate bar, made for runners, before each workout. The bar was an extra snack, and because Joe expended so many calories running and lifting weights, he needed three and sometimes four snacks a day. The snack before his workout gave Joe the energy his body needed. Joe learned that before a workout, not feeling hungry should be ignored because he needed to eat anyway.

- The third time he ate, Joe was attending to his feelings of hunger; he ate when the empty feeling that he'd learned to associate with hunger was at a moderate level. This meant he didn't wait too long and, as a result, he didn't feel like bingeing. Because he didn't wait too long to eat, Joe was also able to notice when he had eaten enough. The feeling of satiation was difficult for Joe to learn to identify. It took him more than one month of keeping appetite training logs to be able to identify his satiation feeling.

Instructions for Your Appetite Training Log: Fill the log out after you eat. Check off whether you ate a snack or a meal. Mark where you were on the hunger scale when you started to eat (with 1 being not hungry at all and 5 being very hungry). Next mark how full you were when you stopped eating. The accuracy of the second rating depends on the resolution of delayed gastric emptying. If you are still experiencing some delayed gastric emptying, you will feel full before your body gets enough nutrition. Continue to do the log and note how this feeling changes. Over time you should notice that it takes longer for you to get the feeling of fullness. Finally, write down any important information (for example, if you skip a meal) and check off the aftereffect. Make copies of the blank Appetite Training Log and continue to keep the log until you feel you have a good understanding of what hunger and satiation feel like to you.

Appetite Training Log
Date: _____

Hunger/satiation ratings						Aftereffect

☐ Snack ☐ Meal

Started	Not hungry				Very hungry
	1	2	3	4	5

Stopped	Hungry				Too full
	1	2	3	4	5

Important information:

☐ Wanted to purge
☐ Purged
☐ Felt satisfied
☐ Felt too full
☐ Restricted later

☐ Snack ☐ Meal

Started	Not hungry				Very hungry
	1	2	3	4	5

Stopped	Hungry				Too full
	1	2	3	4	5

Important information:

☐ Wanted to purge
☐ Purged
☐ Felt satisfied
☐ Felt too full
☐ Restricted later

☐ Snack ☐ Meal

Started	Not hungry				Very hungry
	1	2	3	4	5

Stopped	Hungry				Too full
	1	2	3	4	5

Important information:

☐ Wanted to purge
☐ Purged
☐ Felt satisfied
☐ Felt too full
☐ Restricted later

Reintroducing Exercise

Now that you are weight restored, you can reintroduce exercise into your life. The rule for reintroducing exercise is to *start low and go slow*. Starting low means starting with low-cardio exercise (that is, a workout that doesn't raise your heart rate very much) for short periods of time. Going slow means slowly increasing the amount of exercise you do each month. Follow these rules to safely reintroduce exercise:

Rules for Reintroducing Exercise
■ Check in with your PCP to make sure that you are healthy enough to start exercising.
■ Start with twenty minutes of strength building three times a week for the first month. If your weight drops, it means you are not eating enough to do even minimal exercise. Add a snack or liquid supplement.
■ If your weight is staying within your weight range, add twenty to forty minutes of cardio to your three-times-a-week routine after four weeks. If you have difficulty keeping your weight above your minimum weight, you will need to add calories as Joe did in order to continue to exercise.
■ If you want to exercise more than three to four times a week, you will need to add calories. Try an extra snack right before your workout.
■ For women: If your periods stop, it means you are getting too lean and you need to decrease the amount of time you are exercising and possibly change the type of exercise you are doing. Go back to three times a week for twenty minutes and do less calorie-burning exercise.
■ If you want to pursue a sport, consult with a dietitian who works with athletes to make sure you get enough calories to do rigorous exercise or training.

Treating Comorbid Depression or Anxiety

In chapter 3, you completed the Are You Experiencing Depression or Anxiety? survey. We know that a starving brain will make a person feel depressed and anxious. We also know that most people will experience a resolution of their depressive symptoms with weight restoration, but some will continue to experience depression after achieving a healthy weight. As with depression, much of the anxiety you experienced when your brain was starving may have resolved, but as described in chapter 5, anxiety disorders are common in people with starvation eating disorders, so all of your symptoms may not have disappeared. If after completing the Are You Experiencing Depression or Anxiety? survey again you find that you are still checking off symptoms, it's possible that you have a comorbid disorder. If you think this is the case, see a psychologist or other mental health professional for an evaluation.

Are You Experiencing Depression or Anxiety?		
Depression		
Do you feel down, sad, or depressed most of the time?	Yes	No
Have you lost interest in activities you used to enjoy?	Yes	No
Do you feel more down in the morning than at other times of day?	Yes	No
Do you feel hopeless or think about dying?	Yes	No
Anxiety		
Do you ruminate about things other than food or weight?	Yes	No
Does worry interfere with your sleep?	Yes	No
Do you sometimes feel so panicky that you avoid doing normal, routine things like driving on the freeway or going to the mall?	Yes	No
Do you wash your hands over and over again or check and recheck doors, locks, and appliances many times?	Yes	No

Did you have any "Yes" answers? Compare your answers this time around to your answers in chapter 3. Are you seeing any improvement? It's not unusual to have one or two "Yes" answers after you're weight restored. As with the physical symptoms, it can take some time for all of your symptoms to resolve. It's also possible you have a comorbid depressive or anxiety disorder separate from your eating disorder or that you need to go back and work on cognitive restructuring or anxiety reduction a little longer. Look at the areas you are still struggling with in the following lists to see what your next step might be.

What to Do If You Are Still Experiencing Depression	
Depressive symptoms	**Action**
You feel down, sad, or depressed most of the time.	If you have been weight restored for three months and you are still feeling depressed most of the time or have other symptoms of depression, such as lacking interest, it's time to see a mental health professional for an evaluation for a possible mood disorder. Since you are weight restored, medication may be helpful, but cognitive therapy or cognitive behavioral treatment for depression as well as interpersonal psychotherapy are very good options and can make medication unnecessary. For some people the combination of psychotherapy and medication is the answer.
You have a loss of interest in activities you used to enjoy.	
You feel more down in the morning than later in the day.	
You feel hopeless or you think about dying.	For more information on any of these topics, consider one of the books or online resources from the Helpful Resources appendix that follows chapter 15.
	Important note: If you are having thoughts about dying, you should see a mental health provider right away.

What to Do If You Are Still Experiencing Anxiety	
Anxiety symptoms	**Action**
You ruminate about things other than food or weight.	These symptoms may be indications of a comorbid anxiety disorder such as OCD. Whatever your symptoms, but particularly if you are having panic symptoms that are interfering with your functioning or are feeling compelled to engage in compulsive behaviors like hand washing, you should see a mental health professional so you can be evaluated. If you do have a comorbid anxiety disorder, medication, psychotherapy such as cognitive behavioral therapy, or a combination of psychotherapy and medication can help you recover from your anxiety disorder.
Worry interferes with your sleep.	
You feel so panicky that you avoid doing normal, routine things like driving on the freeway or going to the mall.	For more information on any of these topics, consider one of the books or online resources from the Helpful Resources appendix that follows chapter 15.
You wash your hands over and over again or check and recheck doors, locks, and appliances many times.	

to sum up

By becoming weight restored, you have taken your life back. Weight restoration needs to be followed by weight maintenance and a relapse prevention plan to make sure your starvation eating disorder doesn't take over your life again. This chapter covered eight of the components of a relapse prevention plan. The next chapter will explore the last two components—improving your body image and developing a life beyond your eating disorder.

A relapse prevention plan starts with setting a weight range. Your weight range gives you a guide for knowing when you need to make adjustments in your food intake or exercise in order to maintain a healthy weight. Now is the time to target any residual starvation eating disorder thinking or behaviors because these residual symptoms will give your starvation eating disorder a way back into your life. Developing a plan for gaining weight or losing weight when you need to stay at a healthy weight, and learning what hunger and satiation feel like, are also essential. Finally, if you have a comorbid depressive or anxiety disorder, you should seek treatment for your comorbid disorder.

CHAPTER 15

building a life without a starvation eating disorder

if you have struggled a long time with a starvation eating disorder, it will take some time to live a life without thinking about your disorder or how much you weigh. In fact, you may always be someone who worries more about your weight than your peers do. Despite this, you can have a life where starving, purging, and distorted eating disorder thoughts are not the center of your existence. Before you got well, you were probably thinking about weight, food, and other starvation eating disorder issues all or most of the time. While you have been getting well, you have had to focus on your eating disorder. Now it's time to start developing a life beyond your eating disorder. The first step is to develop a positive body image at a healthy weight. The second step is to expand your relationships and activities. Now that you are well, your relationships with the people around you will change. For example, your relationship with your coach (if you have one) will change, and you and your family members will be able to develop relationships that don't revolve around their anxiety about your health. And in some cases you may need to repair relationships that have been harmed by your eating disorder.

improving your body image

By now you have improved your health by gaining weight, keeping the weight on, and not purging. Your body is healthier, but your image of your body may not be very healthy. Improving your body image will help you stay at a healthy weight and keep the starvation eating disorder at bay. In our Western culture, there are an increasing number of women and men who are dissatisfied with their bodies (Cash 1997). So if you don't like your body, you are not alone. But there is an important difference between someone with a starvation eating disorder and the average person who has poor body image. For the average person, a poor body image may contribute to lower satisfaction with life, but for you, continuing to be unhappy with your body can trigger a relapse of your starvation eating disorder. The good news is that there are steps you can take to improve your body image so that dissatisfaction with your body doesn't undo all the hard work you have invested in being healthy. Let's look at how you can improve your body image with ACCEPT.

ACCEPT
A—Acceptance
C—Caring
C—Compliments
E—Education
P—Pursuit
T—Talking back

Acceptance

Acceptance means that even if you think you look better at a lower weight, you accept that you can't be healthy if you go back to being too thin. Acceptance means that you are willing to learn to like your body at a healthy weight even if you wish you didn't have to. Many people accept things about their bodies that they don't like very much. Most of us, as we get older, learn to accept the wrinkles and other changes that occur with age. We accept these changes because not accepting these things just doesn't work. An acceptance statement is a commitment to learning to like your body at a healthy weight. Let's look at some examples of acceptance statements to see how this works.

> **Joe's Acceptance Statement:** *I want to be at a lower weight because I think I will look better but I accept the fact that my idea of what looks good is distorted. I may not like the way I look at a healthy weight now but I can learn to like and accept that this is the weight I need to be at to be healthy.*

229

Grace's Acceptance Statement: *No matter what I weigh, I need to work on accepting my body. When I was a lower weight, I didn't think I looked good and I was unhealthy, so it's better for me to be at a healthy weight and accept this weight than to go back to being unhealthy.*

Lorrie's Acceptance Statement: *If I don't accept my healthy weight, I won't be able to do what I love. I have always felt like I needed to lose weight regardless of my weight. Accepting that I need to stay at a healthy weight is easier in the long run. If I lose weight, I still won't like my body but I also won't be able to write.*

Amy's Acceptance Statement: *Accepting my healthy weight is accepting my body as a woman's body, a body that can make a baby. Rejecting a healthy weight is like rejecting my body as a woman.*

Now it's time to write your acceptance statement.

Your Acceptance Statement: _____

_____

_____

acceptance card: Put your acceptance statement on a 3 by 5 card.

Caring

Caring for your body can help you feel better about how your body looks. You are already caring for your body by gaining weight and stopping self-harm. You can also care for your body by doing things like relaxation exercises, getting enough sleep, or getting a pedicure. Look over the following list and check off body-caring activities you can do. If you think of an activity that is not mentioned, add it to the end of the list. Commit to doing at least three of your body-caring activities every week.

- ☐ Do relaxation exercises.

- ☐ Get a good night's sleep.

- ☐ Get a pedicure or manicure.

- ☐ Get a massage.

- ☐ Get your hair done.

- ☐ Sit in the sun and enjoy the feeling of the sun on your skin.

- ☐ Use lotions on your skin.

☐ Massage your feet and put on foot cream.

☐ Put on clothes that feel soft on your skin.

☐ Soak in a hot tub.

☐ Masturbate.

☐ Put on makeup.

☐ Have sex.

☐ Go dancing.

☐ Take a hot shower or a bubble bath.

☐ See a fashion consultant to learn how to dress at your new healthy weight.

☐ Other: _____

☐ Other: _____

Compliments

Many of us get compliments about our appearance and then dismiss them. One way to feel better about your body is to let others help you by accepting the compliments that they give you. When you get a compliment about your body, write it down. A body compliment can be anything from "Your hair looks good" to "You look so healthy now." Write down any kind of compliment you get as long as it's not a distorted compliment. A distorted compliment is a compliment that reinforces your starvation eating disorder, one that praises your size when you are not at a healthy weight or that focuses on your ability to lose a lot of weight. Examples of distorted compliments are, "Wow, I wish I was that thin" or "You're thin enough to be a model" or "I wish I could lose weight like you can." Distorted compliments have no place on your list.

Write the useful body compliments you get down in your notebook. The key here is to write down the compliment just as it was intended without adding to or taking away from it. For example, if someone says to you, "You look so healthy now that you have gained a little weight," write it down without taking away from the compliment by adding, "How can she think I'm healthy when I'm so fat?" In other words, accept the compliment as it was given.

Education

Educate your body by saying nice things to yourself. Stand in front of the mirror and talk to your body. You can start by saying nice things about the features you like the best. For example, if you like your hair, you might say, "I have great hair." The education shouldn't be just about how your body looks but should include things like, "My legs feel strong" or "My hands can do a lot of things." To get you started with ideas, let's look at a part of Amy's body education list.

Amy's Body Education List

- *I have nice eyes.*
- *My legs are strong enough to walk five miles.*
- *I like the way my feet look.*
- *I can do many different crafts with my hands.*
- *My neck is nice and long.*
- *I like that my hair is naturally curly.*

Instructions for Your Body Education List: Write down as many things as you can. Make sure to include things your body *does* well as well as parts you think look good. After you have your list, go to the mirror and educate your body by talking aloud to it. It might seem strange at first, but for most people, talking aloud adds to the power of this exercise. Do this once a week.

Your Body Education List

- _____
- _____
- _____
- _____
- _____
- _____
- _____
- _____

Pursuit

Pursuing a healthy body means eating enough and exercising moderately. Extreme behavior is generally not healthy for our bodies, so moderation is the key to pursuing health. Follow these simple rules:

- *Eat regularly:* Eat three meals a day and snacks, as needed to keep your weight healthy. Most people need at least one snack a day.

- *Exercise moderately:* Three to four times a week for one hour is moderate. If you are going to do more, you will have to eat more.

- *Get enough sleep:* Eight to ten hours of sleep each night is ideal for most people.

Talking Back

Talk back to your negative thoughts about your body. Use your cognitive restructuring skills from chapter 12 to rewrite distorted thoughts about your body into useful ones. In his 1997 book, *The Body Image Workbook*, Thomas Cash, Ph.D., lists ten types of distorted thoughts people have about their bodies (Cash 1997, 99–100). Dr. Cash calls the distorted thinking that people have about their bodies *private body talk*. Each private body-talk assumption has a starvation eating disorder spin. Review the types that follows and check off the private body talk you relate to.

- ☐ "Physically attractive people have it all."
  The starvation eating disorder spin: *Thin people have it all.*

- ☐ "The first thing that people will notice about me is what's wrong with my appearance."
  The starvation eating disorder spin: *The first thing people will notice is my weight.*

- ☐ "One's outward physical appearance is a sign of the inner person."
  The starvation eating disorder spin: *If I'm very thin, that will show what kind of a person I am.*

- ☐ "If I could look as I wish, my life would be much happier."
  The starvation eating disorder spin: *If I lose the weight I gained, I will be happy.*

- ☐ "If people knew how I really look, they would like me less."
  The starvation eating disorder spin: *If people knew how much weight I gained or how much I weigh now, they would like me less.*

- ☐ "By controlling my appearance, I can control my social and emotional life."
  The starvation eating disorder spin: *If I lose more weight, I can control my social and emotional life.*

- ☐ "My appearance is responsible for much of what has happened to me in my life."
  The starvation eating disorder spin: *Everything that has happened in my life is about my weight.*

- ☐ "I should always do whatever I can to look my best."
  The starvation eating disorder spin: *I should be as thin as I can be to be my best.*

- ☐ "The media's messages make it impossible for me to be satisfied with my appearance."
  The starvation eating disorder spin: *If I'm not as thin as (or thinner than) fashion models, I won't be satisfied.*

- ☐ "The only way I could ever like my looks would be to change them."
  The starvation eating disorder spin: *I will never like my body unless I lose weight.*

How many private body talk distortions did you check off? For each distortion, write a nondistorted thought that you can use when talking back to the distortions about your body. Remember, if the new thought makes you want to lose weight, it is distorted. If this happens, try again until you write a thought that doesn't increase your urge to lose weight.

Talking Back	
Distortion	Talk back with this
Thin people have it all.	
The first thing people will notice is my weight.	
If I'm very thin, that will show what kind of a person I am.	
If I lose the weight I gained, I will be happy.	
If people knew how much weight I gained or how much I weigh now, they would like me less.	
If I lose more weight, I can control my social and emotional life.	
Everything that has happened in my life is about my weight.	
I should be as thin as I can be to be my best.	
If I'm not as thin as (or thinner than) fashion models, I won't be satisfied.	
I will never like my body unless I lose weight.	

talking-back card: Put the thoughts that work best for you on one or more 3 by 5 cards.

The bottom line is this: improving your body image takes time. Practice some part of ACCEPT every day to improve the way you feel about your body.

taking your life back

Starvation eating disorders take over your life. It's time to start taking your life back. There are two life areas that most people need to work on when they get well. The first area is relationships, and the second is expanding activities and interests. Let's look at relationships first.

Relationships

Relationships often change when people get well, though it might take a little while before the people in your life start to believe that you are really committed to staying healthy. You may even have to repair a relationship that was damaged by your starvation eating disorder. If you have a coach, you should sit down and talk about how your relationship can change. For example, you no longer need your coach to look at food logs, and you may already have shifted the topics you and your coach talk about to things having nothing to do with eating disorders.

If you have been living with a starvation eating disorder for a long time, you may feel that you don't have the basic relationship skills to develop healthy relationships. You may want to take some time to improve those skills.

RELATIONSHIP SKILLS

There are many good resources for learning good interpersonal relationship skills. One resource is dialectical behavior therapy (DBT; Linehan 1993), which was described in the context of DBT distress-tolerance skills in chapter 9. If you want to tune up your relationship skills, DBT can give you a good framework to start with. A DBT skills manual like *The Dialectical Behavior Therapy Skills Workbook* (McKay, Wood, and Brantley 2007) can help you improve relationship skills.

Relationship Skill Tips

■ Use *"I" statements* like "I feel upset" instead of "You make me so upset."

■ Stay nonjudgmental. Don't judge yourself or others.

■ Talk about topics other than your eating disorder.

■ Eat with people without making "fat talk" or talking about calories. If you talk about food, talk about how good it tastes or about the recipe.

■ Learn effective assertiveness skills that get you what you want or need without taking advantage of others.

■ Listen, and learn active listening. Everyone likes to feel heard. Listening without judgment or giving advice is a gift you can give people you care about.

REPAIRING RELATIONSHIPS

Probably the hardest part about changing your relationships with others is repairing relationships that have been harmed by your starvation eating disorder. If your eating disorder has hurt someone you care about, you probably feel some guilt about this hurt. This is helpful guilt because it's justified guilt. Your guilt is telling you that you are a caring person who doesn't like to hurt others. Now that you are well, you can repair the relationships that were hurt by your starvation eating disorder. The first step is to make amends with the people in your life. Make a list of the people you think have been hurt by your starvation eating disorder.

Your Amends List

People who have been hurt by my starvation eating disorder:

■ _____

■ _____

■ _____

■ _____

■ _____

Making amends can be hard and can provoke anxiety, but following these simple rules for making amends can help:

- *Accept your guilt.* Accept that your guilt is normal and justified but don't beat yourself up. Say to yourself, "I have guilt because I hurt someone I care about. I didn't mean to hurt _____ (add the name of the person) but I did, and I need to take responsibility for that hurt."

- *Apologize.* For example, say, "I know you were hurt by my starvation eating disorder and I am very sorry. I know my behavior was hurtful to you and I want you to know I take responsibility for what I did."

- *Commit to not hurting the person again.* For example, say, "I am working very hard to stay well. I am committing to staying at a healthy weight for myself and for all the people I care about. I know that if I get sick again, I will hurt you, and I'm committed to not doing that."

- *Listen.* If the person wants to tell you how you hurt him—listen. Don't defend yourself. Even if he is angry, listen without commenting. When the person is done, tell him you appreciate that he was able to share his hurt with you and that you want to repair the relationship and build it in a way that doesn't revolve around an eating disorder.

- *Let it go.* Once you have made amends, let it go. It might take time, but if you are patient, you will be able to build a new relationship with the person you care about.

Remember that making amends is not something you repeat over and over again with the same person. If you find that you are apologizing every time you see the person—stop. Once you make amends, it's important to move on. If the other person can't move on, give him some time. Once you have made amends, the ball is in his court.

Activities and Interests

Now is the time to take an inventory of the things you have missed out on because of your eating disorder. What have you always wanted to do but didn't because you were spending so much time dealing with your starvation eating disorder? Perhaps it's time to go back to school or learn a new hobby. Joe went back to school. He had always wanted to get a college degree but until he got well, he was too wrapped up in his starvation eating disorder to finish his AA degree. In the following list, write down the things you put on hold because of your eating disorder. Write down as many things as you can think of. If you have trouble coming up with ideas, go back and review How Your Eating Disorder Interferes with What Is Important to You in chapter 6 for ideas. Not all of the things on your list need to be big things like going back to school. Grace put "Host Thanksgiving at my house" on her list, and Amy put "Go to lunch with my friends" on hers.

Things You Have Always Wanted to Do
■ _____
■ _____
■ _____
■ _____
■ _____
■ _____
■ _____
■ _____

Here are some other ideas that can help you develop new interests:

■ Join a club or civic organization.

■ Do volunteer work.

■ Learn a hobby.

■ Get a pet.

■ Join a dating service and start dating.

one last story

It has been my pleasure to tell you about some of my patients. Grace, Amy, Joe, Lorrie, and the other people I have known with starvation eating disorders have all inspired me. I would like to tell you about one more patient it has been my privilege to know. Terry is the oldest patient I have ever treated. When I first saw her, she had been struggling with a very serious starvation eating disorder for more than thirty-five years. The truth is, it was miraculous that she was still alive. In and out of the hospital many times, Terry came so close to death several times. When I first saw her, she was just out of the hospital's intensive care unit and her BMI was dangerously low. When I saw her physical state, my first reaction was to think she needed to go back to the hospital—that's how sick she was. Terry and I set to work, and while it took more than eighteen months for her to get weight restored, she did it. While working on weight restoration, Terry had many panic attacks. Her anxiety about eating left her sick to her stomach and feeling shaky. Terry's chronic purging continued for many months. When she was finally weight restored and had controlled her purging, she started building a life without an eating disorder.

Terry's starvation eating disorder had kept her from working or having a family. She was scared to meet people, and a life without her eating disorder seemed impossible. But with courage that inspires me to this day, Terry took a risk and started doing volunteer work. She got a dog and reintroduced some moderate exercise into her life by walking her dog. For a little more than a year after she was weight restored, Terry struggled with fear and occasional dips in her weight and a few brief episodes of purging. But she didn't quit. Along the way, her life got fuller. The volunteer work became very important to her, and she not only developed friends through the work but started to see that there was a big world beyond her eating disorder that was waiting for her.

Terry has been well now for more than five years. She works part-time at a nonprofit agency and spends her free time with her elderly mother, her dog, and a man she has been dating for two years. Terry has accepted her healthy weight and rarely has the urge to lose weight or purge. Terry's body and brain are no longer starving, and she has a life—a good life. I hope Terry's story is as inspirational to you as it has been to me. You can have a life too—a full life, a life without a starvation eating disorder.

helpful resources

there are some very good self-help books and online resources that can help you decrease your anxiety and improve your mood, self-esteem, and body image.

anxiety disorders

To learn more about anxiety disorders commonly seen in people with starvation eating disorders, try the following self-help books:

Hyman, B., and C. Pedrick. 2005. *The OCD Workbook: Your Guide to Breaking Free from Obsessive-Compulsive Disorder*, 2nd ed. Oakland, CA: New Harbinger.

Markway, B., C. Carmin, C. Pollard, and T. Flynn. 1992. *Dying of Embarrassment: Help for Social Anxiety and Phobia*. Oakland, CA: New Harbinger.

Zuercher-White, E. 1998. *An End to Panic*, 2nd ed. Oakland, CA: New Harbinger.

improving your mood

Take advantage of the following resources if you are experiencing symptoms of depression:

Burns, D. 1999. *The Feeling Good Handbook*, rev. ed. New York: Morrow.

Knaus, W. 2006. *The Cognitive Behavioral Workbook for Depression: A Step-by-Step Program*. Oakland, CA: New Harbinger.

Pettit, J., and T. Joiner. 2005. *The Interpersonal Solution to Depression: A Workbook for Changing How You Feel by Changing How You Relate*. Oakland, CA: New Harbinger.

improving your body image and self-esteem

To improve your body image and self-esteem, consider these resources:

Cash, T. 1997. *The Body Image Workbook: An Eight-Step Program for Learning to Like Your Looks*. Oakland, CA: New Harbinger.

Burns, D. 1993. *Ten Days to Self-Esteem*. New York: Morrow.

McKay, M., and P. Fanning. 2000. *Self-Esteem*, 3rd ed. Oakland, CA: New Harbinger.

dialectical behavior therapy (DBT)

DBT is helpful for mood regulation and improving your communication and relationships with others. There are many DBT resources available; the resources here are two of the most helpful DBT resources I have found for learning DBT skills:

Marra, T. 2004. *Depressed and Anxious: The Dialectical Behavior Therapy Workbook for Overcoming Depression and Anxiety*. Oakland, CA: New Harbinger.

McKay, M., J. Wood, and J. Brantley. 2007. *The Dialectical Behavior Therapy Skills Workbook: Practical DBT Exercises for Learning Mindfulness, Interpersonal Effectiveness, Emotion Regulation, and Distress Tolerance*. Oakland, CA: New Harbinger.

eating disorders

The following are eating disorder resources that can supplement the information in this book:

Heffner, M., and G. Eifert. 2004. *The Anorexia Workbook: How to Accept Yourself, Heal Your Suffering, and Reclaim Your Life*. Oakland, CA: New Harbinger.

Lock, J., and D. Le Grange. 2005. *Help Your Teenager Beat an Eating Disorder*. New York: Guilford Press.

online resources and support groups

Academy for Eating Disorders (AED)—an international professional organization of eating disorder specialists and researchers (including physicians, psychologists, and academic researchers). AED provides information about eating disorders on its website and has an online directory of eating disorder specialists: www.aedweb.org

Anorexia Nervosa and Related Eating Disorders (ANRED)—an online forum: www.anred.com

Eating Disorders Anonymous (EDA)—an online forum, offering support and information on how to apply the 12-step approach to recovery from an eating disorder: www.eatingdisordersanonymous.org

International Association of Eating Disorder Professionals (IAEDP)—a professional organization for psychotherapists interested in treating eating disorders. Provides a referral service on its website: www.iaedp.com

MyPyramid.gov—provides ideas for how much you need to eat to gain weight or to maintain a healthy weight once you reach your target BMI. You can also use this website to expand the list of the types of foods you are eating: www.mypyramid.gov

references

American Psychiatric Association. 2000. *Diagnostic and Statistical Manual of Mental Disorders*, 4th ed. Text Revision. Washington, DC: American Psychiatric Association.

Bachner-Melman, R., A. Zohar, and R. Ebstein. 2006. An examination of cognitive versus behavioral components of recovery from anorexia nervosa. *Journal of Mental and Nervous Disorders* 194:697–703.

Benninghoven, D., N. Tetsch, S. Kunzendorf, and G. Jantschek. 2007. Body image in patients with eating disorders and their mothers, and the role of family functioning. *Comprehensive Psychiatry* 48:118–123.

Birmingham, C. L., and P. Beumont. 2004. *Medical Management of Eating Disorders: A Practical Handbook for Healthcare Professionals*. With contributions by R. Crawford and others. New York: Cambridge University Press.

Birmingham, C. L., and S. Gritzner. 2006. How does zinc supplementation benefit anorexia nervosa? *Eating and Weight Disorders* 11:e109–e111.

Bissada, H., G. Tasca, A. Barber, and J. Bradwejn. 2008. Olanzapine in treatment of low body weight and obsessive thinking in women with anorexia nervosa: A randomized, double-blind, placebo-controlled trial. *American Journal of Psychiatry* 165:1281–1288.

Bowers, W., and L. Ansher. 2008 The effectiveness of cognitive behavioral therapy on changing eating disorder symptoms and psychopathology of 32 anorexia nervosa patients at hospital discharge and one year follow-up. *Annals of Clinical Psychiatry* 20:79–86.

Burns, D. 1993. *Ten Days to Self-Esteem*. New York: Morrow.

———. 1999. *The Feeling Good Handbook*, rev. ed. New York: Morrow.

Cash, T. 1997. *The Body Image Workbook: An Eight-Step Program for Learning to Like Your Looks*. Oakland, CA: New Harbinger.

Crane, A., M. Roberts, and J. Treasure. 2007. Are obsessive-compulsive personality traits associated with poor outcome in anorexia nervosa? A systematic review of randomized controlled trials and naturalistic outcome studies. *International Journal of Eating Disorders* 40:581–588.

Currin, L., U. Schmidt, J. Treasure, and H. Jick. 2005. Time trends in eating disorder incidence. *British Journal of Psychiatry* 186:132–135.

Dunican, K. C., and D. DelDotto. 2007. The role of olanzapine in the treatment of anorexia nervosa. *Annals of Pharmacotherapy* 41:111–115.

Fichter, M., N. Quadflieg, and S. Hedlund. 2006. Twelve-year course and outcome predictors of anorexia nervosa. *International Journal of Eating Disorders* 39:87–100.

Frank, G., U. Bailer, C. Meltzer, J. Price, C. Mathis, A. Wagner, C. Becker, and W. Kaye. 2007. Regional cerebral blood flow after recovery from anorexia or bulimia nervosa. *Internal Journal of Eating Disorders* 40:488–492.

Frisch, M., D. Herzog, and D. Franko. 2006. Residential treatment for eating disorders. *International Journal of Eating Disorders* 39:434–442.

Garner, D. 1997. Psychoeducational principles in treatment. In *Handbook of Treatment for Eating Disorders*, 2nd ed., edited by D. Garner and P. Garfinkel. New York: Guilford Press.

Godart, N., S. Berthoz, Z. Rein, F. Perdereau, F. Lang, J. Venisse, O. Halfon, P. Bizouard, G. Loas, M. Corcos, P. Jeammet, M. Flament, and F. Curt. 2006. Does the frequency of anxiety and depressive disorders differ between diagnostic subtypes of anorexia nervosa and bulimia? *International Journal of Eating Disorders* 39:772–778.

Gorwood, P., A. Kipman, and C. Foulon. 2003. The human genetics of anorexia nervosa. *European Journal of Pharmacology* 480:163–170.

Heffner, M., and G. Eifert. 2004. *The Anorexia Workbook: How to Accept Yourself, Heal Your Suffering, and Reclaim Your Life*. Oakland, CA: New Harbinger.

Herrin, M. 2003. *Nutrition Counseling in the Treatment of Eating Disorders*. New York: Brunner-Routledge.

Hoek, H., and D. van Hoeken. 2003. Review of the prevalence and incidence of eating disorders. *International Journal of Eating Disorders* 34:383–396.

Hyman, B., and C. Pedrick. 2005. *The OCD Workbook: Your Guide to Breaking Free from Obsessive-Compulsive Disorder*, 2nd ed. Oakland, CA: New Harbinger.

Key, A., C. George, D. Beattie, K. Stammers, H. Lacey, and G. Waller. 2002. Body image treatment within an inpatient program for anorexia nervosa: The role of mirror exposure in the desensitization process. *International Journal of Eating Disorders* 31:185–190.

Knaus, W. 2006. *The Cognitive Behavioral Workbook for Depression: A Step-by-Step Program*. Oakland, CA: New Harbinger.

Linehan, M. 1993. *Skills Training Manual for Treating Borderline Personality Disorder*. New York: Guilford Press.

Lock, J., and D. Le Grange. 2005. *Help Your Teenager Beat an Eating Disorder*. New York: Guilford Press.

Lucas, A., C. Beard, W. O'Fallon, and L. Kurland. 1991. 50-year trends in the incidence of anorexia nervosa in Rochester, MN: A population-based study. *American Journal of Psychiatry* 148:917–922.

Marks, I. 1997. Behavior therapy for obsessive-compulsive disorder: A decade of progress. *Canadian Journal of Psychiatry* 42:1021–1027.

Markway, B., C. Carmin, C. Pollard, and T. Flynn. 1992. *Dying of Embarrassment: Help for Social Anxiety and Phobia.* Oakland, CA: New Harbinger.

Marra, T. 2004. *Depressed and Anxious: The Dialectical Behavior Therapy Workbook for Overcoming Depression and Anxiety.* Oakland, CA: New Harbinger.

McIntosh, V. V., J. Jordan, S. E. Luty, F. A. Carter, J. M. McKenzie, C. M. Bulik, and P. R. Joyce. 2006. Specialist supportive clinical management for anorexia nervosa. *International Journal of Eating Disorders* 39:625–632.

McKay, M., and P. Fanning. 2000. *Self-Esteem*, 3rd ed. Oakland, CA: New Harbinger.

McKay, M., J. Wood, and J. Brantley. 2007. *The Dialectical Behavior Therapy Skills Workbook: Practical DBT Exercises for Learning Mindfulness, Interpersonal Effectiveness, Emotion Regulation, and Distress Tolerance.* Oakland, CA: New Harbinger.

Miller, K., E. Lee, E. Lawson, M. Misra, J. Minihan, S. Grinspoon, S. Gleysteen, D. Mickley, D. Herzog, and A. Klibanski. 2006. Determinants of skeletal loss and recovery in anorexia nervosa. *Journal of Clinical Endocrinology and Metabolism.* 91:2931–2937.

Mitchell, J., H. Seim, E. Colon, and C. Pomeroy. 1987. Medical complications and medical management of bulimia. *Annals of Internal Medicine.* 107:71–77.

Nordbo, R. H., E. M. Espeset, K. S. Gulliksen, F. Skarderud, and A. Holte. 2006. The meaning of self-starvation: Qualitative study of patients' perception of anorexia nervosa. *International Journal of Eating Disorders* 39:556–564.

Norris, M., K. Boydell, L. Pinhas, and D. Katzman. 2006. Ana and the Internet: A review of pro-anorexia websites. *International Journal of Eating Disorders* 39:443–447.

Pettit, J., and T. Joiner. 2005. *The Interpersonal Solution to Depression: A Workbook for Changing How You Feel by Changing How You Relate.* Oakland, CA: New Harbinger.

Powers, P., Y. Bannon, R. Eubanks, and T. McCormick. 2007. Quetiapine in anorexia nervosa patients: An open label outpatient pilot study. *International Journal of Eating Disorders* 40:21–26.

Puxley, F., M. Midtsund, A. Iosif, and B. Lask. 2008. PANDAS anorexia nervosa—Endangered, extinct or nonexistent? *International Journal of Eating Disorders* 41:15–21.

Raney, T., L. Thornton, W. Berrettini, H. Brandt, S. Crawford, M. Fichter, K. Halmi, C. Johnson, A. Kaplan, M. LaVia, J. Mitchell, A. Rotondo, M. Strober, D. Woodside, W. Kaye, and C. Bulik. 2008. Influence of overanxious disorder of childhood on the expression of anorexia nervosa. *International Journal of Eating Disorders* 41:326–332.

Silber, T. 2005. Ipecac syrup abuse, morbidity, and mortality: Isn't it time to repeal its over-the-counter status? *Journal of Adolescent Health* 37:256–260.

Silverman, J. 1997. Anorexia nervosa: Historical perspective on treatment. In *Handbook of Treatment for Eating Disorders*, 2nd ed., edited by D. Garner and P. Garfinkel. New York: Guilford Press.

Strober, M., R. Freeman, C. Lampert, and J. Diamond. 2007. The association of anxiety disorders and obsessive compulsive personality disorder with anorexia nervosa: Evidence from a family study with discussion of nosological and neurodevelopmental implications. *International Journal of Eating Disorders* 40(Supplement):S46–51.

Sunday, S., and K. Halmi. 2003. Energy intake and body composition in anorexia and bulimia nervosa. *Physiology and Behavior* 78:11–17.

Tucker, T. 2006. *The Great Starvation Experiment*. New York: Free Press.

Vesper, B., K. Altman, K. Elseth, F. Haines, S. Pavlova, L. Tao, G. Targan, and J. Radosevich. 2008. Gastroesophageal reflux disease (GERD): Is there more to the story? *ChemMedChem* 4:552–559.

Vocks, S., A. Wachter, and J. Kosfelder. 2007. Look at yourself: Can body image therapy affect cognitive and emotional response to seeing oneself in the mirror in eating disorders? *European Eating Disorder Review* 16:147–154.

Wagner, A., B. Barbarich-Marsteller, G. Frank, U. Bailer, S. Wonderlich, R. Crosby, S. Henry, V. Vogel, K. Plotnicov, C. McConaha, and W. Kaye. 2006. Personality traits after recovery from eating disorders: Do subtypes differ? *International Journal of Eating Disorders* 39:276–284.

Zuercher-White, E. 1998. *An End to Panic*, 2nd ed. Oakland, CA: New Harbinger.

Doreen A. Samelson, Ed.D., MSCP, is a licensed clinical psychologist and eating disorder specialist. She practices in a large health maintenance organization, where at least half of her clinical work consists of treating patients with eating disorders. She presents continuing education workshops several times a year on the topic of eating disorders.

Foreword writer **Robert Graff, MD,** is chair of the department of psychiatry at San Joaquin County Behavioral Health Services.

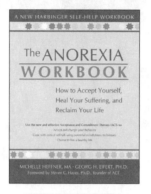

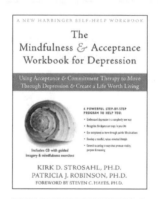
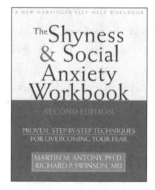